# MEXICAN ROOTS,
# AMERICAN SOIL

# MEXICAN ROOTS,
# AMERICAN SOIL

## A Quest for
## the American Dream

## ERNIE BRINGAS

**PHANTASM PRESS**

Published by:
Phantasm Press
PO Box 20461
Mesa, AZ 85277

Cover and interior design by Frame25 Productions
Cover photographs © Sander van der Werf c/o
Shutterstock.com and Bob Orsillo c/o Shutterstock.com

Visit the author at:
*ernie.ripchords.info*

ISBN: 978-0692721582

10 9 8 7 6 5 4 3 2 1

Printed on acid-free recycled paper
in the United States of America

# CONTENTS

# DEDICATION

I believe it was the actor Dustin Hoffman who comically stated that the inscription on his tombstone should read: "I couldn't have gotten this far without my parents." That was funny. From a more serious perspective, however, the truth of that statement resonates on many levels. Accordingly, I thankfully dedicate this work to my parents and grandparents who with courage and tenacity forged a new life in America, not only for themselves, but also for those of us who followed thereafter.

I also wish to dedicate this work to the millions of immigrants still struggling against difficult odds in their efforts to achieve the American dream.

# ACKNOWLEDGEMENTS

I will simply say this straight out: My proofreader and copy editor, Pat Joynes, was my most invaluable asset in bringing this work to its completed end. I have never had anyone review my work with such thoroughness and precision. Her careful read made all the difference in ferreting out numerous errors on the part of this writer. Furthermore, her creative editing and helpful prompts were essential in helping to shape the final draft and the ongoing quest for publication. I am indebted.

I also want to acknowledge Jonathan Friedman, president and owner of Frame25 Productions. His cover design was beautiful and creative, and his arduous formatting of the text was thoroughly professional. Additionally, it was a pleasure working with someone who was willing to accommodate all of the idiosyncrasies that an author brings to the table. My sincere thanks, Jonathan.

In a more generalized way, I want to thank the many friends not mentioned herein who have touched my life in so many meaningful ways. In this respect I have certainly been most fortunate.

# WHY THIS STORY?
## ¿POR QUÉ ESTA HISTORIA?

MY MOTHER WAS BORN in Mexico and I was born in the USA. My father was born in Texas but his father was born in Mexico. These are my roots; I am a Mexican American. However, up until recently, I didn't call myself a Mexican American, a Latino, or a Hispanic. I simply thought of myself as an American. What else could I possibly be?

To think of myself as anyone other than an American has *never* entered my mind. True, I look more like the Gingerbread Man than the Pillsbury Doughboy, but my students say I look more like Barney Fife. Whatever the case, I'm an American through and through. My life's journey certainly reflects that reality. Although my autobiographical sketch will be the main act that is played out on this written stage, don't think for a moment that you'll be looking at a dry memoir. I've been a teacher, a preacher and a rock & roll feature. My life has been interesting and somewhat of a roller coaster ride; sometimes I'm in the roller coaster and sometimes I'm under it (ouch). Ride with me from the tough streets of Watts in LA to the palm tree-covered streets in Beverly Hills, not to mention the investigative hunt for a serial killer, and much more. But I'll save it for later.

So why do I now finger my way across the computer keyboard? *Why this story?* Well, recent events have brought me back to think about my Mexican roots. Although it was never my intention to write about my family's background, I find myself compelled to do so. My purpose is threefold. Hear me out.

In recent times, the sheer number of immigrants crossing into the United States from Mexico has caused considerable consternation based on the fear that the USA—at least our western border states—will soon be taken over by aliens. Here's a recent email I received that illustrates that point.

> *A U.S. Navy destroyer stops four Mexicans rowing towards Texas up the Gulf of Mexico.*
>
> *The Captain gets on the bullhorn and shouts, "Ahoy, small craft. Where are you headed?"*
>
> *One of the Mexicans puts down his oar, stands up, and shouts, "We are invading the United States of America to reclaim the territory taken by the USA during the 1800s."*
>
> *The entire crew on the destroyer doubles over in laughter.*
>
> *When the Captain finally catches his breath, he gets back on the bullhorn and asks, "Just the four of you?"*
>
> *The same Mexican stands up again and shouts, "No, we're the last four. The other 12 million are already there!"*

Whether or not this humor is politically correct is not an issue for me. However, it does illustrate the popular perception held by many Americans that immigrants are a threat to our way of life (*"We are invading the United States of America to reclaim the territory taken by the USA during the 1880s."*) Americans, of course, wouldn't take this literally as a loss of territory back to Mexico, but more as a loss of American culture to a foreign culture. Not surprisingly, misinformation, disinformation and, let's not forget xenophobia, stoke the fires of this flawed perception. The 2015 confusion over the immigration of Syrian refugees only exacerbates the issue, not to mention Trump's rant against Muslims and Mexicans.

Also consider what happened when people opposed to immigration gathered at a rally on Capitol Hill in Washington, July 15, 2013. Ken Crow, former president of the Tea Party of America, got up and defined for the group what he considered to be "well-bred Americans." He stated that great Americans, such as Thomas Jefferson and George Washington, had incredible bloodlines. "You came from them," he said. "And the unique thing," he continued, "about being from that part of the world, when you learn about breeding, you learn that you cannot breed Secretariat to a donkey and expect to win the Kentucky Derby." In other words, Ken Crow has concluded that he and others like himself are the offspring of racehorse DNA, while people from other cultures have the genes of a donkey. (This is not an isolated incident of convoluted bias, and I will illustrate that fact with other examples in the Epilogue.)

Such rhetoric is not only repugnant, but it is also deceitful, mean-spirited, insulting, and certainly reflects an attitude of animus toward the Mexican people. It is obvious from the above statements that venomous rhetoric and prejudicial feelings run deep in some segments of our society. I came to realize that these derogatory comments should not go unchallenged. They slander not only my heritage, but also the very people at the center of my life; that is, both my nuclear and extended family.

*Therefore, my first purpose for writing is to help mitigate the prejudicial attitudes that prevail.* It is prompted by what I consider to be a direct assault against the Hispanic people, most notably, against Mexicans (for the purpose of this work, the term Hispanic or Latino refers to people of Mexican descent). I hope my family's story—fleeing from the battlegrounds of the Mexican Revolution in 1916 to the USA—will help other Americans recognize the positive contributions made by immigrants that have woven their unique threads into the American fabric. That's one of the great values of immigration. It's the bloodline that keeps our nation from becoming anemic, and stagnant. From top to bottom, the social, musical, athletic, professional, and intellectual contributions made by the constant flow of immigrants are incalculable.

Until Americans come to appreciate this reality, the bitter arguments over immigration will continue to be an exasperating problem. Our citizens need to consider the Seal of the United States that carries the Latin phrase, E PLURIBUS UNUM. It means "Out of many, one," or alternatively translated as "One from many." Traditionally, it was understood to mean that out of our many colonies, a single nation emerged. Recently, its meaning has come to suggest that out of many races, ethnicities, religions and heritages, a single people and nation has emerged (illustrating the concept of the melting pot). E PLURIBUS UNUM reflects the unifying outcome of many peoples thrown together, people that have been flocking to our shores for centuries. Incidentally, in the 1939 film, *The Wizard of Oz* (one of my favorite films), the Wizard gives the Scarecrow a certificate from the Society of E PLURIBUS UNUM.

Like it or not, America continues to be a great melting pot or, as some would say, a salad bowl. I still consider the "melting pot" to be the best metaphor. There is certainly integration in a salad bowl, but it lacks assimilation. The salad bowl metaphor might work if you were willing to put the salad in a blender.

We must be mindful that the benefits of immigration are a two-way street. I will simply say that I am eternally grateful to my family members who had the vision for a better life, and had the tenacity to make that better life possible by crossing the Mexican/American border. I still marvel at their courage and foresight.

On the other hand, I can point with pride to what this country did for me and for our family as a whole. With open arms this nation provided all the opportunities needed for the pursuit of happiness, including education and job opportunities. We, in turn, gave back with service, dedication and loyalty. That will become evident as our story unfolds.

I know that my/our story reflects only one of millions of stories that could be offered, but it's the one I know best. I also admit that our family name doesn't have household recognition. Therefore, any appeal here has obvious limitations. And unless this writing makes the NY Best Seller list—wouldn't that be a hoot?—that reality is not about to change. Nevertheless, I am confident that these few words will help slow down, be it ever so slightly, the present onslaught of prejudicial obsession.

*My second motive for writing is to help all immigrants and refugees to understand the importance of integration and assimilation (fully explained in the Epilogue).* Maybe my story will resonate more closely with those who are struggling through the entry level in search of hope, in search of the American Dream. What if you're an emigrant parent or the child of an emigrant? What happens to Mexican emigrants—like my mother—when they come to this country and what happens to their children growing up in this country (as many of us did)?

New arrivals must not become isolationists by clinging to their own social and cultural networks. Without integration there can be no assimilation. All minority groups must gradually adopt the customs and attitudes of the country to which they migrate. To be absorbed into the American *mainstream* is vital if one is to reap the full benefits of what this magnificent country has to offer. I hope that reading about our/my journey will help immigrants understand the importance of that assimilating process. To do otherwise threatens their ability to realize the American dream. There is no doubt that integration and assimilation have been the key components that have led to the success of all our ancestors, regardless of their country of origin. People from all over the world in all walks of life have traveled this same path of cultural integration, adaption, adoption, and finally, total assimilation—assimilation that is usually achieved over the course of one or two generations (it doesn't happen overnight).

This should not imply that one must abandon all ties to the past. I understand the desire to maintain cultural traditions. But family traditions should never be preserved at the expense of the future. Never!

*My third reason for writing this work is even more personal.* At this point in time (June, 2016) I am now 76 years old. I'm reminded of the doctor who informed one of his patients that he had only ten to live. The patient anxiously responded: "Ten what? Ten years, ten months, ten weeks . . . what?"

The doctor replied: "10, 9, 8, 7 . . ."

Anyway, I thought I'd better get all this down in print before I disappear. As Joan Crawford so aptly put it in the 1956 movie, *Autumn Leaves*: "The future comes a lot sooner than it used to." I trust that these words will serve as a brief historical account for my nieces, nephews and also their offspring who, for the most part, have absolutely no understanding of their historical roots.

The reader may wonder how the following details can be accurately recalled after the passing of so many decades. My pre-birth accounts have obviously come from grandparents, mother, and other family members. As for my personal recalls, the simple answer is that I wrote many of these notes in my confidential log as they unfolded back in the day. These accounts and entries have proved invaluable in the writing of this work. Other entries are conscious memories. Also, rest assured that the following accounts are not exaggerated; they are stated with candor to the best of my knowledge and recollection. I apologize to family, friends, and old lovers who are not mentioned herein. The numbers prohibit such an inclusion, especially the lovers (LOL).

In closing: I am first and foremost an American; my Mexican heritage doesn't change that; it only adds to it. For what it's worth, herein is our/my story of integration, assimilation, and the successful quest for the American Dream; ergo, *Mexican Roots, American Soil.*

NOTE: I like Wikipedia's take on the American Dream:

> The AMERICAN DREAM *is a national ethos of the United States, the set of ideals (Democracy, Rights, Liberty, Opportunity, and Equality) in which freedom includes the opportunity for prosperity and success, and an upward social mobility for the family and children, achieved through hard work in a society with few barriers. In the definition of the American Dream by James Truslow Adams in 1931, "life should be better and richer and fuller for everyone, with opportunity for each according to ability or achievement" regardless of social class or circumstances of birth.*
>
> *The American Dream is rooted in the Declaration of Independence, which proclaims that "all men are created equal" with the right to "Life, Liberty and the pursuit of Happiness."*

# Chapter 1

# THE EMIGRATION
## LA INMIGRACIÓN

*Mexico to America*
1916

IT WASN'T THE BEST of times, and it was going to get worse. In 1876, Porfirio Diaz was elected as the so-called president of Mexico and ruled until 1911. Under his 35 years of dictatorial reign, the people of Mexico suffered immensely, especially the lower classes who constituted 96% of the population. There was great disparity between the haves and the have-nots. President Diaz favored the rich at the expense of the peasantry. The exploitation and appalling treatment of workers was unconscionable. Living conditions became intolerable. In one-way or another, most families were under the gun.

From a personal perspective, this story begins with Guadalupe Guerrero (aka Lupe). She is my grandmother on my mother's side. She was born on January 12, 1887, under the regime of Porfirio Diaz, and passed away at the age of 97, on April 28, 1984. Lupe was born in Zacatecas, Mexico, but eventually came to live in Torreón, Mexico. She had at least two sisters and one brother but I know very little about them.

Note: I do not have any good photos of my grandparents but, strangely enough, the following photo of Lupe's sister—my great aunt Francisca (Guerrero) Fillette—survives.

This part of the narrative derives from my grandmother's recollections to me in my younger day. She spent most of her childhood in the small (ranching/farming) northern community of Torreón, Mexico, about 772 miles south from the border town of El Paso, Texas. Her mother was born in Mexico; and to the best of our knowledge, all generations prior to her mother were born in Mexico. My grandmother would sometimes boast that the family carried Aztec blood. Who knows?

My great aunt Francisca
(Guerrero) Fillette (1920s)

When Lupe was a child, her family enjoyed tremendous wealth at a time when most Mexican families were hard pressed to make ends meet. Her parents were landowners controlling vast acres of farmland that included a beautiful, spacious, luxurious, ranch home. She remembers the abundance of chickens, cows, and some horses, and plenty of good Mexican food. But the Guerreros and other wealthy landowners constituted only a small percentage of the population. There was no middle class to speak of, only the very rich and the very poor. Those that were fortunate enough to have jobs working the land that someone else owned, earned meager wages. In contrast, the Guerrero family was at the top of the pyramid.

Around 1896, this privileged status vanished under the land-grabbing policies of the Diaz administration, even though most aristocrats did not suffer this fate because Diaz favored wealthy landowners. The unjust seizure of their property put the Guerrero family into free-fall. They lost everything. As we would say today, they joined the ranks of the homeless. It was a cruel twist of fate and a life-changing traumatic event for a child who was only nine years old.

In 1898, at the age of 11, Lupe had little choice but to begin hard labor as a means to help support the family. She worked twelve hours a day, six days a week, in a sweatshop that paid the lowest of wages. Child-abuse laws of any sort were nonexistent. In the winter it was freezing cold; in the summer, the sweltering heat was unbearable.[1] And so it was by necessity that her childhood evaporated under the harsh conditions of misfortune.

In 1901, at the age of 14, she caught the eye of the manager where she worked; he was 15 years her senior. She got more than just a slight raise in pay; she got married. That's a bit of a stretch if you're only 14. Actually, historically speaking, the age of consent for girls was much lower than 14. For example, in 1275 England, the age of consent was 12 years of age. In 1863 France, the age of consent was increased to 13.[2]

Lupe's husband, Francisco Arellano (October 8, 1872 - 1948), was a good man of Spanish descent. He was a man of many talents and dabbled in the arts outside of his regular job. He and Lupe lived a moderate and stable life in Torreón during those early years. Soon after their nuptials, Lupe Arellano became pregnant. Painfully, at 15 years of age, her first pregnancy ended in a miscarriage. Shortly thereafter she became

---

[1] As one indication, climate data for Torreón (1951 – 2010) had a high of 109 (F) and a low of 17.6 (F).
[2] Stephen Robertson, *Age of Consent Laws*, University of Sydney, Australia.

pregnant again and, at the age of 16, delivered her first healthy baby boy October 22, 1903. *That was the beginning of the Arellano family.* My uncle Johnny was up and crawling. In 1905, he was followed by my uncle Jesús (nicknamed Chewy) and my aunt Mary, November 5, 1909. By this time, the population of Torreón had swelled to 34,000 and had gained city status.[3] Life was still hard, but the young family was getting on. Then all hell broke loose.

## The Mexican Revolution

In 1910, Mexico exploded. Death and mayhem rolled across the Mexican terrain. President Diaz, as I mentioned earlier, was not a friend of the people. His biased and unwise judgments—like throwing his competitors into prison when they challenged him to a democratic election—triggered what came to be known as the Mexican Revolution (1910 – 1920). Francisco, Lupe, and their three children found themselves caught up in the middle of a revolution that eventually metamorphosed into a civil war. Even after Porfirio Diaz was ousted in 1911, the warring factions continued their bloody battles until 1920. It was a dangerous and deadly time. According to most sources, out of a population of 15 million, between one and two million lives were lost. (That would be the equivalent of at least 45 million dead Americans by U.S. population figures today.)

## The Battle of Torreón, 1913

The city of Torreón was a major garrison for the Federal troops. Although Diaz was no longer around, the Federal troops still

---

[3]By 2014 the population had swelled to 700,000 (from Wikipedia). Also: According to the *Huffington Post* (June 20, 2013), the drug cartels have made it the second highest homicide region in Mexico (second only to Acapulco).

represented the old regime with a new president that was equally disliked. These troops were a natural target for the resistance fighters. History records the conflict as the Battle of Torreón, September 29–October 1, 1913.[4] The ominous dark clouds that gathered over the city of Torreón that day in northern Mexico were the harbingers of death and destruction. The battle was led by one of the most prominent Mexican Revolutionary generals, Francisco Villa (nicknamed Pancho Villa). On the third day of the assault, Villa, with an army of over eight thousand men, cavalry, and two cannons, stormed the city and eventually broke through enemy lines. The city of Torreón fell to Villa and his men. The victory was complete. (The 1976 song "Fernando"—sung by the Swedish pop group ABBA—reflects the Mexican Revolution of 1910; it has a haunting melody that always takes me back to that era.)[5]

The Arellanos were now living under the thumb of the revolutionists. Truthfully, however, they favored these insurgents over the Federal troops since the Mexican government still remained corrupt at its core. Besides, the Villa forces, with the exception of a few executions of government sympathizers, were sensitive to the needs of the people.

In spite of the surrounding turmoil, life went on. Less than a year after Villa's victory, my uncle Eugene (aka Gene) was born in Torreón (July 27, 1914). The children now numbered four. But there was a problem. Francisco Arellano (my grandfather) was musically talented and played several of the horn

---

[4]Exact dates for the battle of Torreón vary in several sources.
[5]According to Wikipedia, "The song was to become ABBA's best-selling single of all time, with six million copies sold in 1976 alone. It is one of the fewer than forty all-time singles to have sold 10 million (or more) physical copies worldwide."

instruments. He also composed music and conducted a band sponsored by the Mexican government. That was unfortunate for my grandfather because Pancho Villa had declared that all government workers were traitors and should be executed on sight. So even though my grandparents sympathized with Pancho Villa and other anti-government forces, my grandfather was guilty by association, and Villa's firing squads were well greased. My grandparents took great caution to conceal that governmental connection.

As a young boy, I remember my grandmother relating two stories about the war. One had to do with her chance encounter with Pancho Villa. Evidently she was standing near one of the shops with some other ladies when Villa and his men rode up. For whatever reason, she did not go unnoticed by the general. He engaged her in conversation but quickly broke it off when he discovered her marital status. Perhaps his code of honor, along with his many victories, was one of the reasons he was such a hero in the eyes of the people. My grandmother said that he tipped his sombrero to her as he walked away.

The most telling story was about a young, frightened Federalist, who was running for his life during the Battle of Torreón. He burst into my grandparents' house and begged my grandmother for help. She did not see him as an enemy combatant, but as a human being in dire need. At the risk of putting her own life and the lives of her children in jeopardy, my grandmother daringly hid the terrified youth in a small space not readily exposed. It was none too soon as Villa's troops pushed their way into the house for a quick search. Obviously they didn't find him. The young lad left under the cover of darkness and, presumably, made his way to safety.

However, that spine-chilling close call set the wheels in motion for considering a possible departure from Mexican soil. They had kids to worry about. Also, the threat to my grandfather because of his former musical involvement with the government, continued to be a cause for concern. But the timing wasn't quite right for launching into immigrant status; my grandmother was pregnant once again.

The last one to be born in Mexico (Torreón) was my mother (September 27, 1915 – March 5, 2009). She was bestowed with the customary elongated handle: Maria del Refugio Gabriella Arellano. She came to be known as Refugio (Ruth) Cristina Arellano. I don't know why or when this partial name change occurred. The children now numbered five.

The battles that continued throughout Mexico were disconcerting and a serious threat to human welfare. Furthermore, Francisco was tipped off that his arrest was imminent; the insurgents had gotten wind of his former association with the government. This led my grandparents to a monumental decision. It was time for the family to "get out of Dodge." They quickly headed for the border. [Patas pa que son?][6]

## Refugees

My grandparents and their five children (which included my 4-month-old mom)[7] escaped the Mexican Revolution when they legally emigrated from Mexico into the USA (February 9, 1916). My grandmother had the presence of mind to for-

---

[6]This is an old, humorous Mexican saying: "What are feet/legs for, anyway?" (It loses something in translation.)
[7]According to her Certificate of Baptism from the Sacred Heart Church in El Paso, she was baptized on October 8, 1916, under the name of Maria del Refugio Gabriella Arellano. As I mentioned earlier, she came to be known as Ruth Cristina Arellano.

mally register the family when they crossed the border.[8] This was extremely important because it provided some protection against future deportation.

They ended up in El Paso City, by the Rio Grande (shades of the country singer/writer Marty Robbins's 1976 #1 hit, "El Paso City"). That song harkens me back to the beginning of my mom's Mexican roots in American soil. It was the beginning of assimilation for the Arellano family. Eventually, all of the Arellano children would become US citizens.

Evidently my grandparents were quite healthy and very Catholic. Stereotypically, they had 11 children, but only seven of the 11 survived childhood. Remember, we're talking early 1900s. Of the seven survivors, five were born in Mexico, two in the USA; my uncle Francisco (aka Frank) March 1,1918, and my aunt Lilia (ca. 1919) were born as American citizens in El Paso, Texas.

As was the case for most immigrant families seeking sanctuary, or a better way of life, they were a poor lot. Most people don't realize how much you leave behind, especially when you're hurriedly forced to flee your homeland. The implementation of such an arduous flight would be a daunting challenge for anyone. It's a burdensome sacrifice. Not only must you give up your livelihood and all of your tangible possessions, but you must also endure the loss of friends and family members, along with regional and national attachments. Beyond those painful losses lies the demoralizing fear of the unknown (a new country, a new government, a new flag, a new culture, a new language).

---

[8]This is the date given on the certificate of immigration from the U.S. Dept. of Justice, Registration #A 3 013 205. Also, my grandmother's date of birth is listed as 1889, not 1887 as her Death Certificate states. I have no way of knowing which b. date is correct.

How does one walk away from everything cherished and familiar without a sense of anxiety? Emigration would be difficult enough for one person, let alone an entire family with five children ranging in ages from four months to 12 years. Scary.

But hey, it beats getting killed. Right? I guess that's the clincher for most refugees on the run. Incidentally, the First World War in Europe (1914-1918) was raging when my mother was born and when she and my grandparents crossed the border to get away from the Mexican Revolution. The estimated deaths for the Mexican Revolution range from about 1 to 2 million. In contrast, according to Wikipedia: "The total number of military and civilian casualties in World War I was over 37 million; over 16 million deaths and 20 million wounded, ranking it among the deadliest conflicts in human history." [Tragically, WW II would far surpass these figures.] But let's refocus on 1916.

## Childhood in El Paso

The Arellano family had found safety in the United States but their poverty was ever present. My mother's childhood was flooded with disheartening scarcity and discomfort. They had a roof over their heads, but it's not an exaggeration to say they were dirt poor; everyone slept on a dirt floor in a one-room "house." No privacy, no running water, no bathroom. Going to the outhouse about 200 feet behind their abode was always an edgy challenge. A floral bouquet it was not. The winter days and nights were especially difficult as they sat shivering on a makeshift, ice-cold toilet seat that felt like sandpaper.[9] The females suffered most of all, and the why of it needs no explanation.

---

[9]According to the National Weather Service, the lowest recorded temperature for El Paso was -8(F); the max monthly snowfall was 25.9 IN.

As for the Christmas season, forget hanging stockings on the fireplace for they had neither. On Christmas Day, my mom recounts that the children were most fortunate to get an apple, and they celebrated that gift with gusto. Slim pickings for sure, but the family remained devoted. The universal glue that held them together was the binding power of love and affection. This they had in abundance. My mom and her siblings also had the advantage of being kids, a congenital condition that *sometimes* softens the harsh realities of life.

Being Catholic, they opted for a Catholic school where the nuns started to teach the children some English. Of course, Spanish was spoken at home, and that would always be the case since my grandparents never came to grips with the English language. The language barrier is symptomatic of many immigrants that reach our "shores." Their kids are the ones who usually end up being integrated and assimilated. Not unlike *Star Trek*'s Borg: "Resistance is futile." Accordingly, all of the Arellano children became naturalized American citizens with the exception of my aunt Lilia (1917) and my uncle Frank (1918 – 2007); they were American citizens by virtue of having been born here in the US two years after my grandparents crossed the border in 1916.

Chapter 2

# CALIFORNIA HERE WE COME
## CALIFORNIA ALLÁ VAMOS

*El Paso to Los Angeles*
1922—1925

AMERICA IS KNOWN AS the land of opportunity. Chasing that American dream started when my mom's oldest brother, Johnny,[10] set out from El Paso in 1922 for the Golden State of California. This was the crucial linchpin that would eventually start the rest of the family down the Yellow Brick Road to a better life in the Emerald City called Los Angeles. The plan was for Johnny—who was only 19—to get settled in California. Thereafter he would send for the rest of the family. He rode the rails and hitchhiked across the western states. (Shades of Woody Guthrie's early years when he left his Texas family for California.)[11]

Reaching Southern California, Johnny hustled for work. He was a real go-getter, very industrious. Proudly, he claims to

---

[10]My uncle: John Honorato Arellano; October 22, 1903 – 2002.
[11]Woodrow Wilson "Woody" Guthrie (July 14, 1912 – October 3, 1967) was a famous American singer/songwriter and folk musician. His best-known song is "This Land Is Your Land."

have worked in some Hollywood films as an extra that included the 1925 classic, *Ben-Hur*, starring Ramón Novarro.[12] He also worked as an extra in a few Charlie Chaplin films.[13]

*My uncle Johnny Arellano with wife Mercy (1920s)*

Eventually, he saved enough money to bring the family out to Los Angeles. It was an entirely new beginning for everyone, including Nero, the family dog. However, before moving out West, the family endured two catastrophic jolts.

As noted, the Arellano family had crossed into the United States in 1916. Two years later, in 1918, there was a worldwide pandemic referred to as the Spanish Flu.[14] It was an unusually severe and deadly strain of the H1N1 (swine flu) virus. Fifty to 100 million people perished worldwide. When you compare that to the number of deaths in WWI—22 million—you get a good idea of the flu's destructive magnitude. In America, the estimated death toll was 675,000. One of those casualties belonged to the Arellano family. My grandmother's second eldest child

---

[12]Ramón Novarro (1899-1968) was a handsome, Mexican leading Hollywood actor in the early 20th century. In a failed robbery attempt he was brutally murdered in his home by two young men.

[13]My uncle Johnny's daughter, Lillian Moss (my cousin), recounts these escapades here.

[14]The term "Spanish Flu" is a misnomer because it did not originate in Spain. The origin is still unknown although several theories have been suggested.

Jesús (Chewy) died of the Spanish flu in 1920 at the age of 15. It's a wonder the whole family didn't succumb to this disease.

Additionally, my grandparents' youngest child—five-year-old Lilia—was playing in the front yard with her siblings when a young motorcyclist speeding down the street lost control of his bike; he careened over the sidewalk into the yard, and horror of horrors, hit and killed the little one (ca. 1922). My imagination cannot envision the heartbreak. Only a mother and father who have lost a child can understand the hellish depths of the grief endured. But here they lost two children within a span of two years.

The young motorcyclist was up for manslaughter. His mother went to my grandmother and pleaded for mercy. Magnanimously, she did not press charges.

### The Road to California

Johnny sent my grandfather enough money to buy a used Model T Ford (aka the Tin Lizzie). That's how they would make the trip to California. In the spring of 1925 the family, with the pooch in tow, set out for Los Angeles. Hauling food and water, a dog, a few sentimental belongings, not to mention the whole kit and caboodle of Arellanos, was a sight to see. It conjures up an image akin to that of a slow, piled up, rumbling Tin Lizzie that we often see in old pictures or cartoons (reminiscent of the opening introduction of that former TV show: *The Beverly Hillbillies*).

Driving on the dirt roads in the wide-open spaces of western America at the beginning of the last century was a bold venture. Sometimes these dirt roads were planked (covered with long wooden boards, especially between Arizona and Southern California). But most of the time, families rumbled across bumpy, dusty, dirt roads, hoping that the ominous clouds above wouldn't mire them down by way of even the slightest rainfall. Worse yet, a sudden thunderstorm could create a deadly flash flood if they were unluckily caught in a low-lying area. What else could possibly go wrong?

Aside from the fact that the Highway Patrol was nonexistent, there was always apprehension about the Model T. How do you keep that radiator from boiling over? Got water? Flat tires were a common problem. Would one spare tire be enough? Just getting the car started up in the chilly mornings was a predictable unpredictability. Is there a mechanic in the house? For the most part, the old Model T Ford was built rugged to travel over rough terrain. But problems were inevitable. While crossing New Mexico, the old Lizzie sputtered out and left them stranded. The following day, the kindness of strangers got them back on the road. As noted earlier, there was nothing easy about cross-country traveling. (Of course, it beat the heck out of traveling by covered wagon in earlier days.)

Furthermore, the landscape was not dotted with McDonald's restaurants and other fast-food places (or slow-food places, for that matter). Also, the scarcity of so-called gas stations, motels, rest stops, and other conveniences that we take for granted today were nearly nonexistent. This made the journey somewhat uncertain and, at the very least, uncomfortable, especially when it came time to relieve oneself. It wasn't just the kiddies piping up every now and then: "I need to go!" It would have helped immensely if these pilgrims could have synchronized their nature calls. Fat chance.

And so it was that traversing 803 miles to Los Angeles would take several uneasy days. Under ideal conditions, the top speed of a Model T—with a tailwind—was 45 mph. Most people drove them no faster than 35 mph. Driving against a strong headwind would slow the T down to a crawl. A gust of wind hitting the 1200-lb Lizzie broadside could blow it off the road altogether. (The average U.S. car today is tipping the scales at 4000 lbs; even the smallest compacts weigh around 3000 lbs.)

Driving at night was not an option because my grandfather, being the only driver, had to get some sleep. Besides, night driving has never been a good idea. Statistics prove it to be the most dangerous time to be on the road (even today). But stopping in the middle of the desert, especially on a moonless night, brought its own set of difficulties. Most notably, the landscape was pitch-black. If you've ever doused your headlights out in open spaces away from city lights on a moonless night, or you've been in the inner bowels of a cave, you'll know exactly what I'm talking about here. If you are freestanding in the absence of any light, just keeping your balance will be a challenge (the elderly usually topple over, and I'm not kidding).

Using the car's lamplights was helpful in finding some suitable ground to spread their sleeping blankets. But the lamplights couldn't be left on indefinitely. All too soon, lights out, meant lights out. Thereafter you were as blind as a bat without sonar. Sit yourself up and you couldn't even see the ground beneath you, or the person lying beside you, or even your hand in front of your face. A pitch-black environment could be unnerving. Was it true that scorpions are nocturnal critters, swapping the day's heat for the cooler hours of the night? As for Nero the dog, he was tethered to the front tire. He might otherwise stray off into the desert and fall prey to the coyotes they heard howling in the inky darkness that surrounded them.

Sleep did not come easy but not always without reward. My mother, lying back and looking straight up at the star-studded sky, recalls the Milky Way as a wonder to behold.

When the Arellano clan finally rumbled into Los Angeles, they were thoroughly exhausted.[15] Thankfully, Johnny had a decent house rented at 354½ E. 33rd street, not too far from the downtown area. Although it was a modest dwelling, it looked more like a palace when compared to the humble dwelling they had left behind in El Paso. More astonishing, this LA house featured indoor plumbing. The American dream was on the upswing. I'm not sure about the following photo that I found after my mother passed away, but it's family back in the day.

My mom and her older sister Mary were back in school. Unfortunately, a national and personal setback was looming.

---

[15]REALITY CHECK! In no way do I mean to imply that these difficult experiences are commensurate with the painful trials endured by the pioneers in covered wagons who traversed the hazardous terrain of the west, or refugees around the world who struggle to survive in war-torn environments (many times unsuccessfully). As my mom would often say, "We've been blessed."

Aunt Mary, being six years older than my mom, made it through high school. But the Great Depression that started in August of 1929 soon torpedoed my 14-year-old mom's educational pursuits, along with those of her other siblings. She got no further than the ninth grade (John Adams Jr. High). With the exception of my aunt Mary, no one in that immigrating family ever graduated from high school. Everyone had to work in order to make ends meet. Even if the younger ones couldn't work, keeping them school bound was not financially feasible. These were tough times, and the Depression would run for roughly another ten years. However, the family had already been tempered by the austerity experience of El Paso.

## Deportation

Aside from the Depression woes, the family faced a much more serious threat—deportation. Sometimes ethnic discrimination is brought on by social unrest. Such was the case with the economic upheaval of the 1930s' Great Depression. In Texas, Colorado, and California, for example, the Mexican American population suffered a great injustice. Federal and local governments panicked because of job scarcity. In the western states, the Mexican minority became the perfect scapegoat. *From 1929 to 1939, the American Government deported (or allowed to be deported) between one and two million legal residents of Mexican descent; 60% of these were American citizens!* In Los Angeles, where the Arellano family lived, the deportation issue was acute. As noted, many Mexicans, even those who had crossed legally, and even some who were American citizens, were either coerced to leave or bodily expelled. I have no idea how our family dodged that bullet.

Sometimes the term "repatriation" was used instead of the term deportation; the word repatriation was clearly a euphemism to evade the deportation laws of the United States. This travesty was undoubtedly one of the worst shameful blots on American history, even more so than the illegal relocation of Japanese Americans to internment camps during World War II. Historians are just now beginning to recognize the magnitude of injustice and suffering created by ill-conceived and unwarranted bigotry against Mexican Americans in the 1930s. In 2005, the State of California passed an official "Apology Act" to those forced to relocate to Mexico, an estimated 1.2 million of whom were U.S. citizens.[16]

In 1935, midway through the depression, my 19-year-old mother-to-be would marry 26-year-old Ernesto Bringas. Before I explain how that all unfolded, I need to say a few words about my father and his family, the Bringas family. Jumping Jehoshaphat! Compared to the Arellano family we're moving from rags to $$$$$.

---

[16]See: Mexican Repatriation – Wikipedia.

Chapter 3

# THE BRINGAS EMPIRE
## EL BRINGAS IMPERIO

*From Mexico to America*
1885

THE BRINGAS FAMILY—originally from Spain—was one of Mexico's wealthiest families. There's no better way to describe it: They were and still are filthy rich. The Bringas name in Mexico was the equivalent of the wealthy Bill Gates name in America (adjusting for inflation). It is rumored that at one time the Bringas family owned half of Mexico City. (If you Google "Bringas Billionaires" you'll find a number of them listed.)

From childhood, I too had heard about the Bringas wealth in Mexico and our *direct* connection to it. The information came from my mother, my aunts and my uncles. Supposedly, we were in line to inherit a part of the Bringas fortune. Here is the story as it has been handed down to me through various family members.[17]

---

[17]I will not attempt to trace all my cousins and family members. I couldn't even if I tried because I don't have all the information. I will list only those that have somehow weaved their way into the tapestry of my life.

I begin this saga with my grandfather, Manuel Bringas II, who was born in Mexico, ca. 1885. To the best of my knowledge, he was the first Bringas to cross over into the United States. Actually, we believe he was fleeing Mexico for reasons unknown. *Rumor* has it that he was on the lam.

Crossing the border around 1903 at the age of 18, Manuel settled in El Paso, Texas, and met a woman named Maria (?) with whom he fell in love. His father in Mexico was not at all happy with the arrangement and warned his son that if he married this woman, he would be cut off from any inheritance. As in a romance novel, Manuel defied his father and married her anyway. In so doing, he forfeited the Bringas fortune, not only for himself, but all future progeny. That's a lot of money to give up for the tender trap. (As a sidelight, this whole romantic episode is reminiscent of King Edward III when, in 1936, he abdicated the throne of England in order to marry the American socialite, Wallis Simpson.)

Manuel and Maria had five children that included my dad, Ernesto Bringas (b. 1908).[18] All were born in El Paso. Unfortunately, their marriage was short-lived. My grandfather (Manuel II) died of diabetes in his 30s, shortly before the discovery of insulin in 1923. Around 1925 the remaining family left El Paso and came to settle in San Diego, California. (It's a notable coincidence that this was about the same time the Arellanos were arriving in Los Angeles, 125 miles north of San Diego.)

Even if I could, it's not my intention to expound on all of Manuel and Maria's five kids. Before I say anything about my dad (Ernesto) I will, however, say a short word about his older

---

[18]Ernesto, more often than not, was aka Ernie. However, to avoid confusion with my name, I will continue to use Ernesto in reference to my father.

brother, Manuel III (b. 1906), because he had firsthand information about the Bringas fortune in Mexico.

Manuel Bringas III married Olga Rodriguez in 1928 and had a son that they predictably named Manuel Bringas IV (aka Manny). This cousin of mine was born September 10, 1929 (10 years prior to my birth). When we were both adults, he alluded to the Bringas wealth as told to him by his father. Evidently, the Bringas family in San Diego was not about to forget the Bringas riches in Mexico City, regardless of the disinheritance legacy.

My cousin Manny told me on several occasions that when he was 16 years old, his father actually took him to Mexico City to meet some of the family in 1946. When he tells me this story, his eyes widen and he sets his jaw. He emphatically recounts that he was taken to a room about 8 x 12, and swears that the room was stacked with gold bars reaching from the floor to the ceiling three to four feet deep. His dad whispered to him and said, "Someday some of this will belong to you and your cousins."

Of course, this sharing of the inheritance never happened because we were on the wrong side of the border. Disconnected from the Mexican powers that be, we were seen as a pariah and ultimately disenfranchised. No one was about to share any wealth with us short of going to court. The issue became perilous when it was made clear that unintended consequences might occur if anyone from the USA ventured into Mexico to make any claim of entitlement. Everyone decided it would be too risky to fight against the insurmountable odds of unlimited money and power in a foreign land. It might even be life threatening. You think!

Accordingly, the Bringas family on this side of the border would have to start from scratch (a work ethic already in progress). Nobody minded. Many years later my mother told me that when someone asked my dad about the fortune in Mexico, he would simply say, "I have my wife and kids, these two good arms, and that's all I need."

Good grief, I'm well into this autobiography, and I haven't said much about myself. As you probably guessed, that's because I haven't been born yet. But I'll be along shortly. First, we've got to get my mom and dad into the same restaurant. Literally!

Chapter 4

# ERNESTO BRINGAS MEETS RUTH ARELLANO

## "I WANT TO HOLD YOUR HAND"
## YO QUIERO AGARRAR TU MANO

1933

SEPARATED BY THE 125 miles between LA and San Diego, it was highly unlikely that Ruth Arellano (my mother-to-be) and Ernesto Bringas (my father-to-be) would ever cross paths. But they did. Here's the gist of it.

My grandmother, Lupe Arellano, had a sister (see photo p. 2) who married a well-to-do husband. They owned a restaurant in San Diego. During the depression jobs were scarce. So my grandmother in LA asked her sister in San Diego if she could send her daughter (Ruth) down south to work as a waitress in her restaurant. The answer was yes. Wouldn't you know it—it was the same restaurant that Ernesto Bringas would occasionally visit.

Before going further with this story you've got to understand that the Arellano guys and gals were extremely good-looking. Of course, that's my opinion, but I have already shown some family photos to bolster that viewpoint. The following photo of my aunt Mary is but one more example). (It goes without saying that their great looks did not carry over into my DNA. Rats.)

*My aunt Mary Arellano (1940s)*

## Chances Are

Anyway, one day when Ernesto wandered into the restaurant and got a gander at my mom, he went from being an occasional patron to a frequent flyer. To paraphrase Jimmy Buffett's 1977 monster hit, "Margaritaville," my mom was a beauty, a Mexican cutie. It was love at first sight, at least from my dad's point of view because my mom was not at all impressed with Ernesto. To make matters worse, my mother complained that he was not a good tipper (rookie mistake on his part). Nevertheless, he was so infatuated with my mother that he became a persistent customer at the restaurant. My mother considered him to be somewhat of a pest. Nevertheless, persistence paid off and they eventually went out together (but not alone). Not alone? This calls for clarification.

This may sound strange but I heard this from both my mother and my grandmother. Back in the day, it seems that in some circles of the Hispanic culture, a young woman was never allowed to be alone with her suitor (that still may be true in some cases). And so it was that my mom and my dad were chaperoned through their entire courtship. My mom states that they were almost never alone as a couple until they got married. Incredible! She does admit, however, that my dad bribed ($) a few of the chaperones in exchange for some alone time (some things never change).

To keep the story short, they fell in love and got married in May of 1935 (she was 19, he was 26). Soon thereafter, Ruth became pregnant. First born was my sister Martha (February 19, 1936 – February 12, 1999). Ernesto was disappointed because he wanted a boy. Let's try this again. Second born was my sister Virginia (April 4, 1937 – February 15, 2016). Ernesto was disappointed because he wanted a boy. Let's try this again. Finally, he lucked out with another familiar cliché, "Third Time's a Charm." Here I am!

## Here I Am

I was born at the San Diego Mercy Hospital on September 19, 1939. In those days, when a baby was born, the doctor would hold the child upside down by the ankles, and then slap the little one on the rump to activate the breathing process. But when I was born, I was so ugly the doctor slapped my mother.

Back then there was no ultrasound to scan the fetus, and men were not allowed in the delivery room. I've been told that my dad went nuts when learning firsthand from the nurse that

I was a boy. Finally, he had a boy (that is, his wife did). In traditional mode he ran around the waiting room handing out cigars to all who were receptive. I have never understood his obsession about having a boy. In the Hispanic culture, I think it has something to do with passing along the family name. Or, maybe it had something to do with his grandfather, father and brother, who all shared the same name of Manuel. Perhaps my dad was anxious to start his own dynasty since I too would now be known as Ernest (aka Ernie) Bringas, Jr. Who knows? Anyway, I was off and running (or should I say crawling.)

*Ruth Arellano & Ernesto Bringas wedding (1935)*

Chapter 5

# HELLO WORLD

## HOLA MUNDO

*In the Beginning—En El Principio*

*San Diego, California*
*1939*

As already noted, I was born in 1939, on September 19th in San Diego, California. It was the same month and year that WW II started (aka the Second World War). The war officially began when Germany invaded Poland on September 1, 1939— 18 days prior to my birth. Welcome to planet Earth. Although the majority of countries worldwide were eventually dragged into the war, including the USA, hostilities never reached the American mainland. For that reason, American casualties were substantially lower than those of other major countries. Consider, for example, that the USA lost around 407,000 combatants while the USSR (within their 1939 borders) lost about 27 million, and more than half were civilians. The Germans, who started this dreadful loss of life, suffered between five and seven million dead. Overall, the Second World War resulted in 60 million to 85 million fatalities. At least 38 million of them were civilians (some estimates go much higher). A few examples of civilian mass murder would include the Holocaust, the firebombing of Dresden and Tokyo, and the use of atomic weapons on Nagasaki and Hiroshima. Although casualty figures may vary, the estimated number of dead makes World War II the deadliest conflict in human history.[19]

## American Soil

Fortunately, I was born on this side of the globe; that is, American soil.[20] I shudder to contemplate the fate of my counterparts who were born in the war-torn countries of England, Poland, Italy, Germany, Japan, Russia, and the Philippines, to name a few. During my childhood, the estimated number of children killed in the war overseas runs into the millions. These numbers seem so abstract. But they represent breathing little souls who never had a chance; some of them dying in the most grisly manner. Parental love and prayer was no match for the gas chambers of Auschwitz, indiscriminate bombings, random killings, and atomic bombs.

## Anchors Away

I was too young to take notice of the war until its ending in late 1945. It was then that I became cognizant of my mom's younger brother (my uncle Gene; born in Torreón, Mexico, July 27, 1914) who served in the Navy. He was aboard the destroyer *USS Smith* (DD-378).

---

[19]These statistics were taken from Wikipedia (2015).
[20]Technically, that makes me a first generation Mexican American since my mother had been born in Mexico, but with second generational advantages since my mother came to America as a child.

*The WWII Smith Destroyer (1940s)*

On October 26, 1942, the *Smith* had been attacked by a formation of 20 Japanese torpedo planes. Twenty minutes later, a Japanese kamikaze[21] crashed into the forward part of the ship causing a heavy explosion. The forward part of the ship was engulfed in a sheet of smoke and flame, and the bridge had to be abandoned. Fifty-seven sailors were killed, and 12 were wounded. In spite of the carnage, chaos, and loss of steering, *Smith* retained her position with all serviceable guns firing. *Smith's* gunners downed six Japanese planes. Appropriately, the *USS Smith* was awarded the Presidential Unit Citation for heroic fighting against the enemy.[22]

Of course, when the war ended on August 15, 1945, we were not privy to all these details. All I knew as a youngster was that the entire family was prayerfully thankful that my uncle

---

[21]The word kamikaze means "divine wind." These were Japanese pilots who loaded their planes with explosives and then made a suicidal dive on an enemy target.

[22]The information herein was taken from the U.S. Department of the Navy and Wikipedia sources.

Gene had survived the war and was headed home. Not until I was middle age did I actually talk to my uncle about his war experiences. Like most veterans who have seen action, he never encouraged the exchange. On one occasion his eyes grew misty as he recounted the visual horrors of body parts hanging by shreds of skin from jagged pieces of twisted steel, the result of successful kamikaze attacks that he witnessed on several occasions. I can look back with great pride knowing that my uncle Gene was part of what eventually came to be known in America as "The Greatest Generation."[23] To be sure, he wasn't the only Mexican American involved in this heroic struggle.

*My uncle Gene Arellano*
*with wife Margaret (1940s)*

My father, having three children and working in the aircraft industry, was exempt from the draft.[24] Trying to make ends meet, he also worked part time as a butcher in a poultry shop. Furthermore, during the war years, he served as an

---

[23]"The Greatest Generation" is a term coined by journalist Tom Brokaw to describe those heroic Americans who grew up during the Great Depression of the 1930s and then went on to endure the sacrifices of World War II (both on the battle field and on the home front).

[24]The draft was a compulsory requirement of all healthy young men for military service in the United States from 1948 until 1973. Men were drafted to fill vacancies in the armed forces that could not be filled through voluntary means.

air raid warden for the city of San Diego because Americans believed that the West Coast might be subject to Japanese air raids or even a land invasion. In hindsight, such prospects sound a bit farfetched, but at the time nobody knew for sure. The attack on Pearl Harbor had created an atmosphere of hysteria. In fact, the U.S. government prohibited any large public gatherings on the West Coast for the duration of the war. As a consequence, the 1942 Rose Bowl game originally scheduled to be played in Pasadena, California had to be moved to Durham, North Carolina. That was the first and only time that the Rose Bowl was played elsewhere. (Oregon State defeated Duke 20-16 at the stadium on the Duke University campus.)

Every time I think of a college bowl game, the World Series, or the Super Bowl, I'm always reminded of one of my pet peeves; super pop stars trying to outdo each other when they sing our national anthem. Why can't they sing it the way it was written? All we hear anymore is an abrasive evolution of vocal gymnastics. I'm starting to turn off the sound when the song is being sung. It's almost like fingernails on a blackboard. We need to form an American Society for the Prevention of Cruelty to the National Anthem (ASPCNA).

As a newborn, of course, I had no knowledge or concerns about the global violence erupting in most regions of the planet. My beginnings in life, barring any unforeseen catastrophes, looked quite promising. In retrospect, I can only pity my European and Asian counterparts. But life, even in the best of circumstances, is fraught with difficulty and danger. If you take a serious look at St. Jude Children's Hospital today, you'll get the gist of what I'm saying.

## The Wizard of Oz

Aside from the start of WWII and my coming-out party in 1939, that year was one of great significance (you may rightly argue the significance of my birth, but my parents didn't). Anyway, several other whoppers occurred that memorable year, and I'm not talking about Burger King (founded in 1953). The 1939 whoppers I speak of are *Gone with the Wind*, *The Wizard of Oz*, *Stagecoach*, *Mr. Smith Goes to Washington*, and many other films that made their smashing debuts in theaters across the nation.[25] More importantly, it was during that same year that Dr. Howard Florey, a future Nobel Laureate, and three colleagues at Oxford University were able to demonstrate penicillin's ability to kill infectious bacteria. That was a game changer! It was the beginning of antibiotics. It was called the "wonder drug." By 1942 it was being mass-produced. As a consequence, thousands of soldiers were spared the death sentence from bacterial battle wounds. Eventually, millions of people worldwide would owe their lives to this antibacterial revolution. This was a good war waged against an unseen enemy. In fact, antibiotic warfare has saved more lives than all the warring conflicts in human history combined. And yet, why is it that I've always known about Hitler, Clark Gable, Judy Garland, John Wayne, Jimmy Stewart and the Scarecrow, but I can't say the same about Dr. Howard Florey? Whatever the answer to that question, one thing is for certain: I would have been a

---

[25]If you don't know any of these movies, you have certainly not been assimilated into the American culture.

dead duck several times over had it not been for antibiotics (more on this later). So, as it turned out, here I am with a story to share (thanks in part to Florey and colleagues). By the way, do you know why anteaters never get sick? Because they're full of little anti-bodies! (Sorry, I just couldn't help myself.)

Before I lay out my life's journey, I need to clarify my cultural heritage and my nationality. Who or what am I? Obviously I'm an American citizen because I was born in America. My nationality, therefore, would be American. But what is my ethnic origin (ancestry)? My mother and her mother's family were indigenous (native) to Mexico. My father was born in Texas, but his father (Manuel II) was born in Mexico.[26] Therefore my ethnic roots are Mexican (and also European because the Bringas name hails from Spain). Whatever the mix, I'm not an Irish American, Italian American, or African American. I am the son of an immigrant Mexican mother and a first generation Mexican father with Spanish ancestry.

Technically, therefore, I am a first generational "Mexican American" because my sisters and I were the first generation to be born in America (on my mother's side). I use the word "technically" because although my mother was born in Mexico, and I was born in San Diego, California, you will remember that she came to the USA as an infant. One could argue, therefore, that in reality it was my mother who was a first generational Mexican American even though she wasn't born here, and that I would be more accurately described as a second generational Mexican American. Furthermore, my dad

---

[26]We believe his wife Maria was also of Mexican descent. However, she remains a bit of a mystery.

was a first generational Mexican American before I was since his dad—Manuel II—emigrated here from Mexico.

As a result, it seems that I'm caught somewhere between first and second generational status. I have no problem with this distinction. In fact, this differentiation may help to demonstrate the evolving process of assimilation that occurs from one generation to the next. Second generational benefits almost always supersede those of the first. I had far and away more advantages than my parents or my aunts and uncles. They were the ones that truly blazed their way into the USA. The road they paved for me made my assimilation almost effortless. Because of them, my Mexican roots have been so deeply planted and fully nourished in American soil that I have to mentally remind myself about my Mexican/Spanish heritage. Having said this, however, you must keep in mind that my early upbringing was Mexican oriented. This is due to my mother and her side of the family's influence (to be explained shortly).

Not unlike my mother and her siblings, neither my sisters nor I could speak a word of English when we first entered kindergarten. That's why today I'm somewhat bilingual. Although my first acquired language was Spanish, my mother tongue became English and I have no accent. Thank God they didn't have bilingual education when I was a child. There's no substitute for immersion (learning a language by the exclusive use of that language). There is no substitute for early exposure to a native vernacular. That's probably why my mom, aunts, and uncles had virtually no accents either. There's nothing wrong with having an accent. But an accent, or a language deficiency, may, in subtle ways, cause you problems within the cultural mainstream. I seriously doubt the outcome of my present path had I not "mastered" the English language. After all, "When in Rome, do as the Romans do." But let's face it—it's not simply doing as the Romans do when you're in Rome; it's equally important to speak as the Romans speak.

# Chapter 6

# MY CHILDHOOD YEARS
## MIS AÑOS DE INFANCIA

*San Diego, California*
1939—1945

DURING THE FIRST SIX years of my childhood I experienced several traumatic events that I will now share with you. We begin this journey by backtracking to the very first year of my life. Many incredible things happened to me that first year. Unfortunately, I can't remember any of them so let's move on.

Ditto for the second year. Bear with me.

Finally, a few things come into focus regarding the third year of my life. Some of these happenings I remember outright; others have required a bit of fill-in from my mom.

Aside from the unremembered slap on the butt when I was born, I sustained a memorable experience at the age of three. This was my first vivid memory (emphasis on the word "vivid"). This experience revolves around a metal bobby pin.[27] I was sitting on the floor with this little thin gadget when I

---

[27]Back in the day before we had plastic, the bobby pin was a small, metal, double-pronged hairpin that slid into a woman's hair to hold it in place.

spotted what I now know to have been an electric wall socket. (Some of you parents can guess what's coming next.) I've always been curious. So naturally, I made my way over to the wall and proceeded to shove this little double-pronged object into the wall socket. It was a perfect fit. Yeow!

I can clearly remember the shocking results (an obvious pun). I kid you not, that sucker blew me away, literally. The force generated by the marriage of those two items lifted me off the floor and threw me halfway across the room, not to mention the fact that my right arm suffered second-degree burns up to the elbow. Let me tell you in no uncertain terms, electricity really smarts. (I'm probably one of the reasons we have safety covers on these electrical outlets today.) My mother came running at the sound of my frenzied screams. Not knowing much about electricity (and very little about theology), the story in our family was that it was my guardian angel that tossed me away from the danger zone. I grew up thinking it so until I got older and started grappling with "cause and effect" issues. Unfortunately, this was the least of the traumatic experiences our family would suffer during my formative years. Many more momentous happenings would overtake us soon enough. Of course, World War II was raging on the other side of the planet, but I was much too young to know about it.

## Highway 101

Sometime between the age of three and four, my mom and dad gathered us kids up for a trip to go visit my grandmother (my mom's mom) who still lived in LA. In 1942, getting from San Diego to Los Angeles took some doing. It wasn't a straight two-hour shot on the Interstate 5 like it is today. Before the Interstate, one had to travel up the winding, scenic, coastal

Highway 101. This main route was a two-lane road that passed through quaint little towns that slowed vehicles down, and made the trip much longer, albeit more interesting. It was also somewhat hazardous because there was nothing but a double-striped white line separating two-way traffic between towns. No safety dividers like we have today. Those double white lines couldn't stop a chicken from crossing over. (That reminds me: do you know why the chicken only traveled halfway across the road? Answer: because she wanted to lay it on the line!) Sorry.

I'm not sure what kind of car we had but it was certainly pre-40s. That means we didn't have bucket seats, seat belts, air-bags, drink holders, car seats for us kiddies, and certainly not any of the electronic goodies we enjoy today. These toys and utility items were far off into the future. At least the windshield was laminated (safety glass), but not at all to the standards that went into effect after 1966. That 60s additional built-in safety glass was designed to withstand three times the impact velocity of the earlier windshields. Still, our old car didn't have *plain glass* as featured in the earliest automobiles. Can you imagine?

It was a blustery day as we sped along 101. The wind was horrific and it was pouring rain like crazy. The back and forth rhythmic wipers struggled to keep up with the unrelenting rain-drops that splattered against the windshield. My dad remained focused behind the wheel while my two older sisters romped around in the back seat. My mother sat quietly in the front, somewhat nervous about the blinding rain and the gusty wind that pressed against us like an ominous hand. In fact, due to the stormy weather, my mother had argued with my dad against taking this trip in the first place, but to no avail.

I was small enough to be standing between my mom and dad, and no one seemed worried about my precarious position (child abuse by today's standards). But I felt perfectly safe standing between the two people who loved me the most as we unsuspectingly rumbled along. That feeling of loving security was quickly dispelled when a drunk driver speeding along from the opposite direction, crossed the double line and hit us head-on. (Rumor has it that he was trying to avoid hitting a farmer's chicken that had wandered onto the highway.)

I do remember some of what happened on impact, but only vaguely. Most of what transpired has come from my mom. My sisters were unscathed but badly shaken. The rest of us were not so fortunate. My mother and I were hurled into the windshield like a fastball into a catcher's mitt. That I do remember. The glass shattered and we were cut to pieces. I would have been ejected completely through the windshield if my mother hadn't grabbed me at the last second and hung on for dear life. Nevertheless, I hit that glass like a battering ram. It swelled my head but it could have been a lot worse. My main injury was a severe laceration across the left side of my face. Blood was everywhere. My mom fared no better. Aside from the cuts she suffered, she sustained a broken hand and a few broken front teeth. My poor dad had been slammed against the steering wheel and suffered some broken ribs, along with some cuts from the fragmented glass. What a mess!

The situation got worse. Because of the blinding rain, several cars hit us from the rear. I have been told that a total of nine cars crashed into the pileup. They didn't hit us full bore or we'd all be dead. They were obviously trying to brake at the last moment on the wet pavement but couldn't avoid sliding into the pile. Some of what I'm relating here could have been embellished over the years. All I know is that numerous ambulances were on the scene to whisk our family and others to the hospital. Sirens galore; I do remember them.

As for the inebriated driver, he got the worst of it. Although he was not seriously injured by the collision—a common outcome for many drunk drivers—he made the mistake of getting out of his vehicle. Traffic had not yet come to a standstill, and cars were zooming every which way trying to avoid hitting us. As he staggered around, he was mowed down by another auto. If that didn't kill him, the next car that ran over him did. Aside from his gruesome demise, we all survived in good stead. I don't know what happened to the chicken.

A few years later I would need additional surgery to eliminate some of the scarring on my nose and cheek. Other than that, we were all pretty lucky (or "blessed," as my mother would always say). But being "blessed" in no way guarantees immunity from the slings and arrows that life throws your way. I'm not telling you anything you don't already know. Sooner or later we must all come to grips with this unpleasant reality. In our case, it was sooner than later. Not long after the car accident, our family suffered an unthinkable catastrophe. I will take the following account from one of my former publications.

**The Last Goodbye**
It was April 24, 1944. Our nation was embroiled in the bloody conflict of World War II. But it wasn't the war that ended the life of my father, Ernie Bringas. No, it wasn't the war; just the insane act of a killer gone mad in the otherwise peaceful city of San Diego, California.

That fateful day had started with my dad's unassuming routine of an "I'm off to work kiss" for my mom, and the wild goodbye squeals of a four-year-old boy and two older sisters who were now six and eight. The heartfelt grief that was yet to unfold that day would be borne primarily by my mother, although the consequences for all of us would be permanent. The final report of the *San Diego Tribune* would read:

> *. . . Ernie Bringas died early this morning from cerebral head trauma caused by multiple blows to the head by an unknown assailant . . . police have not found the murder weapon. A fellow employee found Mr. Bringas, the father of three children, lying in a puddle of blood trying to speak on the telephone . . . robbery is suspected as the main motive.*[28] [The killer was never apprehended.]

*The three surviving Bringas children (early 1940s) L-R; Martha, Virginia, and Ernie*

---

[28]Ernie Bringas, *JESUSGATE: A History of Concealment Unraveled.* Faber, Virginia: Rainbow Ridge Books, 2013, p. 54. (Original quote from the *San Diego Tribune.*)

I was only four when all this took place. In hindsight, of course, I can visualize how horrific this was for my poor mother who was now a widow left with three fatherless children to raise.

I hardly remember anything about the tragedy. I suppose I was kept out of the loop because of my age. I'm sure I have repressed the feelings that surrounded his sudden disappearance from my life. I was, after all, the apple of his eye, and I do remember being exceedingly loved by him. I must have mourned his absence on some level but I have no recollection of it. Only a smidgen of memory recalls my two older sisters and I sitting on my mother's bed while she tried to explain the horrid situation to us. Even so, I successfully buried any emotional response I might have had at the time.

It wasn't until 1993—49 years later—that an overdue epiphany caught up with me. It was triggered by country singer Doug Supernaw's 1993 version of "I Don't Call Him Daddy." The song blew me away. I found myself sobbing uncontrollably and I didn't know the why of it. The song is about a divorced father whose ex-wife has since married another man. His young son assures his father that he doesn't call his stepfather, "Daddy." As you can see, the song really didn't pertain to me, so I couldn't figure out why it was pulling this almost uncontrollable emotion out of me. On close analysis, I realized it was the line in the song about the boy giving a little wave goodbye to his father that jerked me back to a forgotten memory—a memory of waving goodbye to my daddy as he went off to work that fateful day. I would never see him again. It was our last goodbye.

## Schooling Begins

During the same year of my father's death (1944), I started kindergarten in September a few days short of my fifth birthday. I hardly spoke any English because my mom and dad spoke mainly Spanish at home even though they were English fluent. Anyway, my opening experience in kindergarten was dramatic. I well remember the incident. Here's what happened.

I'm sitting on the floor with all the other rug rats. We're all playing with various toys that are scattered about. Unfortunately, every kid in the room wants to play with the same gadgets that I do. I get really frustrated. My brain cells begin to percolate: How can I play with the toys I want for as long as I want? Make a plan! Our room had a self-contained bathroom. I figured that if I could slip into the bathroom just before our class let out at 3 PM, I could hide in one of the stalls until everyone left, and then I'd have the toys all to myself. This could work.

When it was almost three o'clock, I put my plan into motion. I entered the bathroom, slid into a stall and waited for the closing school bell to ring. It finally did. I knew the teacher would come in shortly to check the bathroom as a precaution. She always did. I also knew—because I had seen her do this before—that she would stoop down and look under the stall doors to ensure everyone was out. However, I had never seen her open the stall doors. So, I put the toilet seat down and climbed on top of it so my feet and legs would not be visible to her when she peeked under the stall door. Sure enough, she came in, checked under the stalls for kiddie legs, and saw none. She left. So far so good, my plan was working. I waited a few minutes until there was complete silence, and then I slowly emerged from my hiding place and walked out into a completely empty room. The door was closed and the blinds facing the courtyard had been shut tight. I was alone. I actually remember feeling quite satisfied with my cleverness. There were toys galore and I had a blast.

But all good things must come to an end. Besides, I knew my older sisters would be looking for me. Time to go. I reached for the door and discovered to my dismay that I couldn't get out.

Now, before I go further with this story, it's very important that younger readers understand what being locked up inside a building (or house) actually meant in 1944. It meant you couldn't exit the facility because the doors had keyholes that could only be opened or locked with a "skeleton" key. That is, once a door was locked, you could not open the door from the inside (or the outside) unless you had the key that locked it in the first place. How was I to know? Let's get back to my escapade of which I still have detailed memories.

Naturally, I panicked when I discovered I couldn't get out. My kindergarten brain was not able to rationally understand what I thought was a catastrophic predicament. My world was coming to an end. All I knew for sure was that I couldn't get out and I was never going to see my mother again. The tears started to flow, and flow, and flow. At least I was smart enough to open the blinds. It took but a few minutes for a crowd of kiddies to gather outside of the window, as they pointed their fingers in my direction with looks of bewilderment and curiosity. I pressed my tear-stained face flat against the window as if I might get closer to the outside world. By this time, I was sobbing uncontrollably. My older sister finally appeared with a look of disbelief and concern. I couldn't get out and no one could get in. She was yelling at me from the outside, but I was crying so hard that I couldn't understand her. Then she started to walk away and disappeared. I didn't know she was just looking for the janitor. I thought she had abandoned me. I went into a frenzy and started banging on the windows. Some of the kids got scared and backed away. Finally, my sister reappeared with the janitor in tow. He had the key. I was never so happy to get out of that place. When the janitor asked me how in the world I got into this mess, I simply told him the truth: I was in the bathroom when the teacher dismissed the class, and she locked the door behind her not knowing I was still there. It wasn't my fault.

## A Monumental Move

I didn't finish the school year because in early 1945 my mom moved us from San Diego to Los Angeles to be with her side of the family. This was big. We lived with my grandparents (Lupe & Francisco) and my aunt Mary—my mother's sister—in a duplex at 324 East 80th Street, a somewhat lower, middle class, "totally" white suburb. The house was small, well-worn, but sturdy and utilitarian. It was an old neighborhood with wood-framed houses, unique in their structure; the sterile tract housing of suburbia was yet to come. The cement sidewalks were cracked in places, but the area was clean and most of the houses were neatly attended. Our street was narrow, but we were only half a block away from San Pedro Street, a major north-south thoroughfare; bus lines, schools, theaters, grocery stores (no chain stores) and little shops were all within walking distance from our home. It was a welcoming neighborhood, and we came to know most of our neighbors up and down the block. This was the place where my most cherished childhood memories were shaped. I don't have any good photos of my grandparents, so this faded copy will have to do.

I couldn't know it at the time, but this move away from San Diego would create a huge separation from the Bringas side of the family. That's why this story revolves primarily around my mother's side of the family (Arellano). In fact, I wouldn't see my cousin Manny Bringas for another 68 years. On the one hand, that doesn't sound very positive. But on the other hand, I think the separation spurred my assimilation.

My grandparents Francisco & Lupe Arellano (1940s)

At the very beginning of this work I spoke about the importance of integration as a conduit for assimilation, and I will touch on this again in the Epilogue. I think that the most important part of my Americanization was the fact that both my grandparents, and subsequently my parents, didn't live within the Mexican barrio (a poor neighborhood populated by Spanish-speaking people). Of course, my mother and aunt were virtually Americanized already because they came across the border as children. Somewhere along the line they integrated into the mainstream. I give my family great credit for the courage to integrate accordingly. In the early years it certainly took them out of their comfort zone, but it was the best thing that could have happened to them and to the rest of us who came afterward. I think that is the foremost reason I've never thought of myself as anything other than an American, even though I've always been aware of my Mexican heritage.

My mother and grandparents were born in Mexico, but I never saw or heard anything about a piñata. That doesn't mean we were devoid of everything Mexican (as I'll explain shortly). But once we started school and mastered English, our dominant exposure was to Main Street America. Unfortunately, most immigrants, regardless of the country from which they come, migrate to their own cultural havens and are cloistered away from mainstream society. These native havens (barrios) slow the process of integration and, therefore, hinder the process of assimilation into the conventional culture.

As I stated earlier, my grandparents—who spoke no English—lived in white "middle-class" suburbia. My aunt and my mother knew English, but they always spoke in Spanish because of my grandparents. With the exception of my family, however, I was totally surrounded by non-Mexicans. At the beginning of my schooling, this did create some problems. For example, after moving from San Diego to live with my grandparents in LA, I still couldn't speak very much English. When I re-entered kindergarten at LA's South Park Grammar School in the spring of 1945, I did hit a speed bump. My one memorable moment from that K-class was a slap across the face from my teacher (just what I needed, another blow to the head). I don't remember anything about the incident except the slap (and her name, which I carry with me to this very day). In hindsight, I can only conclude—since I've never been a troublemaker—that she must have said something to me in English that I didn't understand, and she took my indifference as an act of defiance; ergo, the slap. The memory is very vivid but, strangely enough, I've never carried any conscious ill feelings about that experience (only her name). Fortunately, my older sister (Martha) was in the third grade, and after a long hard cry, they would take me to her classroom. She was the only one who could calm me down. I spent many a day in the third-grade classroom before I ever got to the third grade.

By the way, for some of you younger readers, it was permissible—back in the day—for a teacher to inflict corporeal punishment. Palms were slapped with wooden rulers (ouch), and butts were popular targets for the wooden paddle (Yeow!). Students in parochial schools were not exempt. Amazingly, corporeal punishment is still allowed in many areas of the U.S., especially in the South. In some parts of Europe, corporeal punishment is neither allowed in the home nor the school.

In the fall of 1945 I would be entering the first grade. Lest we forget, as I mentioned earlier, August of 1945 brought an end to the Second World War. Uncle Gene would be back from the Navy in time for Christmas. The names of all returning service men were read aloud on the radio. I remember the family buzzing around the house waiting for his name to be called out. Everyone cheered and hugged when his name finally filtered in . . . Eugene Arellano!

I also remember hearing radio reports about a strange, new bomb that had been dropped on a Japanese city, the name of which I couldn't pronounce at the time. Supposedly, this bomb was more powerful than all the bombs used during the war combined. For a few seconds I tried to envision the blast knocking over a few trees and some houses. Then I went outside to play, not realizing that approximately 135,000 people had died in Hiroshima and another 80,000 would die in Nagasaki. Nor did I realize that thousands more would die by 1950 from atomic bomb-related diseases or injuries, while I enjoyed the good life.

Chapter 7

# MY CHILDHOOD YEARS
## MIS AÑOS DE INFANCIA

*Continued—Continuado*
1946—1951

IN 1946 I WAS six years old going on seven. Following the tragic years of WW II came the magical years of that decade. The second half of the 1940s was truly amazing (at least from my perspective). This was an incredible time for many different reasons. It was a continuing increase of progress for our family during those years. The war was over. The fruits of science and industrialization were developing mechanical gadgets in machine-gun fashion for those who could afford them—and for those who couldn't, there were always the 5 & 10 cents stores. Not so incidentally, my mother became a naturalized U.S. citizen in 1946.[29]

Sundays I went to church, but on Saturdays I went to the Castle Theatre. The Castle Theatre, about one mile away from our home, was a real source of entertainment. More than that,

---

[29]Naturalization #6636977, United States District Court of Los Angeles, California, January 11, 1946.

it was one of my main conduits into Americana. We didn't have television. It was the silver screen that lit up my imagination. The actors I saw were bigger than life. Western heroes like Randolph Scott, Roy Rogers and Gene Autry, made my Saturdays, along with the war films that featured John Wayne. Additionally, I was really psyched by some of the rerun movies of the previous decade. The reruns included *Bambi*, *Robin Hood* (with Errol Flynn) and Judy Garland in *The Wizard of Oz*, and let's not forget, *King Kong!* We didn't have television so movies were the favorite pastime. Unlike today, we were treated to two motion pictures, a newsreel, a cartoon, and some incredible serial (such as *Rocket Man* or *Flash Gordon*). Every Saturday was Christmas. I couldn't wait. Best of all, we got it all for 20 cents.

For some American families, the transition into the middle class came slowly. In a rapidly changing world, the new and the old mingled throughout. Along with the shiny new automobiles coming down our block, there was also the "iceman" with his wagon pulled by an old, brown horse we used to pet whenever possible. I can still hear the clickety-clack echoes of the old horse's hoofs on the paved street. We kids would run behind the moving wagon grabbing chunks of ice to suck on. Twice a week the iceman delivered huge blocks of ice for those of us who couldn't afford refrigerators. My grandmother would buy this ice and store it in what was called a cooler—a small self- enclosed space just below floor level that kept our perishables fresh (provided enough ice was maintained).

The Good Humor ice cream vendor was another source of excitement. We kids could hear his familiar theme song a block away. All of the neighborhood kids scurried about seeking a dime to pay the piper. In the late afternoons and early evenings, all the neighborhood kids would be out running around playing Hide-And-Go-Seek ("Olly olly oxen free free free"). Of course, playing cowboys and Indians with my next-door neighbors, Jimmy and Johnny, was deliciously fun. When we were called in on account of darkness, I could sit for hours on the linoleum floor playing war games with my plastic soldiers. What a blast. These were the simple joys that filled my life.

Looking back, however, I can't be sure how all this played out for my mother. My dad had been murdered and our lives had been turned topsy-turvy. My mother bore the brunt of being without her husband, living in a new city, and having the full responsibility of raising three little ones (with the help of my grandmother; my grandfather died in 1948).

After taking typing lessons, my mom honed her typing skills to the max. Fortunately, she landed a decent job doing secretarial work at the Hall of Records in downtown Los Angeles. But it was long hours and she often worked overtime. She would board the bus early in the morning on San Pedro Street, about half a block away from our house, and not return until evening. Of course my grandmother was a great asset and watched over us when we returned from school.

Almost every evening, about 7:30 PM, we kids would bunch up around the front door as we peered out through the screen door into the darkness waiting for our mom to return. We could see the bus stopping at our cross streets of 80th and San Pedro, but we couldn't see who had gotten off. It was such a joy when she emerged from the shadows. My heart remembers.

Although my mom often worked overtime, money was scarce. I wouldn't say we were dirt poor—certainly not at all like what my mother had endured as a child. Importantly, I don't remember feeling poor. Sure, we didn't have a car, we never went on vacation, we never got an allowance, but we had each

*My mom Ruth (Arellano) Bringas (ca.1946)*

other and we never felt destitute (because we weren't). We never lacked the necessities of life, and every fall my mother would take us all shopping for the new clothes and shoes we would need for school. Whenever possible, she took us kids to the movies, bought special gifts and books; a set of the *Book of Knowledge* was a tremendous resource of education and entertainment. I must tell you that I always felt loved, wanted, and appreciated by my mom. Never once in my entire life did I ever feel unloved. Even after her death in 2009, her presence remains undiminished.

I would be amiss not to mention the tremendous assistance that the American Government gave us during those early years. The Social Security Act, signed by Franklin Delano Roosevelt in 1935, would inevitably impact our family following my father's death in 1944. Every month, three Social Security (SS) checks for us kids would arrive without fail. That assistance would go uninterrupted until each one of us turned 18 years of age. Having had first-hand experience with the life-saving programs of SS, I have never in my adult life complained about paying income tax. And I will always be grateful to the U.S. Congress for passing the life-changing Social Security Act in 1935.

I think I could write this entire book solely on my childhood days, but that wouldn't accomplish my overall goal.

Nevertheless, I will share a few other notable happenings. Some of these are serious, some humorous, and some of which influenced the trajectory of my thinking.

## The 1946 Fire

One fine day I was home alone with my older sister and grandmother. I was six years old. We were pulling weeds in the garden. As usual, my mother was away at work. Evidently I disobeyed my grandmother in some way that has long faded from memory. Anyway, as punishment, I was locked up in the house while my grandma and sister worked outside. Actually, I considered this so-called punishment to be a stroke of good luck. I still had my toys and an overactive imagination. That sure trumped pulling weeds.

So there I was at the tender age of six wandering around the house trying to figure out how to entertain myself. I had a thought. I knew where they were, I knew what they did—sort of—and I knew what they were called: Matches! But I was too little to reach these red-tipped sticks in the cabinet above. The rearrangement of a nearby chair took care of that problem. With matches galore I set out to explore.

I had seen my mother strike the coarse side of the matchbox to ignite the red tip of the stick, but I had no idea what these colorful beauties did except help light the pilot lights in the stove (which I had seen my mother do many times). What else could they do, I naively wondered? I set about to find out.

I made my way to the bathroom, lit one up, and dropped it in the toilet. All I got was a puff of black smoke and the familiar aroma that came when my mom blew these things out. My first experiment had been uneventful. Next, I found my mother's compact, opened it up, lit the match, put it inside the compact and quickly closed the lid. I scurried away for a moment but then cautiously returned to see what had happened. I carefully opened the lid only to discover a matchstick with a previously red tip turned black and a lingering smell that only a match can give. That second attempt was also a bust. Maybe these things only worked if one was lighting up the stove. I would give it one more try.

I was in my mother's bedroom looking around when I spotted a large cardboard closet standing in the corner. I peeked inside and discovered a large paper bag with some items therein (shoes?). Anyway, I thought this would be a good place to strike-up my final experiment. I obviously had no clue as to what I was doing. And if my experiment did succeed, I had no idea what that meant or what it would look like. Anyway, I scratched the tip of the match and tossed it into the paper bag that was leaning against the side of the closet. Do I need to tell you what happened next? That bag lit up like a Roman candle.

That's more like it, I thought to myself. I stood there mesmerized by the small flickering flame. At last, my experiment was off and running . . . and running . . . and running. I slowly backed away from the closet as the flames started to lick their way up the cardboard closet wall. It didn't take long for me to realize that something was amiss. I don't remember being frightened right off the bat, but the next 45 seconds got my attention. The entire closet was up in flames. I slowly backed out of the bedroom, my eyes fixated on the combustion spectacle that was unfolding before me. I was now becoming a bit concerned as the fire started to ignite surrounding objects. I clearly experienced an "uh-oh" moment. This experiment had succeeded but to what end? By the time I reached the kitchen, the farthest room from the bedroom, I could no longer see the flames. But as I glanced back, I could see the lighted reflections dancing their way into the living room. Instinctively, I knew it was time to vacate the premises. I reached for the doorknob, twisted it all the way to the left, and had a much more emphatic "UH-OH" moment. I had forgotten my lesson from kindergarten! I was trapped again! I couldn't get out without the key. (By the way, this kind of dangerous predicament couldn't happen today because the law now mandates that all doors must be "openable" from the inside. Thanks to me, we now have safety covers for electrical outlets and keyless "unlockable" doors from the inside.)

The thought of dying never entered my mind. I was just too young to realize how precarious my situation was. But I knew I was in trouble if nothing more than a spanking. Meanwhile, back in the garden, my grandmother and sister toiled away. Luckily, at the exact moment I was reaching for the doorknob, my grandmother was instructing my sister to go check up on me. That's what she did (reminiscent of Jimmy Jones's 1960 blockbuster song, "Good Timin'").[30]

When my sister opened the door and entered the kitchen, I still remember my exact words: "Ginny," I said in a serious tone. "There's a strange light coming from Mom's bedroom!"

My poor sister, who was only two years older than me, cautiously walked toward the flickering light emanating from the bedroom. She slowly half-peeked around the bedroom doorway. Within a split second her body jerked backwards as she turned around and started running towards me, screaming uncontrollably with a wild look in her eyes. She scared me

---

[30]"Good Timin'" was a number-one R&B single in the UK Singles Chart in 1960. In the U.S., it went to number three on The Billboard Hot 100 Chart.

half to death. Grabbing me by the hand, my sister urgently scrambled us out of the house while she continued to shriek at the top of her lungs. I knew now that I was in real trouble.

It wasn't long before fire trucks, neighbors, and passersby were on the scene. By this time the duplex was ablaze. Kids and grownups came running from all directions. There was lots of excitement all right. The neighbors on either side of us had their hoses full blast. The fire fighters did their job and we only lost half of the duplex, the side that my mother and we kids lived in. (Excuse the preposition.) Fortunately the structure had not burned down to the ground. I say fortunately because we didn't have anywhere else to go. We slept in that burned-out shell of a home until my uncles were able to rebuild it. Thank God we lived in LA where the climate is usually mild. I still remember looking up at the stars through the missing timbers of the roof as I tried to sleep. Oh yes, there was also that never-ending smell of burnt wood. That smelly memory still abides.

Of course, no kid in his right mind would ever confess to this kind of catastrophic mess. Who, me? Not Me!

I proclaimed my innocence throughout the entire ordeal in spite of the overwhelming evidence against me. They knew I was guilty. The fire department's arson squad pinpointed the exact flashpoint that clearly indicated the fire was no accident. Forget the fact that I was the only one in the house. But I knew little of such things at the age of six. So the claim of innocence made perfect sense to me and it continued to be my mantra. I was naively attached to that now popular cliché: "That's my story and I'm sticking to it." However, they were not about to let me off the hook. I suffered two devastating punishments.

First, I was taken down to the fire station where the fire chief scared the bejeebers out of me. He told me in no uncertain terms that if I ever lit another fire, I would be taken away from my mother and I would never see her again. It was a terrifying thought. That was the perfect threat that derailed any plans I might have had about future bonfires. Even so, my mom wasn't through with me yet.

*"Saint" Ernie Bringas (ca. 1945)*

My second punishment was altogether the most effective. For an entire week, except for the time I was at school or church, I was to sit in a chair and be excused only to go to the bathroom. Since my mother would be at work all day, she left strict orders with my grandmother to make it so, and she did. When I came home from school, I got the chair. Saturday was the toughest. I couldn't go out to play or do anything else but sit there for hours on end. Oh how I wanted to go outside and play with my friends. That was really, really tough. My sisters thought I got off easy. They had no idea. I'll tell you this: You'll never see another kid go to the bathroom as many times as I did that week.

### A Chick Named Fred

We had chickens, lots of chickens and a couple of roosters. This was probably a throwback to my grandma's childhood in

Mexico. But this was the USA, and having chickens running around in the middle of the LA suburbs was a bit uncommon. Nevertheless, these were the first pets my sisters and I ever had. We loved them as almost any child would. I remember Francis as a well-rounded red hen; Blondie was a slender, light colored hen; and Blackie, the rooster, was—you guessed it—black. These were just a few of the several chickens that clucked their way around our backyard (Blackie didn't cluck).

We didn't have to wait for Easter to go egg hunting. Actually, we didn't even have to hunt; our egg-laying hens made regular deliveries during the night while locked up safely in the chicken coop. During many a sunrise I was awakened by Blackie's, "cock-a-doodle-doo," his way of saying, "come get some fresh eggs." I still remember the feel of my small fingers carefully wrapped around those beautiful, beige-colored oval shells that on occasion were warm to the touch. I didn't mind Blackie's sunrise reveille during school days since I had to get up early anyway. But I could have done without those awakenings on weekends.

So what about Fred? Fred was a baby chicken that was given to me by my mom when I was seven years old. I don't remember where she got the chick; maybe Blackie had fooled around in the chicken coop (beyond my understanding at that time). I misnamed

*I'm lovin' a close friend (1947).*

my baby chick Fred because I was too young to realize that Fred was a female. All I knew for sure was that this newly hatched bird was my personal pet and my personal responsibility, and that's all I needed to know. She was this small bitty thing with fluffy yellow plume, and was obviously quite delicate. At first sight, I simply fell in love with this enchanting tiny ball of fur. What's not to love?

About a week after receiving Fred, my first test as a guardian came to pass. It was a blustery Saturday, and the weather had turned chilly. The day grew darker as black clouds slowly blotted out the azure skies of Southern California. I was sitting on the living room floor having a grand time playing with my plastic toy soldiers when I heard the pitter-patter of raindrops hitting the house. It was a light rain and I paid little attention. The house was comfortably warm, I was having fun, and school was a distant thought. I was in my happy zone. My mother's voice interrupted those pleasantries.

"Hijo," (son) she said, "¿dónde está Fred?" (Where is Fred?) "It's starting to rain and she needs to be in the hen house." (Note: My mother and other members of our family would often begin a statement in Spanish, and then finish it in English. That was one of the idiosyncrasies of being bilingual, although we kids never did that.)

"Okay, Mom, I'll take care of it." I got up and made my way to the kitchen window that overlooked our backyard. Sure enough, the rain was picking up. I got a glimpse of Fred moving toward our stand-alone garage that sat about 100 feet behind and to the right of our duplex with a long driveway that made its way to the street. She was obviously not in the hen house with all the other birds and would soon be drenched if I didn't hurry. I grabbed my coat and went out the back utility room. The rain was coming down steadily as I moved toward the garage, but Fred was nowhere in sight. Where did she go?

There are plenty of places for a baby chick to disappear, but I had a pretty good idea where she had gone. There was about a two-foot gap between the right exterior wall of our garage and our neighbor's fence. If she entered that narrow space, I could easily catch her because that two-foot gap, although it was 20 feet long, was nothing more than a cramped dirt path that dead-ended against our backyard fence; and there was no way out except for the way she had entered. Even an adult could easily walk in and get her. I made my way to the outside edge of the garage and peered down the narrow passageway. There she was at the other end of this one-way run. I called to her but she didn't come out. No problem, I thought to myself. I'll just go in and get her. It had to be quick because the rain was coming down harder and there was no covering to protect her.

There was nothing in this constricted pathway except for a very long, wooden ladder that laid flat, although it was some-what warped at both ends. It had probably bowed from past rainfalls, causing both ends of the ladder to be slightly elevated. As I stepped forward into this cramped area, my foot landed on the first rung of the ladder that was about three inches off the ground. The weight of my shoe pressed my end of the ladder flat to the ground. But in doing so, I inadvertently raised the other warped end of the ladder. At this tender age I was not yet familiar with Newton's Third Law of Motion: For every action, there is an equal and opposite reaction.

Anyway, Fred was frightened by the ladder's sudden movement and started to scurry around. As I took my foot off of the first rung, the other end of the ladder came crashing down. To my dismay, Fred had just maneuvered herself directly underneath it and, from where I stood, it looked like she had been struck. My heart sank as I came to realize what had just happened. Did I just kill Fred? I panicked at this possible calamity and started running toward her. In my uncontrolled effort to reach her, everything went from bad to worse because with every step I took, I unintentionally caused the other end of the ladder to spring back and forth like a jackhammer. In short, I was pounding my little friend into the ground. When I finally reached her, I scarce could bear the sight. Small tufts of yellow hair and numerous feathers that varied in size were strewn about, not to mention one flattened little chick, all clearly evident against a background of puddled water turning pink. It started to pour, but somehow that didn't matter anymore. I was utterly devastated. In a zombie-like state, I trudged back to the house as my tears mingled with the rain. Some things you never forget.

## Religion in the Home

I never experienced Catholicism. By the time I was born, my immediate family had become Protestant. I think that's because my mom's sister (Aunt Mary) got divorced, and the Catholic Church was not very accepting of what they considered to be a scandalous outcome. My mom, her older sister and parents had little choice but to bail out of the Catholic Church. All of my mom's other siblings remained Catholic. The Bringas side of the family also remained Catholic. By the time my mom married in 1935, she was Catholic in name only even though she was married in a Catholic church. I think that was the last time she visited a Catholic church. We kids never did. Following the death of my father when I was four, as already stated, we moved from San Diego to Los Angeles. Thereafter, we were Protestants (non-Catholic Christians).

To recap from a former publication, ". . . we lived with my grandmother on 80th street, an almost middle-class neighborhood at that time. During these early years, my mother made sure that we kids made it to church on Sunday mornings. It was a small, conservative, non-denominational church (not that I knew what all that meant). The half-a-mile walk from our house was much longer by short-legged standards, but it was doable. Spiffy is the word I'd use to describe how my mother put us together those long-ago Sundays. Our family was closer to poor than middle class but my mom always made the best of it. I can still visualize my sisters with their pretty flower print dresses, smart shoes, and colorful ribbons in their hair. As for me, a light blue "manly" suit surrounded my undersized frame. Off we'd go."[31]

I'll have more to say about religion shortly. Suffice it to say that my early experience was uplifting. Songs like "The B-I-B-L-E" and "Jesus Loves the Little Children" sounded from my lips with great gusto. My favorite song at Christmas time was "Away in a Manger." I have fond memories of sitting on my mother's lap and seeing the joyful expression on her face as I sang it. It was all so simple then, so beautiful.

Christianity became a central facet of my life. Its impact has been indelible. My religious experiences have been somewhat diverse, even from my earliest years. This last comment provides a perfect segue to a monumental incident that occurred when I was nine.

---

[31]Ernie Bringas, *JESUSGATE: A History of Concealment Unraveled*, Rainbow Ridge Books, 2013, pp. 54-55.

## Little Kathy Fiscus

It was a beautiful balmy day on Friday, April 8, 1949, in San Marino, California (near Los Angeles where we lived). Little three-year-old Kathy Fiscus, her nine-year-old sister Barbara and her cousin Gus were playing and running in a grassy field. Kathy's little legs were unable to keep up with the older two. Tragically, she fell into an abandoned well that was only 14 inches wide. What are the odds?

Noticing that Kathy had disappeared from the field of play, her sister and cousin doubled back toward the faint cries that seemed to come out of thin air. They found the well but could do nothing except run for help.

In a matter of hours the field was awash with trucks, bull-dozers, three giant cranes and 50 floodlights from the Hollywood studios. Inevitably, Kathy's plight made its way to the radio, the most popular means of communication in those days. The fledgling TV station, KTLA, was also on the scene. It was a watershed moment for TV broadcasting, the first TV news telecast of its day on location. The drama was visualized nationwide for the minority of Americans who had television sets. Those who didn't have access gathered in front of TV stores to watch the coverage. The ongoing tragedy via radio and television took the nation by storm. Almost everyone was riveted to whatever set was at their disposal. The site itself drew 10,000 people who stood vigil for the better part of three days as rescue workers tried frantically to reach Kathy.

Again, I was nine years old when this drama played out, and I had no doubt that Kathy would be rescued. My faith in God's power and kindness was unshakable. I prayed with the utmost confidence that she would be saved. How could it be otherwise?

Besides, it was obvious from the radio reports reaching my small ears that the entire nation was praying for her.

The long awaited news arrived when rescue workers finally reached her that Sunday evening. The announcement went out to the millions that were tuned in via radio and television as well as the 10,000 spectators who had prayerfully gathered at the rescue site. The entire nation held its collective breath as the verdict filtered through the airwaves: "Kathy Fiscus is dead and apparently has been dead since she was last heard speaking."

I was stunned. Even now, that unthinkable tragedy continues to reverberate in my psyche. How could God suffer it so?

Ironically, almost 40 years later, a similar story would unfold on October 14, 1987 in Midland, Texas. At the age of 18 months, little Jessica McClure Morales fell into an open eight-inch well. She, however, was rescued 58 hours later and lived to see another day. She is sometimes referred to as the "Miracle Baby."[32]

Although I didn't fully comprehend what the Kathy Fiscus event meant in terms of my worldview, it had reverberating repercussions. Let's see now: I nearly electrocuted myself when I was three, my nuclear family could have been wiped out in a crash on Highway 101, my dad had been murdered when I was four, WW II had resulted in millions and millions of lives lost, I nearly ruined the family by burning down the house when I was six, Fred was dead, and so was little three-year-old Kathy Fiscus. I was beginning to get the picture.

---

[32]NOTE: Aside from my personal memories, some of the rescue details about Kathy and Jessica were taken from Wikipedia. If you search the Internet, you will find extensive coverage, including video, newspaper articles, photographs, etc. Most interesting.

Even the fictional movies I saw as a youngster highlighted the dark side of planet Earth. Bambi's mother was shot and killed by hunters (I cried). Watching King Kong topple off the Empire State Building was no fun (I cried). Frankenstein fared no better as he was chased down and killed by townspeople wielding pitchforks (I cried). As we left the theatre my mom asked me why I was sobbing over Frankenstein. I tearfully replied, "He only wanted to be friends with someone."

## Additional Childhood Memories

### Rita Hayworth

Sometime between the ages of seven and ten, I discovered a 1941 *LIFE* magazine; it featured the movie star/dancer, Rita Hayworth. Madre mia! She knocked me out! I could hardly imagine such beauty. She was kneeling on a bed made up with satin sheets. Her silky nightgown was white, with black lace trimming the low-cut top.[33] I suspect that's almost too young for me to be attracted to the opposite sex, but something about her brought me to attention. I think that was the first time my heart took flight. She remains one of my favorites.

### Radio:

When I was growing up in the 1940s, very few families had television sets. They were just too expensive. As already noted, the radio was our staple for keeping up with the news. But it also provided a fantastic means for entertainment. It allowed one's imagination to soar. I was glued to such shows as *The*

---

[33]From Wikipedia: "In the summer of 1941, just a few months before Pearl Harbor was attacked, *LIFE* magazine ran a black-and-white photograph of an up-and-coming movie actress named Rita Hayworth . . . . " She died from Alzheimer's disease at the age of 68 in 1987.

*Lone Ranger, Inner Sanctum Mysteries, The Shadow, Captain Midnight, Let's Pretend,* and a host of others. It was exhilarating!

I also fell in love with a radio show called *Your Hit Parade* (aka *The Hit Parade*).[34] "Like most kids, I'd sing along with *The Hit Parade's* top hits. It didn't take long to recognize that I had at least a smattering of musical ability. I could sing along with the best of them and add harmonies to boot. My favorite singer was Frankie Laine, even though I didn't sound anything like him. But I liked his songs. I found myself singing, "Mule Train," "Jezebel," and "That Lucky Old Sun." Laine had 36 hits that included title songs for western movies such as *High Noon* ("Do Not Forsake Me, Oh My Darlin'"), *Gunfight at the O.K. Corral, 3:10 To Yuma,* TV's *Rawhide* and, much later, Mel Brooks's *Blazing Saddles,* to name a few.

Since we didn't have a TV, I was glued to the radio. My insatiable appetite for music was spurred on when my mom brought home a new RCA record player (about the size of a car battery). It was revolutionary in that it could play the new 45 rpm records.

As a kid, I always ended up singing the latest songs from *The Hit Parade* in school. My teachers and classmates seemed to enjoy my singing. It was fun and it gave me plenty of practice getting up in front of the class. This continued on through junior high and high school. I was also very active in my church choir and I would often be asked to sing a solo. All of this helped in building my self-esteem.

---

[34] From Wikipedia: "*Your Hit Parade* is an American radio and television music program that was broadcast from 1935 to 1955 on radio, and seen from 1950 to 1959 on television. It was sponsored by American Tobacco's Lucky Strike cigarettes . . . Many listeners and viewers casually referred to the show with the incorrect title *The Hit Parade*."

Eventually, I came to envision myself as a recording star, just like Frankie Laine. I held that dream through my high school years and beyond. I remember watching Dick Clark's *American Bandstand* and thinking to myself: Someday I'm going to be on that TV show; someday I'll be a recording star; someday I'll be on the charts. I knew, of course, any kid with half a voice—and some without—would imagine the same brass ring. Few would be able to grab it. That was not about to deter me. This ongoing dream of stardom would remain front and center. Sometimes ignorance is bliss.[35]

Here is something I could never have predicted or envisioned in my childhood imagination about Frankie Laine. For me this was totally mind-boggling. About 13 years later, at Columbia Records, in 1963, our paths would cross. What are the odds? Walt Disney was right: "It's a small world after all."[36] (I'll have more on this later.)

*Television*

I was nine years old when the very first television landed on our block. The TV resided with Mr. and Mrs. Hansen about five doors down from our home. They opened their doors to us neighborhood kids every weekday evening around 5 PM. What a wonderful gesture. A bunch of us would gather around their 12-inch Packard Bell as we watched a 15-minute puppet show called *Time for Beany.* It originally aired locally in Los Angeles starting in 1949. My favorite character was Cecil the Seasick Sea Serpent who claimed to be 300 years old and over

---

[35]Some of this "radio section" was excerpted from my previous publication, *JESUSGATE: A History of Concealment Unraveled*, Rainbow Ridge Books, 2013, p. 151.
[36]Ibid, p. 152.

35 feet tall. What a hoot. When the villain, Dishonest John, kidnapped Beany, Cecil would always come to the rescue. I can still hear Beany screaming at the top of his lungs: "Help, Cecil, help!" Cecil would reply: "I'm a-comin', Beany-boy!"

According to some sources, even Albert Einstein was a faithful fan. Evidently he interrupted a conference by announcing, "You will have to excuse me, gentlemen. It's *Time for Beany*."[37]

During this time I became very close friends with a new kid on the block who moved in right across the street from us. Tommy Williams and his family had a television. Together, Tommy and I watched what eventually became my favorite TV program, *Space Patrol. Space Patrol* was a science fiction adventure story that started in early 1950 on a local LA TV station. Every evening, we were captivated by the 30th-century adventures of Buzz Corry, Commander-in-Chief of the Space Patrol. The program proved to be very popular and soon became a national broadcast event. I can't prove "cause and effect" here, but I think *Space Patrol* was pivotal in helping me think outside of the box.

Owning our own TV was still a few years off. I was 13 when we secured our first set, an American-made 21-inch (1952-53) Packard Bell. Peering into the set from the backside revealed numerous vacuum tubes. I became very adept at changing out these tubes when they failed. The nearby Safeway market had these tubes for sale. However, not forgetting my shocking experience as a child, I never got into the electrical box. By the way, the *Lone Ranger* on TV never lived up to my radio childhood imaginings.

---

[37]Stan Freberg, *It Only Hurts When I Laugh*, Times Books, 1988.

## Cars and Vacations

Truth is, we had neither. No one in our immediate family (that included my aunt and grandparents) owned an auto. Every one of us got around on the bus, or we walked. My uncles had autos but were seldom available, especially for fun outings. I remember traveling twice by train to see family once in San Diego and once in El Paso. Other than that, I don't remember going anywhere. When I was 13, my aunt Mary bought the family's first car; it was a new 1952 Chevrolet (I think it cost around $1500). That was a milestone (along with the TV that my mom bought around that same time). Still, I never really went on vacation until I was in my twenties.

Having said this, however, I must confess that I look back on my childhood as one of the great adventures of my life. It was a fun time. I don't remember missing out on anything or being deprived in some way. In fact, it was quite the opposite. It's not that I grew up without problems. Deep in my mind's eye is the memory of a bully I had to confront while walking to school almost every morning. Accordingly, I had to face many of the same problems that most kids face in their early years, including self-esteem issues. Angst is a part of everyone's journey. But I suspect that my mom's unconditional love disallowed any intrusion of negative vibes from the outside world to dominate. As I mentioned earlier, I have always felt her sustaining, unwavering love throughout my life. What a woman. She was savvy, had a great sense of humor, was generous to a fault, and had a great love of animals.

## Optometry, Fishing, and Sausages

Dr. Wyman was our family optometrist. He had an office smack dab in the middle of downtown Los Angeles in one of those multistoried buildings. It seemed like we all needed eye care at some point. I guess Dr. Wyman knew that my dad had been killed and that I was not privy to outdoor adventures. He made kind overtures by asking my mother if he could take me deep-sea fishing. She agreed. At the age of eight, I took my first outing with him.

Knowing what we know in today's world, one would never allow an 8-year-old child to spend time alone with an almost complete stranger. But this was 1948 and the world appeared quite different (although in many respects it probably wasn't). In any case, his motivation was probably split between my good-looking mother, and an honest interest in showing me a good time. I really can't say. I can only be glad that his intentions turned out to be honorable. We had a good time fishing off the California coast, a pastime I would now consider repugnant and immoral.[38] Thereafter he took me fishing once a year until the age of 12 when I had the sausage fiasco. Here's the gist of it.

On one particular fishing trip, we stopped for a hearty breakfast that included eggs and sausages. I loaded up on the sausages. Big mistake.

The pilot boat ferried us to this huge barge floating five miles off the coast and then departed. Its return pickup time was 3 PM. We were there for the duration no matter what. We weren't out on the ocean but a short time before my face turned green. I was seasick. I was Kermit the frog before there was a Kermit. That's a tortuous experience I'll never forget. Anyone who has ever been seasick knows exactly what I'm

---

[38]See: Ernie Bringas, *CREATED EQUAL: A Case for the Animal-Human Connection*, Hampton Roads Publishing, 2003.

talking about. I found myself hanging over the side of the barge throwing up sausages and everything else I had ever eaten since birth, or so it seemed. I was trapped and it was miserable. Since that day I have never been back on the ocean nor have I eaten any sausages. Even the smell of them makes me nauseous. By the way, that's not the reason I eventually became a vegetarian. That story can be found in one of my other writings (see footnote on page 72).

### *The 4th Grade Donut Caper*

Aside from the minor detail of having burned down our house, I was generally a well-behaved kid. However, just like almost any other youngster, I had my moments. The following is one such moment.

Our school district didn't have school buses. So, the mile walk to school every morning was never given a second thought. I usually walked with my two older sisters but it didn't always work out that way. On one particular morning I was alone, walking to school via one of the alleyways. Most alleyways are narrow dirt passageways between homes, and almost every house in my neighborhood had a backyard that buttressed up against an alleyway. You could get into the alley through the gate in your back fence. The alleyway I traversed that morning on my way to school was not your usual alley that ran between two backyards on either side. One side of this alley was aligned with the usual array of backyards and fences, but the other side was aligned with commercial buildings without back fences, resting on a busy thoroughfare called San Pedro. One such business was the Helm's Bakery building. Since the alley ran along the back of the building, I could see that their bakery trucks were being stocked for delivery. It was about 7:30 AM.

As I approached, I couldn't help but catch the pastries' aroma that wafted through the air that morning. Delicious! I stood by silently in the shadows and watched as the men loaded their trucks with various trays of fresh-baked goodies.[39] I started timing the in-and-out cycle; that is, how long were the men gone from their trucks when they entered the bakery and then came back to their trucks with another tray of sweets. Not having a watch, I figured that the trucks were left unattended for about 20 to 30 seconds. Time enough, I thought, to grab me a snack or two from the back of one of those trucks. When the coast was clear, I made my move. When I reached the truck, I saw some empty paper bags and numerous flat trays filled with a wide assortment of scrumptious looking donuts. I instantaneously decided that a snack or two was not worthy of the risk I was taking. So, I quickly grabbed a paper bag, filled it with about thirty donuts, and made a hasty retreat down the alley. It was a clean getaway.

I was very proud of my clever maneuver. However, I soon realized that I was now stuck with 30 donuts that I couldn't possibly eat before I reached the school, and there wasn't any place to hide them until after school. I was stymied. I might as well have taken—stolen—only two donuts because now it looked like I would just have to trash 28 donuts. What a waste.

Then it dawned on me: I would take this bag of donuts to my fourth-grade teacher as a gift from me to the entire class. Everyone would get a donut and I would be a hero. I can't remember the excuse I gave her for having all these donuts, but it must have

---

[39]Although Helms baked products were never sold in stores, they were well known by millions of LA consumers. Every weekday morning, dozens of Helms trucks would leave the bakery for various parts of Los Angeles. According to Wikipedia, the Helms motto was "Daily at Your Door."

been a good one because every kid in the class got one. I was king for a day. Still, that evening, I had second thoughts. I knew my mother would have been disappointed if she knew about my shenanigans. I could not tolerate the thought. That was my first and last caper. Even as a youngster, the last thing I would ever want to do is to hurt my mother in any way whatsoever. Of course, I'm not saying I was perfect. After all, I did burn the house down! But honestly, I'm glad to say that those missteps would not be repeated.

My mom was also a great disciplinarian. Kids at my grammar school were using two words that I added to my expanding vocabulary. I can't remember the circumstances surrounding my miscue, but one day I foolishly—although I didn't know I was being foolish—told my mother to "shut up." She quickly moved in on me and without hesitation slapped me across the face. That's when I realized I had crossed the line.

"Don't you ever talk to me that way again," she stated firmly.

The force of her hand was measured, but my surprise wasn't. I was startled to the max. That teachable moment was a lesson well learned. I never again uttered those words to anyone, much less to my mother.

### Christmas Memories

When I was in my single digit years, all I wanted for Christmas was two major gifts, and they had nothing to do with "my two front teeth" (a Christmas song that never made any sense to me). More than anything, I kept asking Santa for a bicycle and an electric train. I would have settled for either one but I got neither. They were just too expensive and I was not the only child in the family. No matter, Christmas time and the holidays that followed were the most exciting times ever. School was out and numerous presents were scattered under a nicely decorated tree. Ah, the wonderful aroma of those Christmas trees is an ever-present memory when Christmas rolls around. Whoever came up with the synthetic Christmas tree was a real killjoy. (Yes, I understand the other side of the argument.)

The excitement of shaking and jiggling unopened packages was a predictable yearly occurrence. I think that's a universal kid thing. The only presents I disliked were those containing clothes. Yuck. That was a real bummer.

On Christmas Eve there was a hustle and bustle throughout the house as an old Mexican tradition took place. My grand-mother, mother and aunt, would set about making buñuelos. They made hundreds of them because aside from us, many of them would be given to other family members. All of my three uncles would come over on Christmas day and make off with a bunch of them. So what are buñuelos?

Imagine, if you will, a round, doughy pastry, not quite as thin as a sheet of typing paper, and a little larger than a Frisbee. It was made from white flour; it was big, round, flat, very thin, with added spices such as canella (cinnamon). They didn't look like cookies, and they didn't taste like cookies, because they weren't cookies. But they sure were good. They came in two flavors: salt and sugar. Making them was no easy task (my sisters would pitch in when they could). I stayed out of the way. I loved eating those things but I didn't see much fun in making them. It was a horrendous effort by all the women folk. Before these buñuelos were fried, they had to be laid out. Remember, these buñuelos were big and required lots of room. Thus, white bed sheets were draped over every piece of furniture in sight. The house was overflowing with white sheets covered with giant white "tortillas." We always had a white Christmas, but it was on the inside of the house.

I never got to bed early on Christmas Eve because the beds had been commandeered to serve as tables for the buñuelos. Every room in the house was used except for the closets and bathroom. What a sight! You should have seen it.

Eventually each buñuelo had to be carefully lifted from its appointed spot and deep-fried in oil. It was a long process, but the end result was worth the exhausting effort (easy for me to say). Each buñuelo ended up as a giant brittle disk. They were easily breakable and had to be handled with care and stacked appropriately. The closest comparison I can offer is for one to imagine hundreds of rounded potato chips—chips that are flat, bigger than Frisbees, and a little crispier than potato chips. Keeping these monster chips from disintegrating when you ate them, or stacked them, was an art. By the way, I favored the sugar buñuelos but it was a close call. The taste was so unique that I have no American example for comparison. I miss this Mexican tradition; I haven't had a buñuelo in decades.

New Year's Eve was another time for Mexican escapades. This time the women folk prepared delicious tamales made from corn meal. Again, the house was turned topsy-turvy, but well worth it. The tamales were delicious. I've never tasted better than those that came from my grandmother's recipe.

### No Allowance

As you might imagine, money was scarce in our family. We kids never got an allowance. We didn't even know what that meant. Thus, I was always looking for a way to make a little dinero (money). At the age of nine I was selling *The Grit*, a weekly newspaper that I could sell in my neighborhood. When I was 11, I was shining shoes on the corners of San Pedro and Manchester in LA (this effort was inspired by the 1950 hit song, *Chatta-nooga Shoe Shine Boy*). At the age of 13, I was hired by my local church to do janitorial work. A few years later (ages 14-16), while still working at the church, I also maintained two paper routes (morning and evening deliveries), made deliveries for the Fuller Brush Man, and also delivered spirits for Murray's Liquor store. I think those liquor store deliveries were illegal because I was underage, but Murray trusted me, and he was evidently willing to take a chance (I realize now I must have made a good impression on him). Obviously, I was no stranger to work as a youngster. But these were all part-time efforts. My first full-time job came after high school. (I have now gotten ahead of my story so let's go back a tad.)

### The Korean War

The Korean War started in June of 1950 and ended in July of 1953. It was all-out war between Communist North Korea and South Korea. Although there was a world effort to help the South after the Communist North invaded, 88% of all ground troops sent to Korea were American. I monitored this war very closely for two reasons.

First, I was only 10 years old when the war broke out and very naively fascinated by it. After all, for most boys that age, playing at war (or cowboys & Indians) was a great pastime. My imagination was captivated by the newly developed jet fighters such as the F-80 Shooting Star, and the F-84 Thunderjet. Then came the F-86 Sabre jet. It was the first swept-wing jet fighter that could counter the Soviet MIG-15 in high-speed dogfights over North Korea. How could a young boy's mind not be pulled in by the adventure of it all, especially after seeing all those John Wayne movies of WWII?

Second, I was prompted by my grandmother (Lupe) to give her a daily blow-by-blow account of the war. She couldn't read English so I would carefully go over the evening newspaper with her. She was actually following the career of General Douglas MacArthur who had long enjoyed iconic status with the American people. In 1942 he was appointed Supreme Commander of Allied Forces in the Southwest Pacific theatre. In 1944 he was promoted to the new five-star rank of General of the Army. And now, he was in command of all military forces fighting in Korea. My grandmother, like most Americans, idolized the man. Reminiscent of her great respect for Pancho Villa.

Unfortunately, there was a falling out between President Harry S. Truman and General MacArthur and, to put it bluntly, Truman fired MacArthur in 1951 for insubordination. Evidently, MacArthur had made public statements about the war that President Truman had instructed him not to make. As Commander-in-Chief, President Truman relieved him of his command. MacArthur was so popular that most people rebuked Truman, including my grandmother who was truly angry with the president. In retrospect, however, most people agree that President Truman made a correct and courageous call. The military must always remain amenable to civilian authority. That is one of our nation's greatest strengths.

## White Flight

In this day and age I think it's very hard for young people to fully grasp the pervasive, racial discrimination that persisted through the 1940s, '50s, and 60s, even in California. I don't remember anyone in our family using the "N" word in conversation, but we kids did naively chant a children's counting rhyme called *Eeny, Meeny, Miny Moe* that did contain that racial slur. The song was used to choose a person to be "it" for games such as tag. Here's the way we chanted: *Eeny meeny, miny, moe, catch a "N" by the toe. If he hollers make him pay, fifty dollars every day.* Throughout my childhood, my sisters and friends repeated this chant with childhood innocence, without any sense of impropriety. We couldn't know that we were being brainwashed through the cultural conditioning of societal bias. Today, that racial slur has been removed. The words now go: *Eeny, meeny, miny, moe, catch a tiger by the toe. If he hollers let him go. Eeny, meeny, miny, moe.* Even so, knowing what I know now, the song makes me uncomfortable upon hearing it.

However that plays out in your mind, the point is, we had virtually no contact with the people we called Negroes in those days. I neither saw them in the neighborhood nor in the grammar school I attended. Any views I had about these folks came through secondhand sources. For example, when blacks appeared in the movies that I saw, they were usually portrayed in the most unflattering ways. I also remember having a book in hand called *The Story of Little Black Sambo*. Some versions of this story pictured blacks in stereotypical fashion (that's the version I had). Eventually the word "sambo" was seen as a racial slur. Modern versions of the work have corrected that discrimination. The older renditions have gone the way of the buffalo, along with more than over a thousand U.S. restaurants called "Sambo's" (a popular restaurant chain of the 1960s and '70s).

My main source of understanding about African Americans came, of course, from my family. I never heard any direct negatives about them from my mom or grandparents, but the underlying tone in their conversations always conveyed a subtle sense of uneasy apprehension and lack of respect. This understated nuance exploded into full-blown anxiety when we got word that a Negro family had moved into the area a few blocks from us. As word of this "calamity" spread throughout our community, it seems that everyone started running for the hills. My family was no exception. I was at the beginning of the sixth grade and my whole world was about to collapse. People started looking for a way out—out of the neighborhood! This is what came to be known as "white flight!"

White flight was no accident. It was cleverly orchestrated and brought about by real estate agents seeking to make a quick buck. If they could get a flood of houses on the market at the same time, property values would drop precipitously. Agents could snatch up the houses at their lowest selling point and resell them later at a nice profit. Their tactic for creating white flight was known as "blockbusting." It was based on fear.

The idea behind blockbusting was to provoke panic in an all-white neighborhood by selling a house to a black family. Of course, there was an unwritten code among whites that they would never betray their neighbors by selling to a black family. But getting around that obstacle proved to be quite easy for real estate agents. They simply supplied black shills with an abundance of cash, thereby allowing them to make an overpriced offering on a house; that is, they made the white family an offer they couldn't refuse. Once that first home was sold, all hell broke loose. Locals panicked! White fright led to white flight. Everyone scrambled to get out of the neighborhood before property values dropped. Heaven forbid that black neighbors flank you on both sides. You had to sell as early as possible, and the only buyers were black because no white person in their right mind would buy a house in a neighborhood turning black. The turnover could happen within a matter of months.

I was smack dab in the middle of the sixth grade when we scrambled away from 80th Street in LA and moved to another all-white suburb in the city of Inglewood (a city adjacent to LA, about ten miles south of Hollywood). There were other youngsters in the area that would eventually take advantage of Hollywood's proximity (as I would do a few years thereafter). The yet-to-be Beach Boys lived a few miles south of us. Sonny and Cher, also living in the area, would eventually team up. In fact, both Sonny and I attended Inglewood High School although not simultaneously (and he never graduated).[40] Aside from his musical success, Sonny would go on to serve in the United States House of Representatives. Not bad for a high school dropout and someone born in Detroit to *Italian immigrants.*

The move to Inglewood at the age of 11 felt like a move to an enchanted kingdom. Was this the city of Inglewood or the Emerald City? It felt like the Emerald City because the difference was ever so graphic from our previous setting. When I arrived at 217 E. Fairview Blvd., the experience was reminiscent of the opening scenes from the *Wizard of Oz* when Dorothy stepped out of her black & white house into the colorful world of Munchkin Land. To begin with, this "new" home was made of stucco, not wood. Compared to the house on 80th street, it looked like a palace. The neighborhood was definitely an upgrade from every perspective, and we now lived on a boulevard instead of a narrow street. This precluded any street

---

[40]We did not attend Inglewood High simultaneously because he was four years older.

football, but other benefits were obvious. It was definitely a move into the upper middle class.

The world I left behind was gone forever and nothing would ever be the same again. Even the new grammar school (Centinela) I now attended (entered January 22, 1951) was demonstratively different. They were light years ahead of any socializing I was accustomed to. When they played "spin the bottle" (a game I had never heard of until then), they kissed each other like the starlets I had seen on the silver screen, and the social pecking order in that school was well defined. Clarence was the top dog (strongest kid), and Ann (prettiest of all) was his lady in waiting. Aside from Rita Hayworth and my third-grade teacher, Ann was the first girl I ever had a crush on, but getting past Clarence was not about to happen. However, at Ann's birthday party I did manage to steal a kiss while playing spin the bottle. It was my first landing on cloud nine. Everyone laughed when I kissed her on the cheek. I just couldn't kiss her on the lips for the same reason that the skeleton couldn't cross the road; neither one of us had the guts.

Chapter 8

# JR. AND SR. HIGH SCHOOL YEARS

JR. Y SR. AÑOS DE ESCUELA SECUNDARIA

*Inglewood, California*
1951 - 1957

**Junior High Days**

I was almost 13 entering junior high school (seventh grade) in September of 1951. Aside from the normal apprehension one has from hearing all the horror stories relating to how we would be treated on arrival by upper classmates, my transition was smooth enough.

My two years at the junior high level were relatively uneventful. Having said that, however, I do recall three standout memories. My first eventful memory revolves around a stolen bicycle. Not to worry, this is not a donut caper with wheels.

As a child, I had always wanted a bike. But my mom's budget wouldn't allow. Fortunately, when we moved to Inglewood, the police department had a program that recycled unclaimed stolen bikes back into the community. In other words, they provided these unclaimed stolen bicycles to less fortunate families at no cost. We got one. It was a beauty, with all the bells and whistles. It looked almost new. Hot diggity.

The very next day I'm proudly off to school with my "new" bicycle. I locked my bike at the bike rack and went to class. I waited impatiently for the close of the school day so I could hop on that two-wheeler and make my getaway. It was a disheartening moment when I returned to find it missing. Great! My stolen bike had been stolen! I felt terrible. I spotted a custodian nearby and quickly informed him that my bicycle had been swiped. He looked at me a bit oddly and then asked me to follow him. I tailed along behind him until we reached the principal's office. The principal wasted no time telling me that one of the students had recognized my bike as the bike that had been stolen from him several months earlier. The expression on his face told me that he thought I was a thief! I tried to explain but they weren't about to take my word. Shortly thereafter, two juvenile officers arrived. That's about as close as I ever came to being arrested ("Book 'em, Danno!").

The irony of this story is that I distinctly remember asking the officer who first gave me the bike, what would happen if someone recognized it once it was in my possession. His response: "Not to worry. We've been doing this for 20 years and that hasn't happened yet."

My second most fascinating junior high memory revolves around sex education; those classes were downright disappointing. We were hoping to get a glimpse of the real thing. But what we got, appeared to be nothing more than a side-view drawing of the reproductive tract. The drawings were totally confusing and were obviously meant to conceal anything real about female anatomy. Without a head-on shot, we couldn't begin to decipher the mystery. Never having seen the real thing, how in the world did they think we could make heads or tails out of half a woman? We weren't even sure it was a woman. We already knew about the birds and the bees; what we needed (or wanted) were some graphic visuals. (Explicit R and X-rated movies and accessible porno magazines were far off into the future, as was the Internet.)

Of course, none of us would admit we didn't know squat about female anatomy. All we could do is pretend that we did, by singing the "I know it all" song, sung to the tune of, 'I'm Looking over a Four Leaf Clover."

> I'm looking under a two-legged wonder
> That I overlooked before
> First come the ankles and then come the knees
> Then comes the … oops that surprises even me
> No use denying this act I'm trying
> It's way-ay beyond degree
> I'm looking under a two-legged wonder
> That even surprises me.

Anyway, the sex education class discussions, and especially the genital depictions, were a real letdown. I don't know about the junior high girls, but we guys were bonobos in heat.[41] Funny how it is: We guys come from the vagina and spend the rest of our lives trying to get back to it. For example, if you give a man a Rorschach inkblot test, he'll usually find a vagina in there somewhere (I kid you not).

My third standout memory is about the junior high dances. They were atrocious. We know that girls mature faster than boys. Guys don't mature until they're about forty-five.

---

[41]A bonobo is an African ape that is popularly known for its high levels of sexual appetite.

As for the girls, when they reach junior high, that's when they really start developing their weapons. They start looking like real women. The boys still look like the scarecrow from the *Wizard of Oz* but only half as tall. We guys were all hot to trot, but most of us didn't look strong enough to pull the wagon. It didn't help my self-image being almost one year younger than my classmates. I was so thin that when I turned sideways and stuck out my tongue, I looked like a zipper.

Maybe kids grow up faster today, but back then, getting us to dance with the opposite sex was like trying to get two porcupines to back into each other. And who was the idiot that put us all in the gymnasium? The expansive floor stretched before us like a virtual minefield. It's hard enough asking a girl to dance that's twice your size, without having to cross no man's land to reach her.

Finally, when the dance is almost over, one musters up enough nerve to take the perilous trek across the great divide. You get halfway there, and you realize that all the girls are scurrying around or hiding behind each other. That's not a good sign. The gym is semi-dark. You're like an errant torpedo trying to hit a moving target. Where'd she go? Now what? There she is! Good grief, why are all these girls so tall?

At last, the moment arrives and then she says "no." That's just great! Now what? You either must hightail it back to the other side with your head hung low, or avoid that embarrassment by exercising the domino approach—you move down the line asking every girl to dance until one of them accepts. There was always at least one girl with enough sympathy to throw you a lifeline. (Thanks to that one, wherever you are.)

## Senior High Days

I started the ninth grade at Inglewood High in September of 1953. I was 13 but would turn 14 later that month.

Unfortunately, the girl drought didn't change for us regular Joes who were not blessed with excessive good looks or athletic brawn. Those who were fortunate enough to have one or both of these qualities were bound for glory days. A good-looking athlete was choice. You know the type: Varsity football and basketball players, wrestlers, and water polo jocks. They stuck out like redwood trees in a lemon grove. Many of us guys were not yet filled out, and the girls continued to bloom at the speed of light.

Fortunately, I was not totally bereft of some saving graces. Although I lacked body mass and my nose was too big, I had a winsome personality and a fair amount of intelligence. But when it came to dating, that didn't seem to cut any ice with the girls. It did, however, allow me to prosper in this angst environment. I did okay and most everyone liked me. Besides, I had an escape hatch that proved to be much more fulfilling than school. It was the church.

It was during my early teenage years that my sisters and I attended the Grace Evangelical United Brethren Church (try and tell that to your teenage buddies). It, too, was conservative, at least in our region (it was part of the Evangelical United Brethren denomination). During these formative years I made a formal declaration to accept Jesus as my lord and savior and to understand the basis of Christian faith. I would never trade the nurturing warmth of this experience although, in retrospect, I must admit to its less enlightened side; there were no alternatives to a Bible incapable of error and a one-way plan of salvation.

Beyond the local church, I reveled in the Billy Graham crusades and the newly released cinema spectacles of *The Robe, Demetrius and the Gladiators, The Ten Commandments* and *Ben Hur*. It was great theatre. These epics played well against my simplistic understanding of Christianity. It all made perfect sense: Jesus, salvation, miracles, and an unquestionable Bible. In time, my educational pursuits would temper that perspective with a much more sobering and rational analysis. But I'm getting ahead of myself.

As I journeyed through my freshman and sophomore years of high school, a new brand of music was beginning to make the scene through mainstream radio channels. It came to be known as rock & roll. My generation was on the ground floor of a musical revolution that gave the world a real jolt. Using '50s slang I'll put it this way: It was a gas! My teenage brain was totally blown. I went ape over singers like the Del Vikings, Little Richard, Chuck Berry, Bobby Darin, Fats Domino, and many others. They were so groovy! Elvis was okay, but these other cats were the most; that is, really bad! If you couldn't dig rock & roll, you were a drag. You certainly weren't hep, daddy-o.

For the most part, I really enjoyed my first three years at Inglewood High. As I stated earlier, most everyone seemed to like me, and there were no problems outside the usual self-esteem bumps we all endured. But in my senior year—my fourth year—my life experience became extremely turbulent, primarily for two reasons. Both were self-inflicted.

First, at the beginning of my senior year I went out for the varsity football team. Although I lacked the bulk, I loved football and had these delusions of someday playing tailback for USC (a university only half an hour's drive from my home). I should have started this venture in my freshmen year, but a newly discovered heart murmur disallowed that initiative. Finally, in my senior year, at the weight of 148 lbs—which included pads, cleats, a helmet, and a stomach full of food— I finally made my way onto the gridiron (albeit without any experience). In a blink of an eye, I was demoted to the junior varsity with the other scarecrows, and rightly so. However, I considered this to be a positive move. Scarecrow facing scarecrow didn't seem so bad. What I didn't realize was that the varsity would scrimmage against the junior varsity. That didn't help matters at all. They used us like tackling dummies. Actually, I did quite well on offense, but playing defense was my Achilles heel.

The only varsity guy that left an imprint on my memory banks—as well as my body—was a bruising 6'6" 235 lb. left end named Lori Belger. (I'm not sure those figures are exactly right; all I know for sure is that he towered over me and was a lot heavier than I was.) When I was playing cornerback and they threw him the ball, I wanted to stop playing and start praying. When he got behind me, as he usually did, I was like a dog chasing a train; that is, what do you do when you catch up with the caboose? Worse yet, when he caught the ball in front of me and then turned up field, he never bothered to go around me. He had my number all right. That train was barreling full speed ahead and this time I was in front of it. To mix metaphors, I was no match for this Godzilla-like creature.

The comedy act started when we collided; a shoe or helmet would generally fly off in one direction or another, and guess whose airborne items those belonged to. My tackling skills were zilch. If I brought him down, it was only by accident. Most of the time he simply tripped over me. This was not fun, but everyone watching this sequence of events thought it was great sport. (I give myself credit for finishing out the season.)

My second twelfth-grade memory is much more searing and turbulent. Julie was not from my school—she went to Dorsey High—but we were very close friends because we attended the same church. At some point, I fell head over heels in "love" with her. Kaboom! It was my first time falling out of the tree house (must have been a redwood).

This fall from normal brain function led to unimaginable bewilderment, not to mention the pain of it all. These discomforts were the result of non-reciprocal responses to my many romantic overtures. Although we were close friends, she wanted nothing further. How could she not return my affection? What's not to love?

*My high school senior year (1956–57)*

Anyway, this first go around, with what I considered to be true love, slowly dissolved into a complete fiasco. Alfred Lord Tennyson, one of Britain's most popular 19th century poets once wrote: "Tis better to have loved and lost than never to have loved at all." Yeah, right! In hindsight I can certainly buy into that lofty line. However, during that adolescent misadventure, nothing could have sounded more absurd.

I was so enamored with Julie and so troubled by her lack of interest that I royally messed up my senior year. I did manage to show up for football practice, but everything else was sacrificed on the altar of love.

I had been an almost straight-A student throughout my first three years, and now I was only making Cs and Ds. I forfeited a possible scholarship to USC. I actually got expelled from school for one week for having eight consecutive days of unexcused absences. I was at school all right, but it was the wrong one; I was at Dorsey, not Inglewood. I just wanted to be near her and maybe be lucky enough to give her a ride home after school. Of course, I was doing all the wrong things trying to impress her; no girl really wants a lapdog for a boyfriend. Now and then she did afford me a mercy date. But hey, a mercy date is worse than no date for the same reason that a wax banana is worse than no banana.

Anyway, it was during the latter part of my senior year that my unrequited love went from bad to worse. Like an idiot, I brought one of my best high school chums, Gunner, to one of our church parties and, as luck would have it, the girl of my dreams and my best friend gravitated toward each other like two dogs in heat. My heart was broken, and my dream of her ever being my girlfriend was shattered. Ironically, Elvis Presley recorded a song in January of that same year (1957) called "That's When Your Heartaches Begin." I always identified with that song because it reflected my situation almost perfectly; that was the end of my girlfriend, that was the end of my friend, and that's when my heartaches began.

I continued to labor with a broken heart as Gunner and Julie continued to float on top of cloud nine. She drove me to drinking. I wasn't very good at it either (one Tequila, two Tequila, three Tequila . . . floor). Alcohol became one of my defense mechanisms. Intoxicating drink doesn't get rid of your problems, but it does diminish their size.[42] In the long run, of course, trying to drown your sorrows is only a fool's solution. Fortunately, that escape route was quickly abandoned.

Gunner was so smitten by Julie that he had already dropped out of school before graduation. She wasn't what you would call a beauty, but there was something about her that drove us both nuts. At least he got to go steady with her.

In spite of my discombobulated senior year, I actually managed to graduate from Inglewood at the age of 17, in June of 1957 (thanks to my Chemistry teacher, Mr. Eliason, who, out of the kindness of his heart, gave me a D instead of an F). Ironically, Julie did go with me to my Graduation Dance; it was a mercy date, sure enough. This story isn't over yet, but we need to take a slight detour for the moment.

---

[42]Paraphrased from the 1958 film, *Some Came Running* (with Frank Sinatra and Shirley MacLaine).

Chapter 9

# POST GRADUATION DAYS
## POSTGRADO DÍAS

(1957 – 1958)

## An Alternative Quest

To keep several overlapping events in perspective, I need to clarify some points. Julie was not the only quest on my radar screen at that time. I was simultaneously involved with another endeavor. Backtracking to my childhood fantasy, I was hoping to land a recording contract with a Hollywood studio. I made plans.

After my graduation in 1957 I decided to take some guitar lessons. Learning to play might help jumpstart my singing career. I searched the Yellow Pages (remember them?) and found a music store that offered the service. I would take my guitar lessons from a man called Ray Pohlman. He was a friendly, soft-spoken man with lots of talent. Neither Ray nor I knew it at the time, but he was destined to be one of the most highly sought out rock & roll bass guitar players in Hollywood.[43]

---

[43]The late Ray Pohlman is considered to be the first studio player to actively use the new electric bass on records. By the early 1960s, Pohlman was the dominant electric bassist in L.A., playing on hundreds of recording sessions, including those for Herb Albert, Jan & Dean, the Beach Boys, and most of Phil Spector's early work. (Redacted from: albumlinernotes.com)

As for me, my attempt at learning the guitar was a bust. I didn't have the patience and I had trouble fingering the frets. Within weeks, I was done (stick a fork in it). However, I did mention to Ray about my singing aspirations. As stated earlier, I had wanted to be a recording star since the first day I fell head first out of my crib. (Evidently the floor wasn't carpeted.)

Ray suggested, as a first step, to make a demo recording (a temporary demonstration record of my voice called a "dub") that I could submit to the recording companies for evaluation. This would require some musicians and a recording studio. He offered to arrange and personally supervise the session.

"How much is this going to cost me?" I politely asked.

"Oh, about $100," he answered, as if I had deep pockets. That was a lot of money in 1957. His response was discouraging. That kind of dough was out of reach because I was still up to my eyeballs in car payments. He was quick to understand.

"We can do it for less," he calmly offered. "Instead of using a whole band, we'll get along with just my guitar supporting your vocal."

"How much will that cost?" I asked, a little more hopeful.

"I charge $20 an hour, and the studio time will be $10 an hour. If we cut the track at Gold Star," he continued, " the whole thing will cost you about 30 bucks, and you can't do better than Gold Star.

When Ray said I couldn't do better than Gold Star, I thought he was talking about a second-rate joint that could give me a cheap price (as if the studio were the equivalent of Monopoly's St. Charles Place). That assumption was totally misplaced. On the contrary, Gold Star was Hollywood's premier recording studio. It was located on Santa Monica Blvd., just off of Vine Street. Despite its unimpressive exterior, its modest interior, and its dilapidated bathrooms, it was the most sought-after independent studio in Hollywood (Monopoly's Park Place property.) Its reputation was unmatched, not only in regard to its custom-made recording equipment (for example, its one-of-a-kind echo chambers) but also for the genius of its recording engineers.

From its inception in 1950 through its closing in 1984, more than 100 Top 40 hits of *various genres* were recorded at this Hollywood facility. The musical spectrum was widespread and well represented. Consider this partial list of notables that recorded at Gold Star: Ritchie Valens, Eddie Cochran, The Chipmunks, The Cascades, "Route 66" composer Bobby Troup, Phil Spector, Brian Wilson (Beach Boys), Sonny & Cher, The Rose Garden, Zane Ashton (aka Bill Aken), Buffalo Springfield, Duane Eddy, Jimi Hendrix, Neil Young, The Ronettes, Dick Dale, The Righteous Brothers, Iron Butterfly, Herb Alpert & The Tijuana Brass, Jan and Dean, Joan Jett, Cherie Currie, Meat Loaf, The Champs, The Baja Marimba Band, Bobby Darin, The Cake, The Who, The Monkees, Tommy Boyce, The Band, The Go-Go's, The Ramones, The Association, Art Garfunkel, Leonard Cohen, Bob Dylan, John Lennon, Tina Turner, Maurice Gibb , to name a few.[44] Enough said.

My big day finally arrived. The session was scheduled at 11:00 AM on a summer day in June of 1957. I was 17 years old and headed for Gold Star Recording Studios. My old Plymouth wasn't that old, but it had worn-out brakes, a leaking radiator, and a sputtering motor. It was about a thirty-minute

---

[44] Notable names were taken from Wikipedia. Google *Gold Star Studios* for a plethora of information or (see: www.goldstarrecordingstudios.com).

drive from Inglewood to Hollywood in a normal car. I left an hour early to allow for the wind.

Having arrived with time to spare, I drove around the movie city until 10:45, and then made my way to Gold Star. Upon entering I was greeted with a businesslike smile from a pert, brunette secretary seated behind the counter. "What can we do for you this morning?" she politely asked.

"My name is Ernie Bringas. I believe Ray Pohlman booked some recording time for us this morning."

"Oh yes," she nodded affirmatively. You'll be in studio A with Stan Ross."

"No," I answered quickly. "I'm supposed to be with Ray Pohlman."

For a moment she was expressionless and then she recouped. "Oh, yes, you will be with Ray Pohlman," she said reassuringly. "But Stan Ross is your engineer." She didn't call me an idiot but that's how I felt. "Just go to the end of the hall," she continued, "make a left and they'll be waiting for you in Studio A."

Shrugging off my miscue, I sauntered down the hall, made the left turn and . . . bingo! Ray was waiting for me. We chatted for a few moments and then he introduced me to the engineer, Stan Ross. I couldn't know it at the time, but both Ray and Stan would become lifelong friends with me. I also didn't realize that Stan Ross was Gold Star's premier engineer. A few words about him are warranted.

It's hard to describe someone who's bigger than life. I suspect that Stan Ross could have been one of those unique Hollywood character actors. He was so animated with the zest of life, aided by a deep voice that gave you the confidence to follow his direction. He reminded me of General Patton as played by the actor George C. Scott, but with a jovial personality. A commanding presence nonetheless. When he stood behind that recording panel, the studio became an ocean liner, and he was the captain at the helm.

In 2011, Stan Ross died at the age of 82. The following excerpt comes from the *Los Angeles Times* article written by Valerie J. Nelson (March 17, 2011).

> "Many of the more than 100 Top 40 hits recorded at Gold Star benefited from Ross' creative inventiveness . . . . The recordings were as diverse as Ritchie Valens' La Bamba,' the Champs' 'Tequila,' Eddie Cochran's 'Summertime Blues,' Iron Butterfly's 'In-a-Gadda-Da-Vida,' Sonny and Cher's 'I Got You Babe' and the Beach Boys' classic 1966 album 'Pet Sounds.' Ross contributed the 'saw' sound on the band's 'Good Vibrations,' said Lisa Sheridan, a screenwriter who worked with Ross.
>
> While Buffalo Springfield was recording the 1967 hit single 'For What It's Worth,' Ross said 'you gotta do this one thing to the drum' and mixed in the sound 'of a guitar pick goin' through a broom, on the straw,' band member Neil Young recalled in the 2007 book 'Tearing Down the Wall of Sound.'
>
> Young considered Ross one of the 'geniuses of the music business,' according to the book."

*(The above sidebar does little justice to Stan's prolific studio work and the impact he had on the music business. The Internet is replete with more information.)*

99

This morning it was just Stan, Ray, and me in the studio. The studio was divided into two rooms unequal in size and separated by a nearly soundproof glass panel. The larger section could hold a full-size band, and more if needed. The smaller room was the actual control room that housed the engineer and recording console. The console had more levers, switches, knobs, and other mechanisms that were overwhelming to the uneducated eye, and neither one of my eyes were educated.

There was plenty of room for pacing and I took advantage. While Ray tuned his guitar, Stan set up the microphones and some other gadgets unfamiliar to me. After a few minutes everything was in place. Stan made his exit into the control room, closing the door behind him. Through the glass I could see him manipulating the many dials and levers on the console. He removed a new roll of tape from a sturdy brown box and lined the tape up with a receiving reel on the Ampex machine. The Ampex tape was huge relative to anything I'd seen before. (Totally outdated in today's digital world.) Stan appeared to be singing but I couldn't hear a thing. Ray was sitting down ready to go. I kept looking back and forth at the two of them as I nervously paced to and fro.

Suddenly, Stan's voice came booming out from a nondescript loudspeaker in the corner of the room. "Ok, Ernie, what are you gonna do first?"

I jumped!

The Wizard of Oz was real, and so I did pay attention to the man behind the curtain (albeit a glass one). Ray and I had worked out a Buddy Holly[45] tune called "That'll Be the Day." I

---

[45]Buddy Holly (1936-1959) was an American songwriter/singer and a pioneer in rock & roll music. Although his year and a half career was brief—died in plane crash—he had a big influence on the rock genre.

looked over to Stan who awaited my response: "We'll start with 'That'll Be the Day'" I said with contrived confidence.

"What?" Stan answered. "What was that? Ernie, speak directly into the mike. I can't hear you otherwise."

I drew close to the mike and repeated the name of the song. "Okay," Stan shot back as his gaze remained on the board. Then suddenly it dawned on me: this was it! With a fair amount of trepidation I turned to Ray and anxiously said: "Start me off, Ray. I'm all set." This was my first time ever singing into a studio microphone.

Without hesitation, Ray strummed his guitar. His music filled the studio. I faced the microphone squarely, timed the beat, and came in on the right note. I sang as though my life depended on it, making every effort to avoid mistakes. We sailed through the first number without a hitch. As far as I could tell, we had aced it.

As I started to congratulate myself, I was brought to attention by Stan's booming baritone voice as it came blasting out of the speaker. "Okay, let's take it again," he said with an air of anticipation.

What? I thought to myself. There was no way I could sing that song any better than I did, I continued to muse. "What's wrong?" I asked anxiously.

Sensing my discomfort, Stan quickly replied: "You were fine, Ernie. But I wasn't recording you . . . I was just trying to get a good balance between you and the guitar. I think I have it now. Let's go through it again. Oh, and Ernie, this time before you begin, I'll cue you in with, that'll be the day, take one."

Just great, I thought to myself. He hadn't recorded it.

Staring at Stan behind the glass panel, I waited transfixed in front of the mike. Then I heard his cue: "that'll be the day, take one." Once again, Ray took off in good fashion but I flubbed my entrance. Everything stopped cold. In a heartbeat and without any notice, Stan restated the cue: "that'll be the day, take two." Ray took off and this time I followed suit without incident.

Waiting for the playback felt like forever although it only took Stan a few seconds to rewind the tape. I was curious as to how I would sound. You just don't know what your voice sounds like until you hear a recording of yourself, especially on professional equipment. Suddenly, Stan's speaker voice blasted across the room "that'll be the day, take two." The sound of Ray's guitar flooded the studio once again, and with a déjà vu sensation, I heard my voice coming in right on cue. I stared at the floor, not knowing whether to be embarrassed or elated.

Ray was the first to speak. ""Hey, that's not bad, Ernie."

"Thanks," I sheepishly replied.

Stan came out of the control room with some added support. "Sounds good," he said. He didn't get any argument from me. I was greatly relieved by their responses. They weren't jumping up and down with excitement, but I measured their comments as sincere. It was a modest beginning and I was satisfied. The rest of the session was equally satisfying. I ended up with three Buddy Holly songs that showcased my voice.

Driving home from Hollywood that afternoon I felt sky-high and couldn't help eyeballing the swanky homes along prestigious Rossmore Boulevard. It was a beautiful day, flooded with sunlight and birdies that sang in the trees shading the limousines sitting in the driveways of luxurious Rossmore mansions. Tomorrow, I would visit the recording companies and lay it on them . . . a brand new singing sensation.

The next morning I was back to Hollywood in search of a recording contract. No need to bother with the smaller studios. I was after the giants. RCA, Capitol, and Columbia beckoned me like the Sirens in Homer's epic poem, *The Odyssey*. But unlike Ulysses who was tied to the mast, I willingly ran wild, sprinkling my dubs (demos) all over Tinsel Town like a modern day Johnny Appleseed (I love mixing metaphors). I'd simply walk into the studio, tell the receptionist my story, and hand her the dub with my name, address, and phone number. She assured me that someone would give it a listen and would contact me shortly. Mission accomplished. I headed home, kicked back, and waited for the offers to roll in.

Two weeks passed before I received my first response; it felt more like two months. It was a letter from Capitol Records. Long before, I had already decided to await hearing from all the companies before deciding which offer I should accept. That was only logical and made good business sense. So here it was at last, my first offer. This was it! I was so excited I almost tore the envelope in two.

When I read the first sentence, my heart sank. What? You won't believe this, but Capitol Records didn't want me. It was a rejection notice (a form letter to boot). I was bummed out. It was so depressing I kissed my dog and went to bed. However, I'm not one who is easily deterred. I quickly recovered. I surmised that the other companies had not yet responded because they were seriously considering my talented offering. But over the course of the next few weeks, rejection notices dribbled in until no possible hope remained. It was the death of a thousand cuts. That alternative quest was over! (Back to Julie and Gunner.)

## The Saga of 1957 Continued

During the summer after my graduation, the whirlwind romance between Gunner and Julie came to an abrupt end. She had never been interested in me outside of friendship and now, she was no longer interested in Gunner. He was so upset he joined the Marines. After going through boot camp he came back in his colorful uniform in hopes of winning her back. It's an old story and sometimes it works; not this time. Game over! At that point he became emotionally unglued and went AWOL. Worse yet, he got it into his head that I was somehow responsible for their breakup (remember that Graduation Dance?). His emotional agony led him to the conclusion that I had created the rift in their relationship. That's when he came looking for me. What happened next was played out on the most primitive level of animal behavior. I can only be thankful that in those days, guns were not the way disputes—real or imagined—were settled.

On a Sunday evening, following one of our church youth meetings, I stepped out into the parking lot and was approached by two Marines. One of them was my high school buddy, Gunner. Unbeknownst to me at the time, he was no longer my friend but my adversary. He was there for payback. Of course, he didn't realize that payback was unwarranted because I had nothing to do with his unresolved breakup with Julie, and she still wasn't interested in me. Nevertheless, his convoluted logic had deteriorated into a vortex of imaginings, and he had to blame someone other than himself. I became the scapegoat of his mental aberrations.

As we were talking, I was visually distracted and turned away momentarily as I watched a vehicle pull into the parking lot. As I turned back toward the two Marines, my so-called friend sucker-punched me. POW! He caught me totally flat-footed. I never saw the punch coming and, therefore, had no chance to back away from the blow. It was that quick, and his aim was true. I would learn later that he had a rock tightly clenched in his fist in order to create a greater wallop. A punch of that nature has been known to kill.

I didn't realize it at the time, but he broke my nose in four places and shattered the cartilage. He didn't floor me, but the blow spun me into a one-eighty, and my nose was pouring blood as if someone had turned on a faucet. Whirling back around to defend myself (or should I say staggering back around), I was greatly relieved to see the two Marines hightailing it out of the area. Any defense on my part would have been an exercise in futility and probably very dangerous since I was already bleeding in waterfall mode. What a mess. And that was just the beginning of the ordeal. The trip to the Daniel Freeman Memorial Hospital was uneventful, but the *four* surgeries that followed over the next few years, were not.

In those days very few patients had private rooms, unless they had big bucks. I was in a regular room with four other patients. The guy to my right was a hoot and we struck up a friendship of sorts. I was still 17 and he must have been around 50 years of age (hard to ascertain). We had a couple of days to get acquainted because the doc couldn't operate on my nose until the swelling went down. It was actually a fun time sparring with this guy. He told me about the sodium pentothal they would administer intravenously (IV), and the happy pill that preceded it to help calm any anxiety I might have. The pill worked. That was my first experience with drugs and they really kicked me into a state of euphoria. I was giggling and acting funny. It wasn't hard to understand why so many people were hooked on illegal drugs as a means for escape.

This first surgery turned out to be the most serious of the four. I was out cold when they brought me back from surgery. After a few minutes, my buddy next to me became alarmed when I started convulsing, gagging, and spitting up blood. He quickly pressed his call button and simultaneously started yelling. A nurse came running in and quickly realized that I was in serious distress. In fact, I was hemorrhaging and choking on my own blood. He told me that the incident had created quite a commotion as doctors and nurses came running from all directions. I was in serious trouble, and they were hard pressed to get the bleeding stopped. Obviously they did. The moral of this story is: If you have to go through something like this, it's best you not know about it. I would endure three more surgeries to "fully" correct the damage. In hindsight, I can see three very positive outcomes—believe it or not—from Gunner's calamitous punch.

First, it didn't kill me (that's always good). Back then we didn't settle our differences with guns; gunplay didn't even enter our minds. Second, I ended up with a much better looking nose than my previous honker. Honest! Thinking back on the nose I previously had, I've come to consider that punch a blessing. Third, I also ended up with a real girlfriend; not the one I had wanted, but the one I came to want.

My unrequited passion for Julie reminds me of a song by country singer, Garth Brooks. The lyrics tell of a guy who has passionately flipped out over his ideal girlfriend. He pleads with God to make it so. He'll never ask God for anything else again if He'll just grant this one wish. But it doesn't happen. Years later he runs into his old dream girl and comes away thinking: "Thank God for unanswered prayer."

This in turn reminds me of Oscar Wilde who said: "There are two tragedies in life: one is not getting what one wants, and the other is getting it." (Ok, let's get back to the new girl in town. Here's how that unfolded.)

## My First Girlfriend

A few months before that one-sided altercation with Gunner, a new missy named Karen, from Ohio, had moved into the neighborhood and started attending my church. She was about a year younger than I was. I was still 17 going on 18; she was 16 going on 17 (there's a song in there somewhere). For whatever reason, she took a strong liking to me. I still had my old nose but that didn't seem to discourage her any (that's when I realized miracles were still possible). But as luck would have it, I didn't feel the chemistry. Julie remained ever present in my psyche. It's almost always about triangles, isn't it? Rats. Nevertheless, I decided to ask Karen out since I wasn't getting anywhere with Julie. What could possibly go wrong? Yeah, right!

I asked a friend of mine who was going steady with his girl if we could double date. He agreed and we decided to take the two girls to Disneyland. Disneyland—in Anaheim—had opened in 1955 and was only about an hour away from Inglewood (by freeway). The four of us piled into my late 1940s Plymouth that I had previously purchased for three hundred dollars when I got my driver's license at the age of 16. The money came from my janitorial work at the church. The pay was $75 a month and, in the 1950s, that was hefty dough for a kid.

Anyway, this was the first time out of the gate with Karen, and I was not at all sure about the outcome. Karen was anything but shy, and she had no reservations about telegraphing her intentions. In those days our cars didn't have bucket seats or dividing consoles to slow down any unwanted advances. Of course, in most cases, the advance was from left to right, not right to left. But if the girl wanted to move across, she could. This one wanted to. I tried to be cool, but as our one-hour drive to Disneyland progressed, she became more and more demonstrative. I remember being thankful for the limited security provided by the steering wheel. But in the end it proved to be as helpful as an ice cream cone in a microwave.

I know what the guys are thinking as they read all this: "Is he crazy? I'd kill for that kind of a problem!"

Ordinarily, so would I. In my case, such happenings are as rare as a hairy-nosed wombat. But for whatever reason, I just wasn't interested. It was a long night at Disneyland, but there were enough attractions to keep us occupied.

In spite of her unwanted attention, the drive back from Disneyland provided some psychological relief since I knew the evening was coming to an end. But my optimism was short-lived. When we pulled up to her parents' home I discovered, much to my chagrin, she was not about to fade off into the night gracefully. Karen had other plans. My buddy and his girlfriend took her prearranged cue and proceeded to excuse themselves for a so-called quick stroll around the block. Karen and I were left alone in the car. It was entrapment, pure and simple.

I politely hinted that it was late and I needed to be on my way. She understood. But first, she boldly requested a goodnight kiss (this girl was ahead of her time). Feeling pressured, I simply told her "no." After all, I wanted to be the "chaser," not the "chasee" (actually, there's no such word as "chasee"). I told her it was up to me as to whether I would kiss her. That's when I discovered her stubborn streak. We argued hopelessly. It was time to walk her to the door. I started to turn so as to exit the car. At that moment she shamelessly threw her arms around me in a crushing bear hug. There I was, pinned against my car door!

I didn't have much wiggle room, and I couldn't get enough leverage to break her grip. Karen was incredibly strong (or maybe I was incredibly weak). I struggled as best I could. That's when I smashed my right knee into the steering column—"ouch!" ("Ouch" is not exactly the word I used.) The battle raged on. The old Plymouth was rocking back and forth as I spotted my supposed buddy and his girlfriend walking by. I signaled in desperation. They looked at me and smiled, then quickly moved away. I would learn later that they mistook our jostling around for something else.

On the promise that she would release me, I finally puckered up and planted one. But after our lips met, she insisted on another. That did it! I was determined to escape. I gave up an arm and was lucky to find the door handle beside me. Thrusting my full weight against the door, I yanked the handle and immediately fell out onto the street. A passing car nearly ran me over! I'll never forget that night. I thought that was the end of it.

A short time thereafter is when I had my confrontation with Gunner that landed me in the hospital with a busted nose. I was there for a week following surgery. During that time I received a bunch of red carnations. Guess who? They were from Karen, wishing me well. I was so impressed by her kindness that I decided to give her a second look. That was one of my best decisions. Eventually we started going steady. I'm not quite sure how that happened, but it did. That Disneyland kiss, along with the flowers, must have worked their magic. Also, I think our mutual interest in Christianity was helpful. We were both very much involved with our church.[46] Neither one of us had any real experience with the opposite sex. Even so, she taught me everything she knew and vice versa (more like the blind leading the blind).

My first intimate experience with Karen occurred one evening at her home. She was hosting a dance for our church youth group in her very spacious backyard. After dancing to a beautiful song called "Stardust," magnificently sung by Nat King Cole, she took me by the hand and proceeded to lead me back into the house. She led me to her bedroom and closed the door. We not only rounded first base, but also flew by second on our way to third. It was my first personal view of what I had longed for since day one of puberty. Let's not forget that back in the day we were almost entirely sheltered from anatomical previews. Thank goodness for the Sears catalogue. Anyway, that evening, I learned very quickly that making love to a woman was like jumping out of a fifth-story window; once you get started, you can't stop.

But I don't want to leave you with the wrong impression. Because of our religious upbringing, we never made it to home plate. Intercourse was not on the table, even if we were, so to speak.

## Collisions Galore

During this time period, like so many other teenagers, I was a daredevil driver. I might as well have been driving one of those bumper cars you see at the amusement park. I hit more cars

---

[46]Some of the Karen episode was lifted—almost verbatim—from my previous 2013 publication, *JESUSGATE: A History of Concealment Unraveled*, pp. 166-68.

than the ocean has waves (or so it seemed). On one occasion I even hit a parked car. But sometimes I got hit. My late 1940s Plymouth got totaled when another teenage driver ran a stop-light and slammed into the old buggy broadside. Karen and I were driving back from Hollywood after seeing a sci-fi movie when the accident occurred. In spite of the serious damage, no one was seriously hurt except for Karen (fractured ankle). It was three weeks before her mother let me take her out again.

I think my worst collision came on a Sunday night after a church youth meeting. This particular evening my buddy Rich-ard needed a ride home to West Covina. That was about a forty-five minute drive on the freeway from our church. But that's nothing when you live in LA. Since my Plymouth was now scrap metal, I borrowed my brother-in-law's Ford station wagon.

It was rather late when we finally got started. Off we went. Richard crawled into the back area of the wagon and fell dead asleep. So there I was speeding down the freeway at about 70 miles an hour when the "sandwoman" came around. I rolled down my window and turned up the radio. Richard remained comatose. I should have gotten off the road. (Even as I write this, my eyelids are getting heavy.) How was I to know that directly in front of us an earlier accident had brought traffic to a standstill? Can't a guy get some shuteye around here without being rudely awakened? At least I saw this one coming, barely. That split second was a lifesaver. I slammed on the brakes full force. I still slid into the pile, but only with half the momen-tum. KABOOM! Richard woke up.

Thankfully, we weren't hurt. Someone claimed whiplash and I got sued for $25,000 but the insurance company set-tled. Unfortunately, my brother-in-law's car was nearly totaled. (Anymore, I try not to go out on Sunday nights.) I still didn't have my own wheels but my uncle Gene, bless his heart, sold me his 1952 Ford Victoria at a steal.

## Decision Time

Following the tumultuous summer of 1957, I decided I was tired of school and opted to take some time off to find a full-time job. I figured one year off between high school and college might do me some good. I could always return to my educational pursuits if I so decided. Besides, I needed some extra money to spend. Karen and I were still going steady and the relationship needed some maintenance. She was entering her senior year at Inglewood High.

Uncle Frank offered me a job at the Kettel Mufflers and Engineering Company where he was the shop foreman. They made industrial mufflers, and I was hired to tag and spray-paint the mufflers. Some of these mufflers were as small as toasters; others looked like whales. Sometimes they'd put me in a sound proof chamber with a jackhammer hanging from the ceiling above one of these metal giants. I had to climb on top and straddle the thing, grab the jackhammer, pull it downward, lean forward, and aim/press the chisel against a slit in the metal to create a half-inch opening when I pulled the trigger. This bending of steel was only possible because the hammer had such tremendous force. It had quite a kick so you had to brace the back end firmly against your shoulder (not unlike a shotgun or high-powered rifle). Like any jackhammer, it was exceedingly loud, and it was necessary to wear earplugs during the process. This pastime was my favorite part of the job. I could spend hours isolated in that room just pretending that I was a hero-soldier firing a machine gun and fighting off the enemy with every blast of that jackhammer. What fun! I was, after all, still a teenager.

Some of the guys from Kettel asked me to go rabbit hunting with them one fine Saturday morning. Anyone who knows me today knows that I'm an avid animal lover. In fact, in 2004 I wrote a book on the subject titled, *CREATED EQUAL: A Case for the Animal-Human Connection.* I'll borrow a page or two from that writing to explain what

*My uncle Frank Arellano (1940s)*

occurred on that hunting trip when I was still a teen.

"The grim specter of hunting has haunted me since my early years. I suspect it all began at the impressionable age of seven when my mother took me and my two sisters to see Walt Disney's *Bambi.* Yes, we all left the theater in tears . . . .

Ironically, alongside these warning signals was my budding love affair with guns. Like most young boys of the 1940s, I was swayed by the Power Rangers of the day—Gene Autry, Roy Rogers, Tom Mix, Red Ryder, and my all time favorite, the Lone Ranger (loved that "William Tell Overture"). Anyway, I can remember the proud sensation of strapping those double-holstered Lone Ranger six-guns around my slim waist. When I was old enough for the real thing, the love of guns remained. I eventually ended up with one rifle, one shotgun, and two handguns.

In spite of my *Bambi* reservations, the lure of hunting overtook me during my 18th birthday, when some of my buddies invited me on a rabbit hunt out on the Mojave Desert. Until that time I had never killed anything bigger than a potato bug. Encouraged by the thrill of the hunt and the testing of my skill, I eagerly awaited the adventure. It would be the epitome of male bonding.

I don't know where in the Mojave Desert we ended up, but we might as well have landed on the moon. It soon became apparent that the jackrabbits were elsewhere. No matter, for the next few hours we amused ourselves by what we thought was some pretty nifty target shooting. Of course, it helped that the targets weren't moving.

Then it happened. I spotted a rabbit on the run. Without a second thought, I raised my bolt-action 22 Winchester rifle and fired one shot. Unbelievably, the shot was dead-center. In a state of euphoria, we all gathered around the now lifeless form with shouts of celebration. For a few moments I was an exalted hero, as if I had just dropped King Kong.

Suddenly rabbits were everywhere. Rifles and shotguns fired in all directions. One of the guys "shotgunned" a rabbit at point-blank range not ten feet in front of us. The blast blew the hapless creature like a rolling rag doll right up half the side of a sand dune. It was pathetic (if you stopped to notice).

Until that moment I had relished this "guy-thing" adventure. But now I found myself totally out of phase with these exuberant efforts to inflict death. Guilt and pain flooded my spirit as I knelt down on one knee to observe the bloody results of our handiwork. It was awful. How could something so negative be sanctioned as anything positive? We had snuffed out the life force of these animals for no better reason than to appease our glorified delusions of "manhood." (I guess men are from Mars after all.)

I spent the remainder of that afternoon trying to make amends by staying ahead of my companions so as to block their line of fire and to warn any unsuspecting rabbits. This was accomplished by yelling and waving my arms while running back and forth across the desert floor. At first my buddies thought I was jokingly nuts. But when they saw I was serious, they became annoyed. Finally, they gave up the hunt and we headed back home—no other fuzz-balls would die that day. Needless to say, my friends were somewhat upset with this turn of events. They never again asked me to go hunting, but I took that as a compliment. You know, even today I carry a deep sadness for having shot that little fella."[47]

After working almost for a year at Kettel, I realized that my self-imposed sabbatical from college was coming to an end. Should I go back to school or continue working at Kettel?

---

[47]Ernie Bringas, *CREATED EQUAL: A Case for the Animal-Human Connection*, Hampton Roads Publishing Company, 2003, pp. 104-06.

After all, there was something very gratifying about working a full-time job that left one tired and filthy at the end of the day. And, hammering away at those huge iron mufflers was a blast. I toyed with the idea of not going back to school. I had money in my pocket, Karen and I remained an item, and life was good.

I made some of these thoughts known to Eddie, one of my co-workers. I thought he was really cool. Eddie was in his early 40s, was married, and had two little ones. He took me aside and said: "Really? You want to end up like me? Is this where you want to be 20 years from now? Ernie, go back to school. If you don't, you'll be stuck in a dead-end job for the rest of your life, with just enough money to pay the bills while trying to raise a family."

It was a sobering comment. Almost immediately I had a college catalogue in hand and got myself registered for the fall semester. In hindsight, it turned out to be a momentous decision. Thanks, Eddie.

I would also be amiss not to credit my mom for my decision to further my education. Throughout my childhood it was always implied, consciously and subconsciously, that I would go to college. Those seeds were planted early on. Thanks, Mom.

---

Before I describe my college years, here is some creative minutia. During my late teens, I took a stab at poetry (at least that's what I call it). My mother's side of the family had a flare for music and poetry. I guess I was just following suit. Here is one of the poems I wrote for our church youth paper. This is not serious poetry by any means (the meter is very elementary). Anyway, it was written just for fun but it has a moral twist.

OLD JOE SPIDER AND A GLASS OF CIDER

An army of ants passing by a dead spider
Said let's take him home and we'll make us some cider.
It turned out this spider was not at all dead,
But the brave little ants knew that they must be fed.

The leader led forward his army to fight,
They battled the spider on into the night.
Joe spider now weary though bigger than they,
Would not see the sunrise the following day.

When the battle had started Joe's legs numbered eight,
And when there were seven 'twas still not too late.
In the heat of the battle Joe got in a fix,
When another ant carried off leg number six.

Finally but five and then only four,
Before he could stop them there weren't any more.
He tugged and he struggled but all was in vain,
'Twould be but a moment before he was slain.

At last ole Joe spider lay quiet and still,
The ants gently chewing their stomachs did fill.
When Joe was half gone they took him in tow,
And dragged what was left to the others to show.

When reaching their dwelling a problem arose,
No part of Joe's body not even his nose,
Would fit in the tunnel that they had prepared,
And so all together they finished him there.

The moral of course is no matter how small,
Together the small make the mighty to fall.
And should a man think he is greater than most,
A cup full of cider to him we will toast.

Okay, here's one more. It's called:

## ON THE WING OF A BIRD

On the wing of a bird I imagined I flew,
As the sun slowly rising made diamonds of dew.
And the world far below me lay quiet and still,
How the sights filled with beauty my soul did refill.

There were rivers and mountains that I'd never seen,
And the valleys were covered with carpets of green.
My heart sang with laughter, what joy if you knew,
On the wing of a bird I imagined I flew.

We flew in the sunlight then under a cloud,
And filtered through raindrops that fell in a crowd.
Then radiant colors majestically flashed,
On the wing of a bird through the rainbow I crashed.

We circled a mountain whose top to the sky,
Brought mist and a roar from the waterfalls cry.
We perched on a branch in the heat of the day,
Then shot through the jewels of the heavenly spray.

On the land, in the air, and out over the seas,
From the deepest of canyons to the tallest of trees,
There was beauty and reverence that took its command,
From the passion and love of the Almighty's hand.

We followed the sun as it moved through the day,
'til the sunlight was fading the earth turning gray.
But perhaps you are wondering or find it absurd,
That I could have flown on the wing of a bird.

Chapter 10

# JR. COLLEGE AND UNIVERSITY DAYS
## COLEGIO JR Y DIAS UNIVERSITARIOS

*California*
1958—1963

I STARTED ATTENDING El Camino Community College (originally termed Junior College or a two-year college) in September
of 1958. I would turn 19 later that month. I still lived in Inglewood and drove 12 miles to the college in Torrance.

The cost of tuition was unbelievably low at about $2.50 a
semester/16 units. That's because the good people of California
had made it so. They made it possible for any kid to get a good
college education. (Shades of President Obama's State of the
Union Address in 2015 when he spoke of zero cost for our young
people.) Today (2016), the annual cost is about $2400, but still a
bargain when you consider the university system. Comparatively,
your freshmen and sophomore years of college are relatively inex-
pensive. Thereafter, you can transfer as a junior into a university,
as I did in 1960—California State University Long Beach—for a
whopping $46 a semester. How sweet it was.

As a freshman at El Camino, Psychology turned out to be
one of my favorite subjects. I also loved my class in Cultural

Anthropology. The comparative study of human societies and cultures around the world was a real eye-opener. As a young American, steeped in my Christian tradition, I was blown away by the diversity of human thought and development. I was forced to contemplate the relative nature of belief and social behavior. As I mentioned earlier, religion had always been a part of my life. Up until that time I had a religious mindset like a steel trap (shut tight and very hard to open). Anthropology was a mind-bender, and was notably the crowbar that helped pry open, albeit slightly, that rigid mindset. This was the first major, critical blow against my religious *absolutism*. It would not be the last, as we'll see later.

When I transferred to California State University Long Beach in 1960, I was now facing my junior and senior years. As for Karen, we remained tight and came close to getting married. Around this time, however, we broke it off. We were just too young and foolish (she was young and I was foolish). To this day we remain good friends.

Also in the summer of 1960, just before my first semester at Long Beach University, I was asked by my church to serve as a counselor for a jr. high summer camp. I was 20 years old but had plenty of experience working with some of the youth in my local church. The camp experience proved to be a defining moment. I discovered my leadership potential. I don't mean to pat myself on the back here, but this particular talent would reverberate throughout my life down to the present day. I was more than good as a leader; I was a natural! I could lead songs, I could tell jokes, I could speak effectively and I could control large groups of people. I didn't realize how unique this talent was. I don't mean to sound braggadocious, but my life's journey will seem more plausible if one knows that I'm an extrovert to the max (but not out of control). Actually, I tend to be rather humble. In fact, it's only my humility that prevents me from telling you of my other virtues. :) Seriously, I guess I had some sort of charisma, although to look at me you wouldn't think so (looks are definitely not my strong suit).

## The Calling

During my junior year at the University of Long Beach, I had what religious people refer to as "a calling." I felt that God was calling me to serve full-time in some ministerial capacity. Although college was very important to me, the involvement with my church remained central. I planned to transfer to a seminary[48] after I finished my university studies. The timing was perfect because that sense of ministerial calling literally kept me out of the Vietnam War. The Draft Board classified me as 4D (women and children first). Looking back, one has to contemplate the possibility that I subconsciously selected a ministerial career to avoid any involvement in Vietnam. But I don't buy it. I remember being naively nationalistic in my youth, and I would have served if the call to ministry had not been sincere. That reminds me of the late George Burns who

---

[48]SEMINARY: Usually a minimum three-year graduate school beyond college for training students to be priests, ministers or rabbis; leads to an M. Div. or some other degree.

said: "Sincerity is one of man's greatest attributes; if you can fake that, you've got it made."

Joking aside, I do know this: Enrollment in seminary schools across the nation was unusually high during the Vietnam War . According to Wikipedia, "U. S. involvement escalated in the early 1960s, with troop levels tripling in 1961 and again in 1962." Makes you wonder.

As already noted, my uncle Gene served on a destroyer during WWII. He made it back. But my 21-year-old cousin took the fall in Vietnam. Xavier Amado Arvizu served as a Specialist Four cannon crewmember in the U.S. Army, and suffered fatal hostile multiple fragmentation wounds. His name appears on The Vietnam Wall with all of the other Americans who paid the supreme price for their country.[49]

Sometime during 1962-63 of my senior year, I was on the Long Beach University campus making my way to class. My attention was drawn to the many students and other bystanders that lined both sides of one of the cemented walkways that ran through an otherwise grass-covered campus. Obviously the crowd awaited someone special, perhaps a dignitary of sorts, maybe a movie star. I approached one of the students and inquired: "What's the skinny?"

Before he could answer, I knew the answer. Walking toward us, with his entourage trailing close behind him, was a man well known to me and everyone else; that is, everyone else who wasn't dead from the neck up. It was none other than the former Vice President of the United States, Richard M. Nixon, who had served with President Dwight D. Eisenhower

[49]A BTRY, 1ST BN, 8TH Artillery, 25TH INF DIV, USARV, ARMY OF THE UNITED STATES. Killed Feb 24th, 1969. The Vietnam Wall: Panel W31, Line31.

for eight years (1953-1961). He ran for the presidency in 1960 but lost out to John F. Kennedy. Nixon was now running for the governorship of California, which he would also lose. But then, in 1968, he would run for president and win. Go figure.

Anyway, as the former VP walked along, his stride was self-assured. Nicely dressed with suit and tie, he waved to the folks on the green that flanked him on either side. The other suits trailing behind him must have been bodyguards (not Secret Service). And yet, as Nixon proceeded down the walkway, there weren't any suits within 20 feet of him. An idea came to mind. So I decided to act (hoping that it was not reminiscent of my kindergarten brainstorm when I hid after school).

When he got to the spot where I was standing, I daringly stepped off the green on to the walkway and matched his gait stride for stride. Walking alongside of him I immediately engaged him in conversation while simultaneously waving to the crowd, as if to indicate that all of this was perfectly normal. I think I caught everyone off guard because no one challenged me. A few of the suits looked at me askance. Not wanting to push my luck, I bailed out after absorbing about two minutes of his attention. Today, of course, I would either be shot or tackled by those surrounding any high-ranking official. Nowadays, almost paranoid precautions are taken to ensure the safety of our leaders. A necessary outcome from the turbulent '60s that saw the assassinations of President John F. Kennedy, his brother Robert Kennedy, and civil rights leaders, Medgar Evers and Martin Luther King; not to mention the assassination attempts on President Gerald Ford ('70s), and President Ronald W. Reagan ('80s).

The question I asked Nixon that day had to do with the failed invasion of Cuba in 1961 (Bay of Pigs).[50] I can't remember what I said exactly and I don't remember what he answered. I do remember, however, that he answered it to my satisfaction.

## Post Graduation

Following my graduation from the University of Long Beach, I was now ready for my seminary education. However, before we dig into my seminary days, a major disclosure is necessary. A life-changing event had occurred smack dab in the middle of my on-going educational pursuit. It requires explanation. The following two chapters will highlight that momentous happening.

---

[50]The Bay of Pigs Invasion, known in Hispanic America as Invasión de Bahía de Cochinos (or Invasión de Playa Girón or Batalla de Girón), was an unsuccessful military invasion of Cuba undertaken by the CIA-sponsored paramilitary group Brigade 2506 on 17 April 1961. (From Wikipedia)

Chapter 11

# ONE MORE SHOT
## UNA OPORTUNIDAD MÁS

1958 – 1962 Supplemental

FOLLOWING MY FAILED ATTEMPT at musical stardom, my broken nose, and my one-year stint at Kettel, I entered college (as I already indicated) in 1958. Early that same fall, on a given day no longer remembered, I was at the malt shop across from my alma mater, Inglewood High. That's when I luckily ran into Phil Stewart. Phil was not a total stranger. We had become acquainted in the mid-1950s during our high school days in the A cappella choir. He was a year ahead of me. Phil was somewhat mature in the way he dressed. He looked more like a businessman wearing that suit coat and pants. He almost never wore a tie, but his look was one of sophistication. Alcohol and cigarettes were frequent companions. Aside from alcohol, he never used any drugs. He was suave, had a way with words, and the ladies seemed to favor his attention. He always reminded me a little of the 1940s American film actor, Dane Clark.

On that particular day at the malt shop, we struck up a conversation and discovered some mutual interests in music. Importantly, Phil played the guitar. He invited me to his house for a jam session. A few weeks later I was there. We soon discovered the sweet spot of complementary harmony in our voices. In the words of the 1942 movie classic *Casablanca*, where Rick (played by Humphrey Bogart) says to Louie (played by Claude Rains): "Louie, I think this is the beginning of a beautiful friendship."

Encouraged by our self-proclaimed greatness, we were determined to secure a recording contract from one of the big studios. But first we needed a dub to showcase our talent. To do it up right, we needed at least $100 to secure some good studio musicians and pay for studio costs. My mom allowed me to cash in on an old insurance policy worth about $100 that she had started for me when I was a child. Thanks again, Mom!

I had partially written a melody called "Raindrops"[51] but Phil finished it by adding the chorus. It was time to record it as professionally as possible. My past go-around with guitarist Ray Pohlman and recording engineer Stan Ross at Gold Star Studios would prove invaluable. I hired Ray as my music arranger and *lead man* (the guy you trust to secure the instrumentalists and make all of the proper arrangements). With Stan Ross as our engineer, we cut "Raindrops" at Gold Star and came out with a very cool-sounding dub.

Accordingly, in the fall of 1958, I was not only in my first year at El Camino College, but I was simultaneously trying to land a recording contract. I knew, however, from the very beginning, that college was a *must* and music was a hobby. No matter how the music angle turned out, I was determined to stay the educational course. Even so, Phil and I were determined to give our music the best shot possible. During this

---

[51]Not to be confused with Dee Clark's 1961 #2 hit "Raindrops."

dual quest (education & music) I never forsook my educational path. But the music side of my efforts proved extremely arduous and time consuming.

From 1958 to 1962, we approached every recording company in Hollywood, starting with the mega studios—Columbia, RCA, Capitol, Decca—but they didn't want us (another deflating shock to the ego). Phil and I decided to hit the lesser known record companies such as: Last Chance Records, Hole In The Wall Records, Loser Records, No Talent Records, and Nice Try Records. Surprise! They didn't want us either. (Our egos were flat, nothing left to deflate). None of them had been nearly as receptive as our relatives had been.

I started to take rejection notices in stride. Besides, I only had my senior year left at Long Beach University and would thereafter be off to United Theological Seminary (UTS) in Dayton, Ohio, for an additional three years of study to secure my Master of Divinity degree (M.Div.). Still, I had to face the fact that my dream of becoming a recording artist was now null and void. After four years of pounding the Hollywood streets, Phil and I decided to call it quits in early 1962.

## Turnaround

However, that very same year before I started my last fall semester at Long Beach University, a strange thing happened to me on the way to the You Lose Hall of Fame. I was sitting at my kitchen table sifting through a collection of old 45 rpm records that I had purchased over the years. One of those records by Jan and Arnie caught my attention. But what really caught my eye was the Arwin record label (a record company located in Beverly Hills). At that time, I knew that Jan and Arnie (which later morphed into Jan & Dean) had left Arwin

Records for another record label called Dore (located in Hollywood). In fact, their first record for Dore was "Baby Talk" (it peaked at #10 in 1959). Anyway, I surmised that the Arwin label might be in need of some new artists to replace the now absent duo. So I called Phil and asked if he wanted to go with me to Beverly Hills and explore the possibility. Phil declined, but I decided to give it *one more shot*. I drove the 15 miles to Beverly Hills with our old scratchy demo record ("Raindrops") that we had recorded four years earlier at Gold Star. As it turned out, this shot in the dark to Arwin Records proved to be a defining event.

Actress/singer Doris Day[52] and her husband, Martin Melcher (an American film producer) owned Arwin Records and Daywin Music. Their son, twenty-year-old Terry Melcher, had recently been hired at Columbia Records as an A&R (artists and repertory) producer. (A record producer would be the equivalent of a movie director; they call the shots and put it all together). Terry did not carry his mother's last name (Day). He preferred his stepfather's last name, Melcher. Martin Melcher, in his own right, was a Hollywood magnate. Before his marriage to Doris Day, he had managed the Andrew Sisters. Following his marriage to Day, he produced almost all of her movies before his death in 1968.

Bob Crystal was vice president of Arwin Records. When I brought him our old dub of "Raindrops"—scratchy and old as it was—he listened to the entire recording, the first person to do so since my mother. He saw vocal potential and quickly arranged

---

[52]Doris Day recorded with Columbia Records from 1947 to 1967. With more than 650 recordings, Day became one of the most popular and acclaimed singers of the 20th century. As an actress, she appeared in 39 films and became the top-ranking female box-office star of all time.

for Terry to audition us at Columbia Records; it was part of the CBS complex located on Sunset Boulevard in Hollywood.

In 1962, on a warm summer day in Hollywood, California, Phil and I walked into Columbia Records to audition. We had only our voices and Phil's guitar. The studio was huge with a

*Columbia Recording Studios in Hollywood (1960s)*

first-class layout. It was like everything we had seen in the movies. It was built to incorporate an orchestra that was sometimes used for stars like Doris Day, Andy Williams and other notables. We found ourselves standing in front of a microphone that had no doubt been used by countless celebrities. It was unreal. Terry was behind the glass in the recording booth with the engineer and recording board. His voice popped out over one of the speakers: "Ok guys, let's see what you've got!"

Phil nodded towards me as he often did just before he started strumming his guitar. I could tell he was nervous because his knees kept knocking. I'm proud to say that my knees were perfectly still—they were paralyzed with fear. We sang our hearts out. When it was over, we still didn't know how we had fared. Would we get a contract? They said they would call us. We had hoped for a more definitive sign.

A few days went by. I had just finished my lunch and was getting ready to brush my teeth when I got the call.

"Hi Ernie, this is Terry. Welcome to Columbia Records."

I'll never forget that day. We had just been promised a contract with Columbia Records, the oldest, most notable, and largest recording company in the world. I really got excited; my mom got excited. I had a little dog and she got excited. I was so high on adrenalin that I accidently grabbed the tube of hair styler (Brylcreem) on my bathroom counter—true story—and started brushing my teeth. Two seconds later I was spitting and making with the gasping sounds of ick, yech, and eeew.

At that point in time our moniker was The Opposites. The name seemed apropos at the time because I would be studying for the ministry and Phil was a "private eye" (a tracer). But Phil's mother had concerns because she thought that the name—The Opposites—could falsely imply a positive versus negative image between the two of us since I was headed for the ministry. Therefore, the name The Opposites was changed to the Rip Chords.[53] We were off and running.

---

[53]It had nothing to do with the 1961-63 TV show, *Ripcord* (spelled without the h).

One day, while I was meandering around in the Daywin office, Doris Day came bouncing in. Her magnetic personality was bubbly and vivacious. She was warm and friendly. She knew I was studying for the ministry and she wished me well. This would not be our last encounter.

Incidentally, Phil and I hired Bob Crystal, Vice President of Daywin, to be our manager. His cut would be 20% of our earnings. Bob was a stereotypical character straight out of Hollywood. I told him I might go into missionary work in South America after graduating from seminary. He came unglued.

"You're not going to no South America, baby," he blurted out. "I'm not gonna go cutting through no jungle with a machete looking for you! You're gonna get a church right here in the USA!"

"What are you talking about?" I answered back.

"Look, Ernie," he continued. "You get a church with a big basement, see, and every Friday night we can throw a big Rip Chords dance for the teenagers. They'll pay big bucks to get in and we'll make a killing."

Although my seminary and recording years overlap almost simultaneously, the following section will focus primarily on my Hollywood days. The uniqueness of that experience calls for a broader explanation. Thereafter, I will address my seminary experience (which also was a humdinger).

Chapter 12

# HOLLYWOOD DAYS
## DÍAS DE HOLLYWOOD

*Columbia Records*
1962 – 1965

OUR FIRST RECORDING DATE was scheduled for September 6, 1962. I was 22 years old.

Phil and I drove to the rear parking lot of Columbia Records located near the famous Hollywood cross streets of Sunset and Vine. We parked my old dilapidated 1952 two-tone Ford between a Jaguar and a Porsche. My wreck was a thorn between two roses. This oddity was so obvious it did not go unnoticed. At some point during our time at Columbia, one of the future Beach Boys, Bruce Johnson, couldn't help but ponder this strange anomaly. He wrote a song called "Old Car Made in '52" that eventually became an album cut.

The security guard flagged us in through the back entrance. We met Terry in Studio A. As already noted, Terry was quite young, a couple of years younger than we were. Even so, he had a firm command of the situation and knew his way around the recording apparatus. He had already received extensive training at the Columbia studios in New York City prior to assuming his A&R position in Hollywood.

Terry definitely carried an air of confidence and maybe a touch of arrogance. He was, after all, the son of Doris Day and had been raised in an atmosphere of privilege. No doubt, it was his mother's clout at Columbia that had afforded him the opportunity to become the youngest record producer ever at Columbia. But Terry's ensuing success he owes only to himself. He became one of Columbia's most innovative and successful rock &roll producers. Aside from the Rip Chords, he would go on to produce such groups as the Byrds, Paul Revere and the Raiders and, much later (for another label) the Beach Boys' 1988 #1 hit record, "Kokomo."

Our first recording session with Terry focused primarily on a song that Phil and I had written called "Ding Dong." It was scheduled to be our first release. Unfortunately, none of us were satisfied with the end product. The song was shelved for a possible album cut if needed later. It was back to the drawing boards. Soon thereafter, Terry came up with some other possibilities, and so we re-entered the studio again on December 17, 1962. This time we came away with the "right stuff." But we had lots of help.

## The Wrecking Crew

Phil and I were a vocal group; we were not a band (no musical instruments although Phil played some limited guitar). Accordingly, we needed instrumental backup by studio musicians. These musicians, such as guitarist/singer Glen Campbell, guitarist Tommy Tedesco, drummer Hal Blaine,[54] bass guitar player Ray Pohlman and other prominent instrumentalists, came to be known as The Wrecking Crew. These were gifted musicians. The Wrecking Crew backed many of the '60s groups; such as, The Beach Boys, Simon and Garfunkel, The Carpenters, The Fifth Dimension, Jan and Dean, The Mamas and the Papas, The Monkees, along with many other groups that had chart-topping and Grammy-winning hits.

## First Record Released ("Here I Stand")

Our best effort from the Dec. 17th session was a song called "Here I Stand" (a remake of Wade Flemons's earlier 1958 version on VeeJay Records). Glen Campbell—from The Wrecking Crew—really gave "Here I Stand" a great lift with his lead guitar. Recent remix attempts have watered down his contribution, but on the original release of "Here I Stand," the imprint of his electric guitar is indelible (as was the case with many of the groups for which he recorded).

L-R; Ernie Bringas & Phil Stewart (1963)

Columbia released the single in early 1963. I sang the lead, the falsetto, and also joined Phil with the background vocals. (We are the only vocalists on this recording.) Our version peaked at #51 on The Billboard Hot 100. In Los Angeles, the

---

[54]According to Wikipedia, Blaine has played on 50 number one hits, more than 150 top ten hits. and has recorded, by his own admission, on over 35,000 pieces of music over four decades of work. Blaine is a member of the Rock & Roll Hall of Fame. Musicians Hall of Fame and Museum, and the Percussive Arts Society Hall of Fame. He is widely regarded as one of the most prolific drummers in recording music history.

song reached #20 (KRLA & KFWB). In Miami and Chicago, the song reached #16 (WQAM and WLS respectively). It was a good showing for our first release. Incredibly, we had made the professional circuit. Getting on the charts was a lifelong dream, accomplished only by the very few, the lucky few. Regardless of your talent—or lack thereof—luck is always an important part of that equation. For example, although Glen Campbell was a premier guitarist, he was also a great vocalist. But as luck would have it, he couldn't get a hit record.

It was during one of our later recording sessions that I had a nice conversation with Glen about his dry run. This was in 1964, three years before he became famous. I asked him why the guys in the studio were ribbing him about his own attempts at getting a hit record out. It seems that Capitol Records had signed him in 1962, and the guys were kidding him about his string of unsuccessful attempts to make the grade. At that time, none of us could have imagined that this incredible, guitar playing studio musician would go on to become one of the great recording artists of that era. In fact, Capitol Records almost dropped him before his successful 1967 hit "Gentle on My Mind" and his 1968 mega hit "By the Time I Get to Phoenix."[55]

I told him that I was sorry for his lack of success and voiced my disapproval at those who were making fun of him in what I considered to be a very insensitive and dismissive way.

---

[55]According to Wikipedia, during his 50 years in show business, Campbell released more than 70 albums. He sold 45 million records and accumulated 12 RIAA Gold albums, 4 Platinum albums and 1 Double-Platinum album. Campbell's hits include "Gentle on My Mind," "By the Time I Get to Phoenix," "Wichita Lineman," "Galveston," "Rhinestone Cowboy," and "Southern Nights." Sadly, Glen has stage 6 Alzheimer's disease, has lost most of his language skills, and has difficulty communicating.

He brushed it off, but I could tell that some of those pointed remarks had hit their target. Of course, he would eventually get the last laugh. Big time.

Our conversation took a turn when he volunteered a humorous note. He said he first heard our initial hit record, "Here I Stand," on his car radio while driving down the Hollywood freeway. He didn't recognize us at first until he heard his lead guitar blasting through the speaker. Glen told me that he was telling all his friends that he played guitar for the Rip Chords. That was his claim to fame at the time. Little did I know that many years later I would proudly be telling all of my friends that Glen Campbell played guitar for us. Life is so unpredictable.

## Touring

Phil and I made several personal appearances to promote our first release "Here I Stand." We appeared as an act with the Tommy Dorsey Orchestra for a charity benefit in L.A.; a DJ rock concert in San Francisco (see next paragraph below); and two personal TV appearances, that included the Wink Martindale and Lloyd Thaxton shows. Prior to our first release, we performed at the famous Hollywood Palladium (located on Sunset Boulevard in Hollywood). This particular appearance (December 8, 1962) featured an unreleased single, "Ding Dong," the precursor to "Here I Stand."

"Here I Stand" had become a formidable hit in most parts of the country. It was especially big in Northern California, so the San Francisco disc jockeys invited us up for a rock concert. Columbia Records saw this as a real promotional opportunity and decided to send Phil and me to the windy city. This would be our first out-of-town gig. Terry would join us as our PR man. All costs, including airfare, motels, and whatever, would be covered by Columbia Records.

On Saturday morning, February 16, 1963, Phil and I drove over to Beverly Hills. We were to pick up Terry—who still lived with his parents—and then head out for San Francisco via the LA Airport. We had agreed to meet at 11 AM, but it was an early 10:15 when we rolled up in front of Doris and Marty's luxurious home. This untimely arrival was actually a ploy that Phil and I had cooked up, hoping to spend some extra time in the home of a premier actress. But we got cold feet. We lingered in the car for a few minutes while Phil nervously puffed away on a cigarette and I chomped on some gum. My old beat-up Ford drew some suspicious looks from nearby neighbors so we decided we should make our move before someone called the police.

We slowly made our way up the walk. The huge, two-story house and palatial grounds could have been fodder for a picturesque postcard. I gave the gold-plated doorbell my thumb. We were greeted by the muted sounds of clanging chimes as they filtered through the door into the morning air. Silence dominated for a few seconds. Suddenly, a gruff, unfriendly, male voice barked out from a nearby speaker. "What do you want?"

Tentatively, I asked: "Aah . . . is Terry in?"

"Who is this?" came another gruff reply.

We had met Marty Melcher before. I was sure he would remember us, so I boldly exclaimed, "It's the Rip Chords!"

Sounding a bit annoyed, he shot back, "Well, why don't you rip on down the street?"

In that moment it became quite obvious that he didn't remember us. It was also clear we had either awakened him and Doris from a sound sleep, or they were not yet fully awake.

I hurried to explain. "Mr. Melcher, my name is Ernie Bringas. Phil Stewart and I are here to pick Terry up. We're flying to San Francisco this afternoon."

"Oh, yeah," came a less abrasive response. "Just a minute."

I could hear Doris in the background laughing—laughing, undoubtedly, at her husband's rude treatment of their current visitors. Phil and I looked at each other with a sigh of relief. We stood silently with anticipation and waited for the gates of the Taj Mahal to open up. Perhaps Doris herself would come bouncing out to welcome us in.

The still of the morning was shattered once again by the now familiar voice blaring out: "You boys have your car here?"

"Y . . . yes, sir," I fumbled disappointingly because I knew what was coming.

"Good. Do you mind waiting in your car? Terry is in the shower. He'll be out in a few minutes."

Our ploy was a bust. We slowly shuffled our way back to my Sherman tank with hardly a word between us. Phil lit another cigarette; I found some more gum to chew. It seemed like forever before Terry emerged. "Phil! Ernie!" he shouted. We scrambled out of the car.

Terry stood at his front door wearing an unassuming white robe. "Come on in, you guys; I'll be ready in ten minutes; How come you're so early?" he asked. Neither Phil nor I answered as we followed him into unfamiliar territory. We were house struck. We were out of our league. My mother's house in Inglewood was rather nice, but definitely middle class. Phil's parents, on the other hand, had moved to Inglewood from West Virginia and were renting a little space you could only refer to as a shack. It was so small and cramped that the mice ran around hunchbacked.

Just as I had expected, but could not fully have imagined, the Melchers' living room was beautiful. The gorgeous, snow-white, wall-to-wall carpeting rose three inches from the floor. Luxurious furnishings and art works were sprinkled about. A huge portrait of Doris Day hung near the entrance way but not in an ostentatious manner.

Neither Doris nor Marty Melcher came downstairs to greet us. That was perfectly understandable in their line of work. They probably had to deal daily with every "Tom, Dick and Harry" that came their way.

Terry would be driving us to the LA airport. Before leaving the area, however, I wrote a short note and stuck it under the windshield wiper of my old jalopy. The note read: "We are friends of the Melchers. Please do not tow."

We jumped into the Melchers' New Yorker station wagon and headed for the L.A. International Airport. Riding with Terry was a breathtaking experience. He was behind the wheel and we felt like we were behind the 8-ball. The kid damn near got us all killed.

We arrived at the airport at 11:50 AM. Our United Airlines Flight 877 was due to take off at 12:05 PM. Terry parked the car in a "No Parking" zone. That explained the numerous tickets I accidentally discovered in the glove compartment.

Flying at the age of 23, would be my first experience in the air (except for the first time in the sixth grade when I landed on cloud nine with Ann). We were flying First Class so we sat in the forward section just outside of the pilot's cabin. This made me a bit nervous because I had heard that if something went wrong, the safest place to be was in the rear of the aircraft. But, gazing about this flying brick, I realized that safety was an illusion; if it ever went down nose first, it wouldn't matter if you were on it or under it.

The flight was uneventful with two exceptions. First, it was a blustery day and every time the plane shook, I shook along with it.

Second, there was a passenger riding with us in First Class that gave me the willies. He was an older man, probably in his fifties. He sat directly in front facing us. He looked exhausted and deeply depressed. His dark, brown, wrinkled coat hung sloppily over his hunched shoulders and paunchy middle. He was balding. What hair he did have hung like strings of spaghetti over his shiny scalp. He sat upright and rigid as if he had been stabbed in the back. Moments later his head would droop, his face would contort, and his body would twitch. I tried to take my eyes off him, but my gaze could not escape the gravitational pull of his menacing body language. Something about this character wasn't right. I leaned over to Terry and whispered, "Hey, Terry."

Sensing my apprehension, he whispered back, "What?""

See that guy in front of us?" I cocked my head toward the man. "Something's wrong with him."

Terry studied the man with curiosity. The old man's eyes were now moist, as if he were about to break out in tears. This guy was making me anxious. Terry, I could tell, was also a little spooked. I glanced over at Phil, and he too appeared to be mesmerized by spaghetti head.

Thinking that the old boy might be a danger to himself or, heaven forbid, a danger to us all, I decided to flag down one of the stewardesses (today we call them flight attendants). But I held my fire when I was startled by the pilot's loud announcement that we were about to land. Honestly, none of us wasted any time getting off that plane.

They say it usually rains in the Bay Area. That day was no exception. I felt the cold, sharp drops colliding with my face as we hurried toward the terminal (no protective terminal amenities in those days). Chuck Gregory, a Columbia distributor, was on hand to greet us. Following the customary introductions, we made our way to his blue Cadillac, threw our baggage in the trunk, piled in, and drove away toward downtown San Francisco.

After a drive that took us up and down a few roller-coaster hills, we finally pulled up in front of our hotel. We had reservations at one of the most celebrated luxury hotels in San Francisco; it was called the InterContinental Mark Hopkins. Situated in the heart of SF, it boasted a breathtaking 360-degree panoramic skyline view of the Bay Area from its 19th floor lounge (known as the Top of the Mark). Columbia had spared no expense. We registered and made our way up to the 19th floor for a look-see. The view was incredible, even during these daylight hours. (My immigrant mother had been born in Mexico, and here I was at the Top of the Mark hobnobbing around with Doris Day's son. What an amazing transition in one generation. That's the promise America offers to all newcomers. As Gary Cooper once said in one of his films: "That can only happen in a country like America.")

We made our way back down to our room on the ninth floor. Looking out from our window, we could see the doorman directly below us at the entrance of the hotel. Terry decided that this was a great vantage point for dropping a water balloon. I wasn't too jazzed about the idea for fear that we might get kicked out of this swanky place. Besides, there were no balloons in sight. Terry solved that problem by filling up one of his condoms. I had no experience with condoms, and I was somewhat surprised that Terry, who was two years my younger, had a slew of these things on hand.

The sun finally descended—along with a few condoms—and it was time to leave for our rock & roll extravaganza. Chuck had returned to pick us up and was waiting in the lobby. His blue Cadillac whisked us across the Golden Gate Bridge into Marin County (located in the North San Francisco Bay Area). The Cadillac rolled to a stop in front of what looked like a large old barn. To this day, I don't know where we ended up, but it looked like we were out in a country-like setting. The rainfall experienced earlier that day had continued into the evening. I opened the car door and stepped right into a mud-hole that swallowed my foot up to the ankle. Not too pleasant when you're wearing your nice slacks and polished shoes.

(In those early days of rock, performers always dressed the part with coat and tie. When the Beatles, who would soon share the Billboard chart with us, came on scene, they were ridiculed for having "long" hair (mop heads) even though they were very neatly packaged. Of course, by today's standards, the idea that the Beatles looked like girls because their hair was too long is now laughable. But back then, boys were expelled from their high schools for trying to emulate them.

No doubt, however, that the Beatles opened the floodgates. What followed after their novel hairdo ratified the slippery slope argument. Those innocent mop heads—in the eyes of some—led to the devolution of a much more uncouth rock genre. No one back then could ever have imagined anyone like the '70s hard rock band Kiss, with their members' black and white face paint and striking stage outfits. Madonna, Lady Gaga, and rap music have also been examples of expanding controversial boundaries. But hey, such controversies are not new. In fact, historically speaking, new expressions have always been looked upon with suspicion (if not total disdain) by the older generations. Even in the early, innocent stages of rock & roll, I can remember my elders calling it the devil's music, especially songs from the likes of Little Richard and Chuck Berry. Of course, the Roaring '20s faced much of the same criticism. (Back to touring)

The interior of the big barn-like structure looked very unsuited for a genuine rock concert. Apparently, this was a small time affair. Nevertheless, this gig was important because the SF disc jockeys had organized it and because they were the ones promoting our record.

But the joint reeked with cigarette smoke, foul language, and noisy confusion. It felt like we had stumbled into Bonnie & Clyde's hideout. Two kids got into a fistfight and the police were called. When the dust finally settled, it was time for us to go on. Evidently, we were the only headliners for the dance that evening. Lacking a live band to back us up, we were going to lip-sync[56] our record "Here I Stand." That was a good thing because there was no way we could reproduce the choir-

---

[56]This is when a singer moves the lips silently in synchronization with a recorded soundtrack.

like recording we had made in the studio. "Here I Stand" was basically me singing a number of high-pitched falsetto overdubs that would be virtually impossible for me to replicate in singular voice (you'll understand if you play the song).[57] More problematic, however, was the antiquated sound system at our disposal. They placed our 45 rpm record on a small, old RCA phonograph player. Obviously, it couldn't carry the sound over the noisy audience, so someone stood there holding a microphone up to the small record player in hopes of redirecting the music over their loudspeakers. Worse yet, the phonograph player they used sounded like it had a straight pin for a needle. But I guess that lack of sound quality really didn't matter because you could barely hear the music over the noise that erupted when they started playing our record.

Aside from all the problems, everyone enjoyed the evening and I got a real taste of celebrity status when all the teens—especially the girls—gathered around the stage. It wasn't Beatle mania by any means, but they were screaming with exuberance as they reached out to grab us while we were on stage. When all was said and done, we had to sneak out the back way. It was crazy.

## Second Single Recorded ("Gone")

Terry Melcher's second effort for the Rip Chords was a song called "Gone," recorded April 26, 1963. The Wrecking Crew was on hand to provide the instrumental background. As was the case with our first release, I sang the lead, the falsetto and along with Phil, the background vocals. Bruce Johnston, a friend of Terry's, added an interjecting falsetto that really

---

[57]Several Internet sites incorrectly credit Phil Stewart as having that soaring Four Seasons falsetto. Phil couldn't sing falsetto, he was a bass singer; I did the falsetto parts on "Here I Stand" and many other songs.

kicked the song into overdrive. Bruce had a very smooth falsetto, especially at the very top of the vocal spectrum. Only Phil, Bruce, and I appear on this recording. (From this point on, Bruce and I will share the falsetto parts).

Eventually, when our group disbanded, Bruce would go on to join the Beach Boys. He would also go on to write the 1977 Grammy Awards Song of the Year, "I Write the Songs." Sung by Barry Manilow. It reached number one on the Billboard Hot 100 chart in January 1976.[58]

Although "Gone" did penetrate The Billboard Hot 100, it did not fare as well as the previous hit, "Here I Stand." However, "Gone" went up the charts wherever it received a decent amount of airplay. For example, in San Antonio, Texas, during the week of August 1, 1963 (on KTSA's top 55 survey), "Gone" climbed up to #2, right above Elvis Presley's #3 song, "Devil in Disguise."

## A Conflict of Interest?

In September of 1963, the same year we had released "Here I Stand" and "Gone," I was scheduled to report to United Theological Seminary in Dayton, Ohio, to pursue my ministerial education. Earlier that year I had graduated from California State University Long Beach. I was now headed for three years of graduate work to earn my Master of Divinity (M.Div.) degree.

My desire, at that time, was to remain as lead singer for our group. I could always fly back from seminary to Hollywood when needed to record. That was my plan. Columbia was on board. But church officials saw it differently. They were

---

[58]I met up with Bruce at a 50th Beach Boys concert in Phoenix, Arizona, in June of 2012. We chatted about old times. It was good seeing him again.

concerned about a possible conflict of interests. In fact, they threatened to take away my probationary license if I did not abandon my musical pursuits. Taking away my license would make it virtually impossible for me to attend seminary. Here is the letter I received from the Board of Ministry:

"The Committee would like to know your attitude especially toward two of the vows given to candidates for ordination which are found in the Discipline. I quote:

'Will you reverently heed, with a glad heart and a willing mind, them to whom the charge over you is committed according to the regulations of the Evangelical United Brethren Church?'

'Will you loyally maintain the doctrines and policy of the Evangelical United Brethren Church?'

. . . your attitude and answers to these [questions] will determine whether or not your license for this year or next year will be validated.

You see, your life is really not your own when you become a minister and thus the things you do affect not only you, but the conference and the local church to which you might be assigned."

❋

Wanting to pursue my educational interest, I informed Columbia that I could not record until I straightened out these matters with church officials. At that point in time it was not at all certain that I would even be allowed to return to the group. As a result, when I left for seminary, several questions remained open-ended. My departure had left Phil without a singing or touring partner. Columbia Records could not afford to leave these issues unresolved. The touring problem was quickly remedied.

## The Touring Rip Chords

Since I was now absent from the group, and my return remained uncertain, two young men (Rich Rotkin and Arnie Marcus) were brought on board to tour with Phil as the Rip Chords. *It is important to note that Rich Rotkin and Arnie Marcus were never vocally involved with any Rip Chords' recordings. Their participation was limited to touring.* Be that as it may, Phil, Rich, and Arnie became the official touring wing of the Rip Chords. Having solved the touring issue, Phil was still without a singing/recording partner. The solution was in-house.

## The Bruce and Terry Vocal Component

Producer Terry Melcher and, now, co-producer Bruce Johnston (AKA: Bruce & Terry) stepped in vocally to fill the void created by my absence. Bruce had already sung with Phil and me on our second single, "Gone." Bruce and Terry would prove to be a significant addition as the Rip Chords prepared to record and release their third single.

## Third Single Released ("Hey Little Cobra")

The third Rip Chords' release was a song titled "Hey Little Cobra"—composed by Carol Connors—and was vocally layered by Bruce and Terry (recorded October 15, 1963). Terry sang the lead in my absence. He and Bruce did the background vocals.[59] By November of 1963, it was obvious to everyone that the "Cobra" record was a huge success as it bounded up the national charts. It would eventually peak at #4 on Billboard's Hot 100 in February, 1964. Had it not been for the Board of Ministry, I would have had the lead vocal on that song (along with some of the background vocals). This was truly a missed opportunity on my part. But honestly, I cannot lay the blame totally on the Board of Ministry. It was, after all, my decision to comply with their ultimatum.

Meanwhile, Phil called me at the seminary that same November to complain about his non-involvement in the recording of the "Cobra" hit. He was having trouble with Bruce and Terry and hinted that I needed to return to the group. I will admit that I had already flirted with that prospect. For me to do so, however, would violate the Ministerial Board's wishes. What to do? I informed Phil that my first semester would be over at the end of November, and I had already made plans to get back to California for the holidays. We could discuss it then.

In the early afternoon of November 22, 1963, I had just finished the last final of my first semester at United Theological Seminary (UTS) and was looking forward to my upcoming California vacation. As I made my way up the dorm stairs to my second-floor room, someone leaned over the banister above and yelled: "The president has been shot!"

"What? What president?" I yelled back in disbelief, "Are you kidding?"

[59]Aside from my own personal knowledge of this event, and the personal testimony from Bruce & Terry, other sources also support this claim, e.g., Jason Ankeny, *Bruce and Terry Biography*, Allmusic.

"No, I'm not joking," came the reply. "President Kennedy has been shot!"

I flew up the remaining flight of stairs, opened the door to my small apartment, and reached for the radio. It was true; President John F. Kennedy had been shot. Shortly thereafter, the stunning announcement came that he was dead. I was staggered. For those of us who lived through that calamity, no words of explanation about how we felt will suffice. For those who didn't, I will simply say that it was terrible; so terrible, it could hardly have been worse. I need go no further with any explanation about the assassination.

**Life Goes On**

One week later I was on a Greyhound bus headed back to California. I had sold my old '52 Ford Victoria before moving to Ohio. Although I had flown out for my first semester, I thought it would be great fun—believe it or not—to travel cross-country by bus during this semester break. Boy, was I wrong. Every time we pulled into a bus terminal, it felt like we were entering a Third World country. That was my last bus trip. But I did meet some interesting people along the way. Other than that, you can keep your bus travel; it's not for me. Yet, here's one good memory: During a rest stop at one of the Texas bus terminals, I was brought to attention when "Hey Little Cobra" was played over the PA system. That was a hoot.

Can you imagine how it feels to hear your voice booming out of a Top-40 radio station? The first time I clicked on a Los Angeles station and heard one of our records, it nearly blew my mind. I was cruising down the boulevard in my beat-up '52 Ford when suddenly a D.J. played "Here I Stand." I almost slammed into a telephone pole. I wanted to jump out of the car and shout to anyone within earshot that it was our song. I was bouncing all over the front seat. I rolled down the window and yelled at the driver alongside of me: "Hey," I shouted, "tune in to KFWB; it's my song." I was delirious with joy. I think I scared him, or he thought I was nuts because he sped off before the light turned green. Once you're an "idol," be it ever so brief, it's an amazing feel. Of course, I can only speak from my success with the Rip Chords, which is somewhat limited relative to the success of many others.

When I mercifully got off the bus in LA, Phil picked me up and we made our way back to Inglewood. We had a long discussion. With Phil's encouragement, I decided to rejoin the group. I would have to deal with the Board of Ministry at a later time, whatever the consequences. Although I had been absent from the studio for almost three months, I was still legally under contract to Columbia Records. Terry, our producer, had no objections with this continuing arrangement. The timing of my return was perfect because "Hey Little Cobra" was still moving up the charts, and Columbia was just getting ready to record the *Hey Little Cobra and other Hot Rod Hits* album as a follow-up to the single.

Initially, of course, when the "Cobra" single was released, Bruce and Terry did not receive any credit for their vocal participation because, at that point in time, they were ghost singers; that is, the public never knew they were on the records. (Definitively, a ghost singer is someone who sings on the recording but does not receive credit; in the literary field we call them, ghostwriters.) Bruce and Terry would remain ghost singers for the remainder of the Rip Chords' journey. Nevertheless, I want to give credit where credit is due; that is, I want to make it clear that the vocal contributions made by Bruce and Terry were a major factor in shaping the Rip Chords' music and to what is now known as the *California Sound.*

### First Album Recorded
### (*Hey Little Cobra and other Hot Rod Hits*)

During my winter break between semesters at UTS, I made the decision to re-enter the music world. Phil and I were now going to cut the *Cobra* album. However, at this juncture, it became obvious—based on the success of the "Cobra" single— that Bruce and Terry should be part of the vocal ensemble. Everyone agreed. This is not to suggest that all four voices are present on every single cut; *none of us* were on all the songs.

Within the first four weeks of December 1963, Phil and I, along with Bruce and Terry, recorded the *Hey Little Cobra and other Hot Rod Hits* album. This was our first time singing together as a foursome, and no other voices appear on this album. *In fact, within this affiliation of four (Terry, Bruce, myself, and Phil) all of the 1960s Rip Chords' music would be hammered out, including background vocals.*[60]

However, this arranged format led to an in-house struggle between the Phil and Ernie "sound" and the Bruce and Terry "sound." Regardless, the *Cobra* album featured an equal smattering of both. For example, when one examines the original

---

[60]For further info on vocal participation and discography, see Wikipedia or my personal web page (ripchords.info).

Columbia issue of the 1964 *Hey Little Cobra and other Hot Rod Hits* album (CS 8951 or CL 2151)—featuring 11 vocal recordings—one discovers that Terry carried 45% (5) of the leads, while I also carried 45% (5) of the leads, and Phil carried 10%. (see Discography:

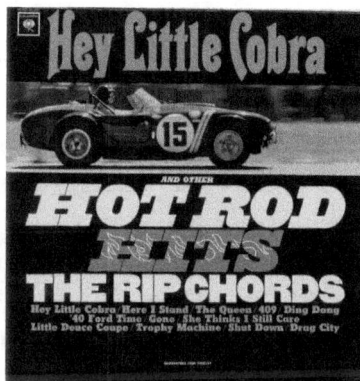

Appendix). Having said all this, I must reiterate: neither Phil nor I deny that Terry and Bruce were major contributors in shaping the Rip Chords' sound. Nevertheless, our signature sound was the end result of all four voices working in tandem. In the final analysis, it was a cumulative effort.

One evening, during a late recording session at Columbia, Terry ordered some take-out food brought into the studio for us. When it arrived, I noticed a few sandwiches, some vodka, and a bottle of orange juice. Everyone knew I didn't drink liquor so I assumed that the orange juice was for me. How thoughtful, I thought to myself as I gratefully drank the OJ. When they finally got around to the vodka, they had a fit; all of their orange juice was gone. Evidently, the OJ had been ordered as a mixer for the vodka (called a screwdriver, as I learned later). How was I to know that they were going to use it as a mixer? Needless to say, they weren't too happy with me. We had a good laugh anyway.

In early January of 1964 I caught a plane back to Ohio. I was going to be starting my next semester at UTS. I was 24.

As I mentioned earlier, the "Cobra" single peaked in February of 1964. The album we had just recorded followed suit and had a successful run. Anyway, it was now time to face the music—not studio music, but time to face the consequence of re-entering show biz without prior consent from the Board of Ministry. It was time to own up and I was unclear about the outcome. But one thing I knew for sure: I would have to pick the right time, the right place, the right person, and the right strategy to have my explanation accepted with impunity. I decided to meet with the highest-ranking church official in my jurisdiction of the Evangelical United Brethren Church, Bishop W. Maynard Sparks.[61] I wrote him a letter requesting a meeting. In his response, he told me that he would not be in Dayton until April but would be happy to see me at that time.

Pursuant to any meeting I might have with the Bishop, I was needed back in Hollywood in mid-January to record our fourth single "Three Window Coupe" (a song co-written by Jan Berry of Jan & Dean). I had just left Hollywood after recording the *Cobra* album in December, and here I was again a month later. Admittedly, I was jumping the gun once again; that is, recording without the permission of church officials. So be it. It was either record, or miss the session altogether. I recorded. However, the "Three Window Coupe" single would not be released by Columbia until the first week in April (64). For the obvious reason of capitalizing on the *Cobra* formula,

---

[61]W. Maynard Sparks (1906 – 1999) was an American Bishop of the Evangelical United Brethren Church (E.U.B.), and the United Methodist Church. The E.U.B. Church merged with the Methodist Church in 1968 to form the United Methodist Church.

Bruce and Terry dominate this single although Phil and I definitely contributed vocally to the end product.

### Fourth Single Released ("Three Window Coupe")

When "Three Window Coupe" was released in April, it was a hit but fell short of the "Cobra" benchmark. The market was a bit soft at the time. Can you guess why? The problem was a seven-letter word called the BEATLES! They were outselling everyone for a while. Nevertheless, our single was a solid hit.

I finally met with Bishop Sparks at the once proud Van Cleve Hotel in Dayton, Ohio on the evening of April 7, 1964 (ironically, the same release week for the "Three Window Coupe" single). The purpose of my meeting with him was singular. I needed his approval for my continued participation as a professional recording artist. Of course, I had already started recording without anyone's okay (the *Cobra* album and the "Three Window Coupe" single), but I held back on divulging that information. Without his support, however, I stood little chance of reversing the ban placed on me by the Board of Ministry. One positive word from him and I would be home free. Those were the stakes. The following is my paraphrased log entry from that encounter.

The lobby of the Van Cleve was bustling and crowded with people. It was upscale and accented by a beautiful red carpet. I made my way to the registration desk and made my presence known. The registrar contacted the Bishop, and I was informed that he would be down shortly to meet me in the lobby. I thought it strange that he did not invite me up to his room. I guess that was standard protocol.

As I sat down to await his arrival, I spotted a young lady behind the concession stand. She was very attractive. Like a bee drawn to a colorful flower, I got up and started across the lobby. It was time to buy some candy. I never made it. The nearby elevator doors opened and out stepped Bishop Sparks. I waved, and he made his way across the red carpet towards me. After a quick handshake and a few verbal pleasantries, we found a suitable place for conversation. From previous encounters with the Bishop at our annual California Conferences, I knew him to be friendly. Nevertheless, the encounter felt somewhat intimidating. After all, we were on the opposite ends of the authority spectrum. Also, I was apprehensive as to how he would regard—let's face it—my rogue status. He knew that the Board had requested I quit recording. He also knew—because I finally fessed up—that I was presently in violation of that request. What I didn't know is how he felt about the situation. I would soon find out.

*I'm hamming it up at a rock & roll youth banquet (1965).*

In hopes of blunting any negative decision on his part, I took the initiative. In the moments that followed, I explained to the Bishop about the many advantages that recording had afforded me. I told him how I had been invited to be one of the guest speakers at a huge youth convention in Philadelphia where more than 2,000 teenagers had gathered. I explained that being part of the rock & roll genre provided a multiplicity of gateways. Opportunities for ministry were almost limitless. I didn't know if he would concur, but I hoped he would. His verdict was at hand.

The Bishop started slowly. His manner of speech was generally deliberate and serious. "I don't think we can condemn you for what you are doing, Ernest," he said. (Bishop Sparks is the only one who ever called me Ernest.)

"We don't always know in what ways God chooses to act," he continued. "We sometimes tend to limit God and feel that He can speak to man only in specific ways."

His words began to put me at ease so I wasn't about to interrupt him.

"Why, you will be able to reach people we never could reach," he went on. "Sometimes, I think the clergy has made a mistake in confining Christianity to the church building. As Christians, we should be striving to reach people for Christ in the real world—the world outside of the church. But too often our Christian witness never reaches beyond the church walls. There is a danger in withdrawing from the world," he said. "I don't believe that this is what God intended. After all, Jesus found people in their habitat, took people as they were and,"— he looked squarely at me—"accepted their differences."

His response couldn't have been better. I was relieved by his objectivity and open-mindedness. But he cautioned me to remember that in spite of his personal views, the Board of Ministry would have to make the final decision. Nevertheless, he assured me that, in all probability, the Board would not raise further objections. I think those were his code words for: "If I'm not against it, they won't be either." He proved right.

At one point in our conversation, the young lady came out from behind the concession stand and strolled across the lobby. She crossed our field of vision several times. I wondered if the Bishop had noticed her. I sure did. In fact, I was too busy noticing her to notice if the Bishop noticed her, or if he noticed me noticing her.

My conversation with the Bishop had only lasted about 12 minutes. But it was a great 12 minutes. He did, however, suggest that I refrain from touring as it might interfere with my studies. I agreed. Expressing my appreciation for his time and consideration, we parted company. Thereafter, I crossed the lobby, stepped out into the cool, night air of Dayton, and caught a bus for the seminary (but not until I had bought some candy).

## Second Album Recorded (*Three Window Coupe*)

With a clear conscience, I flew back to Hollywood from Dayton to record vocals for the *Three Window Coupe* album. I was back in the Columbia studio late in April (or possibly early May). I had secured permission from my instructors to be absent for one week from academic studies. There was, however, one condition: I had to write a term paper on the religion of Jainism for my World Religions class. I didn't see this as a problem because I was well acquainted with the downtown LA library. It was a beautiful, well-stocked library. I would spend some daylight hours there researching Jainism, while recording at Columbia during the evening. It was the best of both worlds. I was on a natural high.

Similar to the first album, the *Three Window Coupe* album (CS 9016 or CL 2216) featured another 11 vocal recordings. On one of those songs, Terry and I shared the lead together ("My Big Gun Board"). I have often thought that the mono version of that song was one of our best ever. I lobbied for its release as a single, but to no avail. Of the remaining 10, Terry carried 60% (6) of the leads, while Phil and I evenly split with

40% (4) of the leads. I mention these facts only because many rock & roll pundits, out of ignorance, continue to foster the false opinion that Phil and I had been vocally sidelined after our first single, "Here I Stand." But these recordings fly in the face of any attempt to downplay our vocal contributions. (See Discography: Appendix)

Furthermore, when it came to the background vocals, at least three of the four of us were almost always involved. Additionally, Bruce and I shared many of the falsetto parts, except when I was on hiatus - this led to the notable exceptions of the "Hey Little Cobra" single and its flip side, "The Queen." At other times, we soloed on falsetto.

The vocals on the *Three Window Coupe* album were cut during the course of one week, primarily in the evening. Sometimes the sessions would run late into the night and into the following morning. I'm not a night owl, but it was impossible to get sleepy, tired, or lose interest. One could not escape the magic of the studio, and the realization that most people would give their right arm for this amazing experience. Even when one was not directly engaged, it was just so exhilarating to hear the playbacks over the loudspeakers again and again as new vocal parts were added to the main track. For example, sometimes I would sing the lead, add some background parts with the other guys (known as overdubbing), or sit back and watch others add the additional parts. There were times when I was singing alone in the

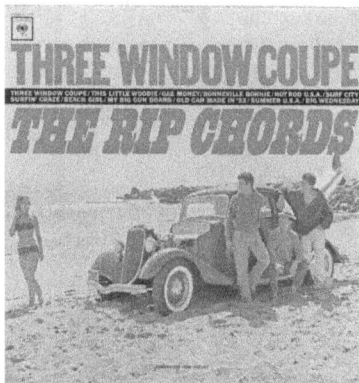

main studio—doing the lead or adding a falsetto part—while the rest of the guys were in the recording booth staring out at me through the glass that separated us. Sometimes those roles were reversed; that is, I'd be staring out through the glass divider at one or more of the guys laying down vocal parts. There was always something to see or something to do. The recording console, the Ampex recorder, and the unique aroma of the recording tape, were all part of studio ambience; it was a magical aura. I never lost sight of how incredibly unique this experience and opportunity were.

Aside from being able to sing, one had to be a quick study when laying down these vocals, be they leads or harmony parts. When Phil and I arrived at the studio, we didn't have a clue about the songs that were on the docket. We went in cold, not even having heard the songs we were going to record during that session. In other words, we couldn't practice our parts beforehand except for a few run-throughs with the instrumental tracks just before we recorded vocally.

This approach may seem careless and haphazard, but there was a practical side to this approach. This wasn't like singing in a duet or quartet where each person learns one part, and that's all they need to know. No, you might be called on to sing numerous parts, and nobody knew for sure how many times you would be called on to harmonize, or double on a part someone else had already sung, and so forth. The multiplicity and possible combinations were numerous. So, you really couldn't prepare for any particular part (you might not even sing at all on any given song). On the spot insights, changes, and improvisations were all part of Terry Melcher's genius in the studio. He did run roughshod over us at times, but all in all, he was a terrific producer. Later, he would add Bruce Johnston as a co-producer. But Terry remained the main decision maker.

Of course, Terry had some strategy mapped out in his head long before we came in to record. Musical arrangements were also pre-planned. The instrumental tracks were laid earlier. Nevertheless, serendipity would be part of the recording equation. In many respects, we were recording vocals on the fly. When singing the background vocals, as one example, one would learn a particular part, record it on tape, and then repeat the process singing a different part or doubling the part just finished. You sang a lead or harmony part over again to give it more body. Again, this was called overdubbing. You could overdub as many voices and instruments as needed as long as the multi-track Ampex tape allowed. It was a blitzkrieg way of recording and it was a blast. But when you left the studio, all of the parts you had sung—except for the leads—were virtually lost to memory.

We had a good idea of what had happened, but we certainly did not know how the final product sounded. That's because after laying down the instrumental and vocal tracks, our producer, Terry Melcher, still had to take the tape into the mixing room to create a master recording. In other words, he had to mix-down the many tracks into one singular track; that is, he had to artfully balance all the many tracks—instruments, harmonies, the lead, and many numerous overdubs—into one master track. He also added echo or reverb, for example, to fine-tune the end result. The vinyl record would eventually be made from that singular, mastered track. Accordingly, it wasn't until Columbia released the vinyl record that one finally got to hear the finished product.

It was the summer of 1964. While I was flying back and forth between Dayton and Hollywood, making records and having a good old time, momentous world events were unfolding. Two epic issues loomed front and center: The Civil Rights Movement and the Vietnam War.

1. In the summer of '64, there was a focused attempt to register as many African-American voters as possible in the highly segregated and racist state of Mississippi. This campaign was known as Freedom Summer (aka the Mississippi Summer Project). These were turbulent times and the young volunteers—mainly college students—were violently opposed by Mississippians, who were not inclined to change their way of life and thinking. It got very ugly.

In fact, three young volunteers were murdered (James Chaney, Michael Schwerner and Andrew Goodman.

2. The Vietnam War was heating up on the other side of the planet. As previously mentioned, I received an educational deferment from serving in the armed forces. The movement against U.S. involvement in the Vietnam War began small. It started with peace activists on college campuses across the country. By 1965 the movement gathered traction and never looked back. Again, these were turbulent times. In 1970, four Kent

University students were shot and killed by the Ohio National Guard.

The point of this sidebar is to illustrate my embarrassment of never having participated in these momentous movements. I really felt like I missed out on some real opportunities to change the world. Thousands of college-age youth were making a big difference. I was almost oblivious to these events. Where was I? What was I doing? I was at Columbia making records or cloistered away at United Theological Seminary. Thankfully, I was not totally absent from these movements (as we shall see).

## The Recording Rip Chords Versus the Touring Rip Chords

Again, although I was back in the studio to record, I did not tour because of my educational commitment and the restrictions imposed on me by church officials. As for Bruce Johnston and Terry Melcher, they had no interest in touring because they were busy as Columbia producers. Also, they were not the Rip Chords, at least not legally and not in the public's eye. But all groups need representation in the field. Accordingly, the arrangement of Rich Rotkin and Arnie Marcus touring with Phil Stewart remained in place until the group disbanded in 1965.

As a practicality, Columbia's powerful marketing machine made no distinction between the recording Rip Chords and the touring Rip Chords. It was the touring Rip Chords (Phil, Rich, and Arnie) that were featured in all of the publicity campaigns. Their names and pictures appeared in ads, interviews, photo shots, magazines, album covers, and so forth. At the risk of being redundant, it is vitally important to remember that this arrangement was necessary; because, even though Rich and Arnie never recorded with us in the studio, they were nevertheless on the touring end of the equation. They, along with Phil, would be the ones showing up on stage.

Accordingly, this touring ensemble was invited to appear on Dick Clark's *American Bandstand*, and toured with him on his 1964 Caravan of Stars (which included The Supremes and other notables). They also performed in the 1965 Hollywood movie, *A Swingin' Summer*, with American actress and sex symbol, Raquel Welch.

As a consequence, to most of the music industry and the public at large, no one realized that the touring Rip Chords and the recording Rip Chords—with the exception of Phil—were not the same people. This confusion was also fostered by both the *Cobra* and *Three Window* album jackets; they correctly listed Phil and myself as vocalists, but then neglected to mention Bruce and Terry, while incorrectly listing Rich and Arnie as vocalists.

Despite these irregularities, Rich Rotkin, Arnie Marcus, and Phil Stewart continued on as the touring arm of the Rip Chords, while Terry Melcher, Bruce Johnston, Phil Stewart, and I made the recordings. This unconventional arrangement would eventually undermine the true identity of our group and the legacy of our music. Who were the Rip Chords, anyway?

It was a wacky situation and, in some ways, more convoluted than Milli Vanilli.[62] I flew in from seminary to record, but I didn't tour; Rich and Arnie toured, but they didn't record; Phil

---

[62]Milli Vanilli was a pop and dance group formed with Fab Morvan and Rob Pilatus. They won a Grammy Award for Best New Artist in 1990. Their success turned to infamy when the Grammy award was withdrawn after it was revealed that the lead vocals on the record were not the voices of Morvan and Pilatus.

recorded and also toured; Bruce and Terry certainly didn't tour although they did record with Phil and me as ghost singers. But no one outside of the studio knew these things. In the words of author Stephen J. McParland, "It was like a cloning experiment in a Saturday morning cartoon gone wild!"[63]

### Our Fifth and Sixth Singles Released ("One Piece Topless Bathing Suit" and "Don't Be Scared")

Our last release of any consequence was the single, "One Piece Topless Bathing Suit" (June, 1964). Terry and I shared the lead. The song managed to break into the national charts, but failed to generate major activity.

Incidentally, it was during the summer of 1964 that I purchased my first new car, a 1964 yellow Mustang. It was the first series of Mustangs produced by Ford and it was a beauty. I drove it back to seminary that fall. It was a real eye-catcher on campus.

In February 1965 a final single was released called "Don't Be Scared." No national chart success ensued. It was the beginning of the end.

### Disbandment and Summary

Shortly after the '65 release, our group disbanded for several reasons. Terry and Bruce sought their own claim to fame by starting their own group. But their success as a duo was not to be. Predictably, however, this divisional distraction was counterproductive. The old axiom that "a house divided against itself cannot stand," proved true. The breakup of the group, in

---

[63]*Summer U.S.A.! The Best of the Rip Chords*, Sony Music Special Products, © & ℗ 2006, Sundazed Music Inc, p. 4. Stephen J. McParland is the editor of California Music Magazine.

any case, would have been inevitable. Personally, I had already made a conscious decision to pursue my ministerial calling rather than my recording career. Bruce was being courted by the Beach Boys (which he eventually joined). Terry had his hands full producing other Columbia artists, and Phil was leaning toward Country & Western (his true love). We all seemed willing to move in these different directions.

This is not to imply that at some points along the way, hard feelings did not ensue. We were all a bit self-centered and impetuous in our younger day. But I don't believe any of us set out to hurt anyone, or deprive anyone his rightful place. Whatever the case, all four of us share responsibility for the group's decline.

Looking back, I know we didn't achieve our full potential as a group. We didn't get it all, but I'm grateful and satisfied for what we did accomplish, and when I say "we," that includes all four singers. But I cannot close this account without reiterating the importance of Terry Melcher (now deceased) and Bruce Johnston. Without them, one wonders at the outcome.

However, I take pride in knowing that our first release, "Here I Stand," featured only the voices of Phil and me, and that was the record that launched the group onto the national charts and paved the way for any future success. Furthermore, in my opinion, the Rip Chords' sound was never so vibrant and expressive as when all four voices registered their influence, which was on most of the recordings. Neither Phil and I as a duo, nor Terry and Bruce as a duo (who recorded their own music under the moniker of Bruce and Terry), ever recaptured the marvelous sounds of all four voices as found on the Rip Chords' albums, especially the *Three Window Coupe* album.

Shortly before Terry lost his battle against melanoma in 2004, I had the opportunity to share with him my personal gratitude for the time we shared together, and his talented contribution to our group. In 2011 I wrote a letter to Doris Day regarding my personal relationship with Terry. In November of 2014, I was contacted by *Closer* magazine. They were featuring an article on Doris Day and her son Terry and were calling me for some input (which I gladly gave them.)[64]

To summarize, we (the Rip Chords) had managed to place five singles on The Billboard Hot 100, a major achievement by any standard. We had also released two albums that reflected the car/surf genre of the

*Actress/Singer Doris Day (1960s)*

day. It was a good run. Stephen J. McParland sums it up this way: "But something as trendy and timely as the Rip Chords' sound and image also had a built-in clock, something like those little pop-up thermometers they used to implant in roasting chickens. When your time's up, you're done."[65] We (Terry Melcher, Bruce Johnston, Phil Stewart and myself) never recorded any music under the Rip Chords' moniker after disbanding in 1965.

---

[64]Lisa Chambers, *CLOSER*: "Closer to the Stars You Love," December 1, 2014, Vol. 2 Issue 48, pp.28-31

[65]*Summer U.S.A.! The Best of the Rip Chords*, Sony Music Special Products, © & ℗ 2006, Sundazed Music Inc., p. 8. Stephen J. McParland, Editor of California Music Magazine.

## The New Rip Chords

Although Rich and Arnie never appeared vocally on any of the 1960s Rip Chords' recordings, they nonetheless toured as the Rip Chords. In the mid-1990s they revived the Rip Chords with additional new members. Today, they tour and record new product calling themselves the Rip Chords with the implied claim that they were also part of the original recording group. However, anything recorded after 1965 under the Rip Chords' banner, is bogus. I repeat: This new group tours extensively, and produces new recordings under the Rip Chords' name. However, none of the original singers from the 1960s are part of this group, or their new recordings. Let the buyer beware.

A few years ago I met with our co-producer, Bruce Johnston, who is now a starring member of the Beach Boys. We met following a Beach Boys 50th Anniversary Tour Concert (July 7, 2012) in Phoenix, Arizona, and discussed this fabricated notion being advanced by the so-called Rip Chords of today. As Bruce so aptly put it: "We did all the singing and they're taking all the bows."

For the average Joe, the Rip Chords' identity crisis matters not. But for rock & roll pundits, the issue remains blurred. That's because it is difficult for anyone to understand the group's original tri-components; that is, (1) the founding/ recording Rip Chords of Phil and myself, (2) the vocal additions made by Bruce and Terry as ghost singers, and (3) the non-recording touring appendage of Rich and Arnie.

However, in 2006, Sundazed Music clearly clarified this puzzle when they issued their final CD Rip Chords' release: *Summer U.S.A.! The Best of the Rip Chords*. (Not to be confused with the CD issued by the new group, *The Best of the Rip Chords... Today*.) The Sundazed CD booklet specifies the fact that Rich

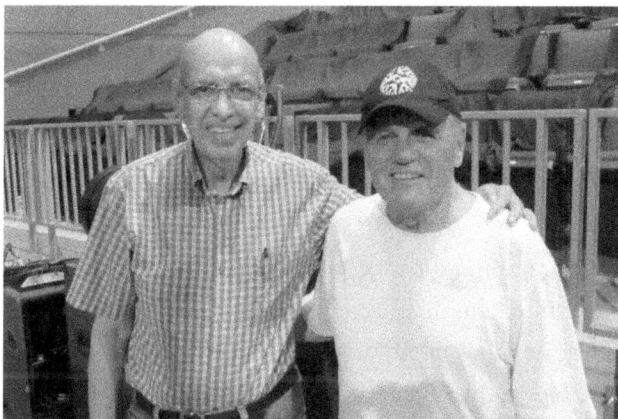

*L-R; Ernie Bringas & Bruce Johnson (2012)*

and Arnie comprised only the touring aspect of the group, but were not part of the recording Rip Chords. The 2006 booklet states: [Ernie] "Bringas, in the middle of his divinity school studies, was slated to attend the United Theological Seminary in Dayton, Ohio and would be unavailable to tour. To resolve this dilemma, two musicians, Arnie Marcus and Rich Rotkin, were hired, *essentially creating two separate groups of Rip Chords; a recording act, and a touring entity.* "[66]

Also, the 2006 CD slipcover clearly identifies the recording Rip Chords: "No group epitomized the sun-soaked California Sound better than the fabulous Rip Chords... Led by legendary producer Terry Melcher along with future Beach Boy Bruce Johnston and ace-vocalists Ernie Bringas and Phil Stewart, these long-board big-guns left an indelible mark on the surf 'n strip sounds of the '60s...."[67]

---

[66]*Summer U.S.A.! The Best of the Rip Chords*, Sony Music Special Products, © & ℗ 2006, Sundazed Music Inc., p. 3.
[67]*Summer U.S.A.! The Best of the Rip Chords*, Sony Music Special Products, © & ℗ 2006, Sundazed Music Inc., on back of slipcover.

NOTE: At this very moment I'm at my computer working on this manuscript while listening to the Sock Hop Oldies station. I'm brought to attention because our song, "Hey Little Cobra," just aired. The memories flood back to Columbia Records and the numerous hours we spent in the studio recording. Here we are 50 years later and our music still pops up every now and then. Believe it or not, I still receive a royalty check from Columbia Records (Sony Music) every six months, albeit quite minimal now. I think the last payment was $1.98. Before I leave this subject of recording, I thought the following two anecdotes would be of interest. Again Disney was right: "It's A Small World After All" (song by Richard Sherman & Robert Sherman).

**Stranger Than Fiction**
Remember Frankie Laine? I loved his music when I was a child (see pp. 68–69) Well guess what? The unimaginable happened while I was at Columbia. Terry Melcher, working with other Columbia artists, asked Phil and me if we would do the background vocals for Frankie Laine. Are you kidding me? Obviously, we jumped at the chance. Phil and I did the background vocals for two of his new recordings. Sadly, I never met the man personally because he wasn't in the studio when we laid the vocals. Rats. Still, the fact that my voice would ride alongside the great Frankie Laine was mind-boggling. Who would have thought it? The one regret I do have is not having logged the information about that recording. I have no memory of what we sang. In any case, I don't believe those particular recordings ever broke on the national scene; that, I would have remembered. Even so, I think of that event with fondness, and

marvel again at the serendipity and coincidental aspects of life over which we stumble.

Before moving on to my seminary experience, I'll share one more incident that occurred during these recording years. It certainly isn't the only story I could relate, but many other reflections can be found in some of my writings and also on the Internet. The incident I leave you with will be reprised almost verbatim from one of my other writings.

## Phil Spector

In the 1960s, Phil Spector was a rock & roll phenom. He was a record producer that specialized in girl groups; that is, vocal groups of young women. Who can forget those blockbuster hits by the Crystals, "He's A Rebel" and "Da Doo Ron Ron"? Let's not forget the Ronettes and their mega hits of "Baby I Love You" and "Walking in the Rain." Spector backed their vocals with his "Wall of Sound," a production technique that utilized reverberation, echo chambers, and a multiplicity of musicians. His Wall of Sound can be clearly heard in the huge hit, which he produced for the Righteous Brothers—"You've Lost That Lovin' Feeling" (according to industry sources [BMI], the most played song in radio history).

Many of Spector's hits were recorded at a little studio called Gold Star, located on Santa Monica Blvd. in Hollywood. The studio had an exceptional echo chamber that helped produce the Wall of Sound. Gold Star was the recording Mecca of many early rock legends, as I previously noted. Accordingly, I was well acquainted with Gold Star. I had been recording there since the age of 17. This was the place I would run into Phil Spector. Here's what happened.

In the summer of 1965, I was back in California for a well-deserved rest from my second arduous year at United Theological Seminary (Dayton, Ohio). One day I happened to be at Gold Star. I was in the hallway when this thin-looking character (whom I didn't recognize) scurried up to me, barking as he approached, "I hear you guys" (meaning the Rip Chords) "have been hitting on my girls while you all were on tour!"

Is he yelling at me? I thought to myself. When it became clear that he was, I responded firmly: "I don't know what you're talking about. I don't know you, and I don't know your girls."

"I'm Phil Spector!" he shot back angrily, apparently more agitated because I had failed to recognize him.

"Listen," I said sharply, "I'm a seminary student home for the summer. I haven't even been on tour with the Rip Chords because I've been cloistered away all year studying, and I resent your accusation. What's your problem?"

I think I startled him. Without a word he spun around and scurried off in the same direction from which he had approached. That confrontational scene was bizarre but evidently not uncommon for Spector. I later learned that he had a nasty reputation for being eccentric and unpredictable. At least that was the scuttlebutt back then, so aside from my own encounter, I really can't say. Nevertheless, in 2003, he drew media attention when he was accused of shooting to death a young woman who was visiting at his mansion. On April 14, 2009, a jury convicted him of second-degree murder. It's likely that he will spend his remaining years in prison—a sad ending to an otherwise illustrious career.[68]

---

[68]Ernie Bringas, *JESUSGATE: A History of Concealment Unraveled.* Faber, Virginia: Rainbow Ridge Books, 2013, pp. 10-11.

# Chapter 13

# UNITED THEOLOGICAL SEMINARY
## SEMINARIO TEOLÓGICO UNIDO

*Dayton, Ohio*
1963—1966

As you already know, my Hollywood days and seminary days overlapped. But if I had to choose between these two incredible experiences, I would keep my seminary days. Fortunately, that's a choice I didn't have to make, thanks to Bishop Sparks.

## The Place
At the age of 23—within a few weeks of turning 24—I arrived at United Theological Seminary (UTS), in Dayton, Ohio, in early September of 1963. The seminary was owned and run by the Evangelical United Brethren Church (EUB Church). Most of the students came from EUB churches. We gravitated there from all corners of the country but most of us came from the Midwest. I was the only one from California.

Prior to coming to UTS in September of '63, I had visited the campus in March of that same year. Having left the beautiful warm weather of Southern California, I had no idea of what to expect in Ohio. I traveled by train—to see the country—and as I got closer to Ohio, I started noticing little patches of snow on the ground from the train window. I didn't think too much about it until I disembarked at the Dayton train station in my short-sleeved shirt. The temperature was two degrees above zero. Yeow! I darn near froze to death!

United had a beautiful campus; it was picturesque. All of the buildings, including the chapel, library, classrooms, and dorms, were placed outside of an oval shaped driveway about one-third of a mile around, and one-fourth of a mile wide. The campus was filled with beautiful green grass and lovely trees that also stretched between and beyond the 20 yards that separated each individual building that rested just outside of the oval driveway. Behind these buildings were acres of green grass and wooded areas. Call it the back lot if you wish, but this is where we had our picnics, football and volleyball games, not to mention a small playground for family kids. When it snowed during the winter, the entire campus and surrounding neighborhood turned into an enchanted wonderland. In many respects, the place was breathtaking. This "Hallmark" setting was all new and very impressive to someone like me who grew up on the snowless, concrete streets of Southern California.

## The Students

Our entering class numbered about 40 and almost half were married. The UTS student body as a whole—Juniors, "Middlers," and Seniors—numbered about 120. I lived in Fout Hall. It was a three-story dorm that sat directly across from the Roberts Hall dorm on the other side of the oval driveway. The majority of marrieds lived in Roberts Hall (a nicer, more modern facility), while all of us singles lived in Fout Hall (an older but efficiently adequate building). The only disconcerting problem we had with our building was the persistent visitation of what our custodians called the "little brown bandits." These "little" brown bandits looked like they were three times the size of a normal cockroach. The scuttlebutt was that they were native to Asia and almost impossible to eradicate. Most frequently, they would make their way up through the plumbing into our shower stalls. You never knew quite what to expect when you pulled back that shower curtain. Sometimes you'd see two or three of these pickle-sized critters scurrying about. They were not at all a pleasant sight. Not so incidentally, all of our custodians were African American with the exception of the head custodian who was, of course, white (remember, this is the early 1960s).

Our dorm was coed. That sounded very inviting to me until I discovered that we only had two women in our entire class,[69] and all the single guys seemed to know in which room and what floor they resided. Today, that gender imbalance no longer exists; it's about a fifty-fifty student body, and that has

---

[69]Ministry was not a profession that women were encouraged to pursue in '60s culture. If they were in seminary, their purpose was almost always to get a degree in Christian Education. This differentiation would be the equivalent of that between a doctor and a nurse in the medical field

made a big difference. Women are now readily accepted as ministers in most Protestant denominations. Reform Jews also accept women as rabbis. Catholics are still resistant to the idea of female priests. Muslims are even more restrictive in allowing women any significant religious authority.

Upon arrival, one had no clue about what kind of people would comprise the student body, except to assume that they would be dedicated Christians of one sort or another. I was really amazed, and in some ways amused, at the varied assortment of characters that showed up. The only non-variable characteristics were that everyone had a college degree, was white, and presumed to be straight (again, this is the '60s). But in reality, we had introverts and extroverts, short and tall, big and small, heterosexuals, homosexuals, wackos and intellectuals. We had honeys, crummies and dummies. We even had a California nut that recorded rock & roll in Hollywood.

With the exception of serial killers, I think almost every personality of the human spectrum was present. There was even a rumor that one of the two girls was a lesbian, but no one could say for sure. She wasn't about to "confess." Nobody back then was brave enough to come out of the closet. Such a disclosure might get you kicked out of school and the ministry altogether. Whatever the case, she sure looked the part (by our naïve and stereotypical standards back then). In *some* ministerial circles today sexual preference wouldn't matter much as long as he or she was capable of professional ministry.

Having said all that, I must admit that some of the finest people I ever met, I met in seminary, including two of my closest, lifelong friends (Dave Bourquin and Dr. Bob Erickson). Furthermore, most students who graduate from seminary make distinguishing contributions to humanity not only in the field of church ministry, but also in numerous other fields such as medicine, psychology, social services, and education. One more point. There was a lot of humor coursing through the religious-oriented veins of the student body. One constantly heard religious jokes of every sort. Here is one of my favorites: "A small rural church, during a given summer week, is conducting its yearly evangelical outreach services. On the front bulletin board outside of the church, printed in big, black, bold letters, are the words: "IF YOU'RE TIRED OF SINNING, COME ON IN!" On closer inspection, one sees that someone has scribbled some additional words underneath the main caption. *"If you're not, call 721 – etc."*

### The Faculty

What an outstanding male faculty. Yes, they were all men except for one female instructor who worked almost exclusively with the female students (we only had two female students). Again, this was back in the '60s and the absence of women in higher education appeared perfectly normal. As stated earlier, today 50% of seminary students are female. Wow, how times have changed. For the better, I might add. Actually, the "modern" push for gender equality started gaining traction about the same month I graduated from seminary. The National Organization for Women (NOW) was started in June of 1966. Although a few laws had been passed forbidding discrimination against women, hardly any were being enforced. Prior to the NOW movement, one rarely saw women in positions of authority; that is, lawyers, judges, ministers, broadcasters, CEOs, doctors, were basically non-existent. The National Organization for Women changed all that; they took society to the mat! As a result, women have made unbelievable progress at every level of private and public life. According to the popular TV program, *Meet the Press*, in 1960 only 18% of women were in college, while today 60% of women are in college (May 10, 2015). However, emancipation is neither universal nor complete. It's still a movement in progress.

In 1972, we got Title IX, a 1972 comprehensive federal law that prohibits discrimination on the basis of sex in any federally funded educational institution. This has led to a large increase in the number of women participating in athletics at all levels of education. For example, according to Wikipedia: Since 1972 "…the number of women in college sports had increased 450% . . . In 1971, fewer than 295,000 girls participated in high school varsity athletics . . . in 2001, that number leaped to 2.8 million. . . . In 1966, 16,000 females competed in intercollegiate athletics. By 2001, that number jumped to more than 150,000, accounting for 43 percent of all college athletes." This late afternoon I watched the USA Women's Soccer team beat Japan's team for the World Cup Championship. An unprecedented third win for any team worldwide. (But I digress. Let's get back to our "all" male faculty at United Seminary.)

All that needs to be said is that these men provided an atmosphere that was enabling on many levels. I guess you might say we were family. We shared meals, personal concerns, and discussed philosophical and theological conundrums. Personal friendships were forged that would last a lifetime.

## When Worlds Collide

My seminary days (actually 3 years) were incredibly rich, not only because of personal encounters, but for the intensity of education received. As I mentioned earlier, my childhood upbringing was quite conservative when it came to religion.

Contrary to what one might think, the EUB Church was very conservative on the West Coast, but somewhat liberal in the Midwest. Looking back, I would classify myself as having been a fundamentalist. By the time I reached seminary, I had mellowed out a bit owing to my university experience in California, but I remained hardcore to the right.

Having made my way east to United Theological Seminary in Dayton, I would spend the next three years trying to elevate my elementary religious KQ (knowledge quotient), to a much more advanced level. I had a lot of work to do for two reasons.

First, my college career had not been a stellar one, to say the least. I had too many outside activities that sapped my time and energy, one of which was trying to land a recording contract, not to mention trying to run a youth program at my local church.

Second, I had majored in Psychology and never took a course in religious studies. Actually, at that time there were not many religion courses being offered. That was a bummer. Following college, therefore, I arrived at the seminary dorm with all the baggage of an opinionated believer. My religious convictions were presumptuous; that is, the only religion of merit was Christianity, and the only way to salvation was Jesus. I was in need of what that song from Hank Williams, Jr. called an "Attitude Adjustment."

It didn't take long to get intellectually and emotionally disoriented because I felt like a Neanderthal who had just been thrown into the 20th century. I ran smack dab into the rigors of biblical criticism (see the sidebar on the following page).

Biblical criticism serves as a catch-all expression that incorporates all the analytical processes of religious scholarship (such as textual criticism, historical criticism, source criticism, form criticism, redaction criticism, and many more). Through harmonious interplay these disciplines help to determine the character, composition, authorship, historical authenticity, and origin of biblical documents; they also help to evaluate the influence of surrounding cultures on the development of Christianity in its early stages. Unfortunately, this term, "biblical criticism," gives the false impression of being negative or critical of biblical writing. This impression is incorrect because the terms "critic" and "criticism" derive from the Greek word *Kritikos*, meaning able to judge or analyze. The word criticism reflects a discipline of scholarly investigation, and should not be associated with the popular understanding as an expression of disapproval.[70] Biblical criticism had a profound impact on my understanding of Christianity. The study of Church History was also an eye-opener.

My first year was a theological mind-bender. Aside from the first year curriculum that hammered away at my calcified beliefs, I remember an incident that was especially helpful in adjusting my religious bias. It all started when I heard from one of my peers that the seminary faculty had invited Dr. Abraham

[70]Ernie Bringas, *JESUSGATE: A History of Concealment Unraveled*, 2013, p. xii.

Heschel to speak to our student body. My first reaction was: "Abraham who?"

Unbeknownst to me, although I was quickly informed, Abraham Heschel was an eminent Jewish scholar, one of the leading Jewish theologians of the 20th century. But I struggled to understand why in good conscience our faculty would invite a Jew to speak to a group of young Christians who were studying for the ministry. It didn't make any sense. I had known since childhood that Jews were headed for hell because they had never accepted Jesus as their Savior. The Gospel of John (14:6) made it very clear where Jesus says: "I am the way, and the truth, and the life. No one comes to the Father except through me." In my uneducated innocence, I thought these were the exact words from the mouth of Jesus. These words from Jesus provided the standard argument for what would happen to people who stood outside of the Christian faith. (This is not to imply that all Christians hold this narrow view.)

I remember sitting in the basement of our dorm, along with other students, faculty, and community leaders awaiting the great Abraham Heschel to arrive. I was, at the very least, curious to hear what this lost soul had to say. At last, he entered the room. What happened next came as an utter surprise, or should I say shock. The following may sound eerie, but I'll try to explain it as best I can.

The minute Dr. Heschel walked into the room, everything went quiet. It was as though we were instantly mesmerized. Even as I think back on it today, I get goose bumps. It's almost impossible to explain. I can't speak for everyone who was there that day, but for me it was an electrical jolt. It felt as if a divine presence had entered the room. The way he looked with his white beard, the way he moved; his overall essence captured my immediate attention. Even before he uttered a single word, I detected a gentleness and a power about this man I had never encountered elsewhere. He slowly made his way to the podium and then proceeded to give one of the most eloquent opening prayers that my ears had ever heard. His voice and the chosen words of his morning message had the flow of divine poetry. It was the coming together of both intellectualism and spiritualism, the likes of which were indescribably riveting.

Upon his departure I was left with an unsettling realization: If this guy was going to hell, what kind of chance did I have? I was left pondering the words of Jesus as found *only* in the Gospel of John: "No one comes to the Father except through me." Something was terribly wrong.[71] For me, this was the beginning of something new that eventually expanded the horizons of my conservative religious mind-set.

However, it was the discipline of biblical criticism (along with the study of Church History) that was the driving force behind my educational experience, and it profoundly changed the trajectory of my spiritual journey. The process of critical thinking, when applied to one's belief system, has serious implications. And trying to escape the consequences of increased knowledge is like trying to dodge raindrops in a rainstorm. It's impossible, unless you want to ignore certain facts and pretend they don't exist. By the sheer weight of the evidence, one's beliefs are reshaped and modified. The end result, as it should be in any field of thought, is a better understanding of reality, a closer approximation of the truth.

And so it was that on my way to becoming a United Methodist minister, I would discover a significantly different

---

[71]Ibid. pp. 137-38.

portrayal of Christianity. It was a Christianity transformed— transformed by the collective knowledge of humankind (both secular and religious), and it was out of sync with what I had been taught at the local level. In other words, it bore little resemblance to what I had learned from family and church. I do not intend to rehash that information here since I have carefully laid much of this material out in other writings (see footnote).[72] Suffice it to say, my belief system was turned topsy-turvy, and rightly so.

## Bits and Pieces

I could share many other anecdotal stories about my seminary years. I'll bypass the temptation. However, I will share three more standout experiences.

### 1. Work!

Although we were in school studying for the ministry, we were expected to get a part-time ministerial job serving one of the local churches in the area. Most of us needed the money to pay for room and board anyway. But doubly important, these jobs also served as an internship. After all, this would provide excellent experience in our chosen field of work. Some of us would serve as pastors, assistant pastors, youth directors, and so forth. Most of the time, the seminary administrators would secure these jobs for us, especially for those of us from out of state since we didn't have any contacts there. Our church employments were usually within a 25-mile radius. But some of the guys served churches

---

[72]See: Ernie Bringas, *JESUSGATE: A History of Concealment Revealed.* Rainbow Ridge Books, © 2013. Also See: Ernie Bringas, *GOING BY THE BOOK: The Past and Present Tragedies of Biblical Authority.* Hampton Roads Publishers, © 1996.

out in the boondocks. That's the main reason we didn't have classes on Mondays. That was nice; every week we had a three-day weekend (albeit we worked on Sundays).

I was hired as a youth worker for the Presbyterian Church in Yellow Springs, about 20 miles from the seminary. That was easy work and lots of fun because I always enjoyed working with youth. I assisted them during Sunday school, and ran the evening junior and senior high programs. The winters were especially challenging because driving on those Ohio roads during a snowstorm could be disorienting. Sometimes the roadway disappeared altogether. Scary.

On another occasion, driving back to the seminary from a youth conference in Pittsburgh, a drunk driver tried to pass me on the driver's side as we approached a hill. No one in his right mind would ever try to pass a car on an uphill grade. We were moving at about 70 miles per hour. Is he nuts? I thought to myself.

So here we are speeding along, side by side, on a two-lane highway that is flanked on both sides by hilly terrain; that is, there's no place to pull off. Sure enough, here comes another car cresting over the hill, barreling down on us from the opposite direction. We were headed for a catastrophic head-on collision. I knew this nut didn't have enough time to get around me so I sped up hoping that he would have enough sense to slow down and squeeze in behind me. Realizing there was no other option for him, he quickly—and I might add barely—got back into my lane as the other car zoomed past us.

However, he and I did not escape unscathed. When he swerved in behind me, he clipped the rear end of my Mustang and spun me around. I turned my wheel into the spin and applied my brakes. I darn near hit the other car as it flew past, and it was a miracle that I didn't flip over. We drove further on until we found a small clearing and were able to pull off to the side of the highway. That's when I discovered the guy was plastered. I was not a happy camper. Harking back to my family's collision on Highway 101, this was my second go-around with a drunk driver.

He gave me a song-and-dance excuse and offered to pay cash for any damage he caused if I wouldn't report this to my insurance company. It seems he was already in hot water for previous drunk driving accidents. Obviously, this guy hadn't learned anything about driving and drinking, and I wasn't about to let him off the hook. I made it quite clear that this would be reported to the police. Of course, out in the middle of nowhere, there wasn't a phone in sight, so that had to wait until my next stop (cell phones were non-existent).

### 2. Fire and Brimstone

Although I was now working every Sunday at the Presbyterian church, and occasionally flying to Hollywood to record, I secured another job working in the notions and pharmaceutical sections of Rikes Department Store in Dayton. I needed the extra cash to help pay for my schooling. Of course, you may wonder why I would need extra money after placing a few hit records on the charts. The reason is quite simple. I wouldn't see the royalty money from the sale of those records for some time. Besides, the real money—the instant money—was in touring. The Rip Chords were making big bucks every week traveling with Dick Clark or getting involved with other gigs. But I didn't tour, so that flow of money was not available to me.

Actually, I had a pleasant experience at Rikes. Most of the time I was putting merchandise on the floor (restocking), and price tagging all the products. All of my coworkers knew I was from the seminary and was studying for the ministry. One evening, as I was stocking the shelves along with one of the middle-age female coworkers, we overheard a customer polluting the airways with foul language while conversing with his pal. After they left, my coworker, knowing I was studying for the ministry, turned to me and she said: "That guy was terrible. Swearing and taking the Lord's name in vain is unforgivable. I think the Bible makes it clear—that man has committed blasphemy! Don't you agree?"

I looked her straight in the eye and answered with firm conviction: "You're damn right! That son of a bitch is headed for hell!"

The look on her face was a mixture of astonishment and bewilderment. Her brain was trying to catch up with my words—words that just didn't compute with what she had expected me to say. Honestly, I did not keep her in suspense and I quickly explained my intention. I suggested that the words he had spoken were not from his heart and were, therefore, not of any real moral consequence. Perhaps his words were careless, impolite or not very thoughtful, but not immoral. As for my crude language, that was just an object lesson in an effort to make a positive point. Being judgmental and jumping to conclusions was not enough exercise to keep anybody healthy. I pointed out that motivation was one of the factors that had to be considered when drawing conclusions about another person's behavior. I'm glad to say she understood. (Here comes my last anecdote for the moment.)

### 3. The More the Merrier

As I have already mentioned, I was a member of the Evangelical United Brethren Church (EUB Church). This Protestant denomination numbered about three million nationwide. Every now and then, the National EUB Board would come up with program ideas to be implemented by the various churches throughout the country. For example, when I was a teenager, one such program was conceived and developed for the purpose of growing EUB membership. The slogan read: *EACH ONE WIN ONE!* Accordingly, we were all encouraged to invite friends and neighbors to our local church in hopes of increasing church membership (or bringing them to salvation through Jesus). The more the merrier. This motto, *EACH ONE WIN ONE!*, was plastered on posters in our churches, talked about from the pulpit, and generally promoted at all church meetings and get-togethers. I did my part by bringing a few of my high school buddies to church. (Stay with me on this; it will all make sense in a moment).

Fast forward to my seminary days. In one of my seminary classes, my assignment was to give a verbal report about the problems of overpopulation and famine. I studied these problems carefully. As I considered the population explosion, the lack of food, and the predicted famine worldwide, I came to the conclusion that "more was not necessarily better." Too many people and not enough resources was a recipe for disaster. It wasn't a good idea to overload the rowboat after all. Bringing more people on board just might sink it. Although somewhat benign compared to overpopulation and starvation, I couldn't help but think back to our big EUB push—*EACH ONE WIN ONE!* Sometimes vibrant movements lose their vitality when they get too big. In any case, pondering the old slogan did provide some insights to the overall problems I was grappling with.

My class report came due. I stood before the class and gave them all the disheartening figures of overpopulation and mass starvation. The facts didn't lie. The world was heading for a population explosion that would create unprecedented food shortages. The prospects were grim, indeed. Before I could finish my final point, the school buzzer went off, signaling the end of our class period. Predictably, everyone eagerly jumped out from behind their desks.

"Wait, Wait!" I shouted. I startled everyone, including our instructor, Dr. Wert. But I had a strong passion for making my final point. Almost reluctantly, everyone slowly sat back down. I continued with my closing comment.

"I've thought long and hard on this issue and I think I found a solution. This is important. Before you leave, I want to share how I think we can solve the problem of overpopulation and scarcity of food." I made my final point!

"All of you are familiar with our old EUB motto, *EACH ONE WIN ONE!* If we tweak it just a bit, we can simultaneously eradicate overpopulation and famine in one fell swoop. We'll call this campaign, *EACH ONE EAT ONE!"* (Uproarious laughter ensued.)

### Summer of 1965

I had just finished my Middler (2nd) year at United and was back in California for the summer. I was one year away from graduation and would be back to United in September to finish my senior year. Unbeknownst to me, at the start of this three-month vacation, the summer of '65 would impact my life in a way that was unimaginable. On the national scene, it would have a pivotal impact on the Civil Rights Movement. Who would have thought it? However, to understand this enigmatic introduction, specifics are in order.

It was August. I was near the end of my summer vacation when all hell broke loose in South Central Los Angeles and surrounding areas. This calamity was termed the "Watts Riots!"

"The Watts Riots . . . was an African-American race riot that took place in the Watts neighborhood of Los Angeles from August 11 to 17, 1965. The six days of racially-fueled vio-

*My seminary days (1963-66)*

lence and unrest resulted in 34 deaths, 1,032 injuries, 3,438 arrests, and over $40 million in property damage. It was the most severe riot in the city's history until the Los Angeles riots of 1992, and is considered by many to be a key turning point in the African-American Civil Rights Movement."[73]

The causes of these riots are obvious. High on the list was residential discrimination. By WWII, 95% of LA housing was off limits to blacks.[74] Thus, they were delegated to the poorest neighborhoods where crime, high unemployment, police

---

[73]Taken from Wikipedia, the free encyclopedia.
[74]Up until the '60s, the term Negro was used to designate Americans of African heritage but is now considered as improper. The term colored people is equally obsolete. Today, African American or black is the usage now generally considered acceptable.

discrimination and brutality were the norm. Accordingly, educational and political opportunities were basically unavailable. As a result, blacks were excluded from high paying jobs, or any jobs for many of them. It was a vicious cycle. Blacks, Hispanics, and Asians (but mainly blacks) had suffered severe discrimination for decades. South LA was a stick of dynamite waiting to explode. On August 11, two police officers made a routine arrest of a black man suspected of drunk driving. An angry crowd soon gathered and the fuse was lit. According to Wikipedia, a 46-square-mile swath of LA would be transformed into a combat zone for the next six days.

Although not in Watts proper, our old neighborhood (80th Street and San Pedro), was very close to the nucleus. Since my family's departure in 1952, most of the area had become almost entirely African American.

My mom's home in Inglewood, where I was staying for the summer, was several miles removed from the turbulence, but nevertheless too close for comfort. We were afraid that the riots might spill over into the white suburbs of Inglewood. We were riveted to the television during those six days—and nights—as we monitored the violence that erupted in the various geographical areas of LA. It was difficult to believe that the events we saw unfolding on TV could be within a 20-minute drive from where we lived.

Actually, we were more concerned for my grandmother (Lupe) and my aunt Mary who, during the late '40s and early '50s white-flight crises, had also moved away from 80th street (as we had). But they lived even closer to the riots than we did (on Crenshaw Blvd. near Florence street, for those of you who know the area). I picked them up and drove them back to my mom's house for "safekeeping." They would remain with us during those days of uncertainty until the situation calmed down. The riot was finally quelled by around 1700 police officers with the help of almost 4000 National Guardsmen. Unfortunately for those who lived in or around the Watts area, many of the buildings were left in shambles. Of course, injury and loss of life were the ultimate tragedies.

A month later I was headed back to Ohio for my senior year at United Seminary. Arriving back on campus, I never gave the previous month's tumultuous uproar in LA much thought. Of course, that incident, along with much of the Civil Rights Movement, was not at the center of my mental radar screen. I knew very little about blacks. I had never seen any of them in elementary, junior high, or high school. The cliché, "Out of sight, out of mind," rang true. And I had no clue about their social plight. I couldn't even imagine that in some southern states, blacks were being hanged just for looking at a white woman or speaking out of turn. It wasn't until much later in life that I even heard of Emmett Till, a 14-year-old African American boy who, in 1955, was kidnapped, brutally tortured and murdered in Mississippi for supposedly flirting with a white woman.

Emmett's mother insisted on a public funeral service and an open casket so that the world might see the ugly results of racism. It was gross![75] But the point was made. Nevertheless, an all-white jury of men found the defendants "not guilty" of the grisly crime, even though the evidence against them was overwhelming. In the South, that was par for the course. In those dark days of our history, white people killed blacks with impunity. What made this story especially wrenching for the

[75]Google this story, if you have the stomach for it.

nation was that the defendants, confident of the *double jeopardy* law, later admitted to killing the young boy.

Of course, in non-southern states, the lethal threat for blacks was a little more camouflaged. Many unwarranted killings occurred under the rubric of law enforcement (we're not totally out of the woods on that one). Other methods of racial discrimination proved pernicious. For example, residential and employment discrimination were two of the underlying causes for the Watts Riots in LA.

## Graduation 1966

Shortly before graduating from United in May of '66, I was approached by my D.S. (District Superintendent) from California. I was 26.

He was on campus to discuss some possible ministerial assignments that the Board of Ministry had considered for me. The D.S. was the go-between. Our Southern California EUB Conference had around 36 churches scattered about. We even had a church near Disneyland in the city of Anaheim. That church would be a nice place to start my ministry.

When you graduate from seminary and return to your home Conference, the Board of Ministry is required to find a place for you to serve in some ministerial capacity (it's called an "appointment"). They may recommend that you take a small church as a senior pastor, or an associate pastor in a large church, or some other form of professional ministry. In short, you're guaranteed a job. And that guarantee holds true throughout your ministry, no matter how many times they may choose to move you (unless you

screw up badly, like getting the church organist pregnant).
As one of my professors so aptly warned us: "Nothing will
get you out of the ministry faster than a stiff prick."

My District Superintendent was Dr. Schaffer. He was the consummate authoritarian religious leader, with a deep-throated voice that commanded your attention. He had come to offer me a very interesting appointment possibility. But he made it clear from the very beginning that I was not obligated to accept the appointment. If I declined, another appointment would be made available. One usually doesn't have this kind of flexibility when coming out of seminary. My curiosity was piqued.

"Ernie," he said, "you have a real knack for working with young people. This has become most evident with the work you did in your local church, and what you've done with our camps and other youth conference programs. How would you feel about working with black youth?"

"Say what?" I unthinkingly murmured.

"We have one church located in an all-black neighborhood very close to Watts," he declared, "and we are hoping that you would be willing to take an associate position in that church to begin a ministry with the black youth in that community."

"You mean we have a black church?" I asked inquisitively. "I don't remember seeing any blacks at our conference youth programs or summer camps, or any adult functions, for that matter."

"Well," he replied, "I guess you might say that's our problem. Either because it's their choice or our fault, there hasn't been much interaction between us. This whole problem of segregation and integration has really come to our attention as the Civil Rights Movement continues to shine a spotlight on racial discrimination. Of course, the Watts Riots in our own backyard last year really made us take notice. That's where you come in. We're asking if you would consider going to 'Watts' to work with our youth."

It was about this time that I realized I might not end up near Disneyland.

"But again," Dr. Schaffer continued, "you would have to be in total agreement with this appointment because we can't pretend there wouldn't be some risk involved. It's been less than a year since the riot. That zone is still a hotbed of unrest and white people usually try to avoid the area. Non-blacks have been viciously attacked on occasion and, frankly, some have been killed, although that would be highly unlikely in your case."

Easy for you to say, I thought to myself. "Is the pastor of that church black?" I asked.

"Yes, he is," answered the DS.

"Are all the church members there black?" I responded.

"Yes," he said without hesitation. "The entire area is pre-dominantly black."

"Where exactly is this church?" I enquired.

"It's near the corner streets of San Pedro and Florence," he answered.

I couldn't believe it. That was about one mile north from where I grew up as a child, just off of the corner streets of 80th and San Pedro. That area had been my old stomping ground. Freemont High School, where we kids and my mom used to go play, was located almost midway between this black church and our old home. It's a small world after all. However, that familiarity could not be the deciding factor in accepting the appointment. There was much to consider. That little white corner of the world that I once knew as a child was now almost universally black. Ironically, I would be headed smack dab into the geographical area that my family had escaped because of the white-flight phenomenon.

As a minster of youth, I would be working with black teenagers in an all-black district. Were black teenagers different than white ones? Could they all sing and dance like everyone said? Would I be accepted? How did I feel about blacks, anyway? Would I have to live in the black community, or could I commute from outside the area? Would I be in harm's way? What about my nose; could it take another punch if it had to?

"Dr. Schaffer," I searched for the right words, "I know I'm good with young people, but I have never worked with black youth, and I don't know the first thing about the black community. Sure, I know about the history of slavery, the Civil War, and today's Civil Rights Movement. But that's about it. Aside from the death and mayhem created by the Watts Riots in LA last year, all I know about these people is Little Black Sambo and Aunt Jemima pancakes. I also know that three young civil rights activists were murdered in Mississippi two years ago.[76] And I'm not even sure how I feel about African Americans since I've never had any experience socializing with them."

"I understand perfectly," he said. "In fact, that's our problem; this is new to us, too. All I can ask you to do is to ponder

---

[76]From Wikipedia: "In 1964 *three civil rights workers were murdered* on the night of June 21–22 in Philadelphia, Mississippi. They were James Earl Chaney from Meridian, Mississippi, and Andrew Goodman and Michael "Mickey" Schwerner from New York City, who were abducted, shot at close range and killed by members of the local White Knights of the Ku Klux Klan, the Neshoba County Sheriff's Office, and the Philadelphia Police Department of that city in Mississippi. The three young men had been working on the "Freedom Summer" campaign, attempting to prepare and register African Americans to vote after they had been disenfranchised since 1890."

this opportunity. I hope your answer will be yes. If so, you'll begin working there next month following your graduation here. I'll be in Dayton for two more days. Let me know what you decide. If you don't accept, we'll have to find someone else. But frankly, I don't know anyone who is more qualified.

Within 24 hours my decision was made. Yes, I would accept the appointment. My reason was twofold. To begin with, I felt obligated to the Board of Ministry for having allowed me to pursue my recording endeavors while attending United. Although I had the okay from the bishop, it was the board members who had the final word. Saying yes to their request would be a good way to show my gratitude. Even without my feeling of indebtedness, I could hardly say no to the Ministerial Board; that would be a heck of a way to start out on one's ministerial career. I didn't want to commit professional suicide. On the contrary, by accepting this deployment, I was demonstrating to the board my willingness to heed their wishes. I was playing the role of the good soldier. This might bode well for me in future appointments. (This all sounds a bit calculating, and I suppose it was.)

Secondly, and more importantly, I quickly recognized the uniqueness and the challenge of such an assignment. I was truly venturing into the unknown, perhaps even a dangerous one. Bravado and excitement tugged at my psyche. The idea of winning souls for Christ was also floating around in my head somewhere, but I don't remember it being the driving motivation behind my decision. I think my passion for that kind of religious directive was on the wane. This developing reserve is usually the result of educational enlightenment. "The heart cannot follow what the mind no longer accepts."[77]

In any case, my decision to go to Watts was a mixture and combination of several driving motivations, some of which I was unaware. Who knows? Anyway, I was on my way to "Watts," nose and all.

[77]This particular quote I owe to retired Episcopal Bishop, John Shelby Spong.

Chapter 14

# THE "WATTS" EXPERIENCE
## LA EXPERIENCIA DE WATTS

*God Calls and Close Calls*
1966 — 1968

As I HAD TOLD the DS, I really didn't know much about blacks. What I did know wasn't very flattering. Like most Americans, I carried many of the stereotype images that flowed through radio, television, and film. With few exceptions, African Americans were portrayed as scaredy-cats, lazy, dim-witted and, at worst, sub-human.

During the earlier days of cinema, even the best of black actors could not escape racial stereotypes. Such was the case with Hattie McDaniel. Hattie McDaniel (1895—1952) was an African American actress. She is best known for her Academy Award-winning role as Mammy in the 1939 film, *Gone with the Wind*. In addition to acting in over 300 films, she was the first black woman to sing on the radio in the USA. She has two stars on the Hollywood Walk of Fame for her contributions to radio and motion pictures. As Hattie became more famous, some in the black community criticized her for accepting, and thereby perpetuating, racial stereotypes by playing a maid. I thought her answer to that criticism was divine: "Why should I complain about making $700 a week playing a maid? If I didn't, I'd be making $7 a week being one."[78] (Note: Back in the day, $700 a week was astronomical.)

## Beginnings

In July of 1966, I drove up to the EUB Church located on the corners of 57ᵗʰ Street and San Pedro. It was an old, stucco, two-story building. It needed a new coat of paint and the front lawn was overdue for a haircut. Everyone walking around in the area was black. Harking back to *The Wizard of Oz*: "Toto, I've a feeling we're not in Kansas anymore." I know that last line has been overused, but it certainly fits the feelings I had when I found myself in an all-black neighborhood that extended for miles in all directions. I thought I was on a different planet. Prior to this time, I had never even met a black person: not in school, not socially, not professionally, not casually, not anywhere. I had never even conversed with one. Looking back, it's hard to believe that segregation was so pervasive and that I was thinking of these people as "those" people.

The living conditions in Watts were mixed, but most people lived in homes that, in many respects, were substandard. Back in the '40s when I lived here as a child, the homes were already

---

[78]This information was taken from Wikipedia.

quite old, but they were decent and well kept. Lawns were green, mowed, and nicely trimmed. A fresh coat of paint every now and then made a big difference. But now, 15 years after the white-flight occurrence, it was obvious that the neighborhood had deteriorated. It wasn't a place you would want to raise a family if you could afford otherwise. I wouldn't classify it as a slum, but it was certainly a depressed area with lots of idle people out of work. Young boys and men hung around the many liquor stores that were sprinkled throughout the area. It wasn't hard to see some of the underlying factors that helped trigger the Watts riots a year earlier. One thing for sure, it was a tough neighborhood, yes indeed. I didn't want to stick out like a sore thumb so I tried to dress and act the part. I learned to walk with some attitude, and I purchased a green, leather-like looking jacket that provided me with a more formidable persona.

I'll cut to the chase. My appointment in "Watts" turned out to be a marvelous experience. The adults were wonderful and the teenagers were engaging. I had a blast. Working with black teens turned out better than anything I could have imagined. We were a perfect fit because they had a wonderful sense of humor. We spent half the time laughing. I discovered very quickly that they enjoyed ragging on themselves (making good natured fun of each other). They chopped each other "down" any which way they could, and loved it. Well, guess what? This type of banter was right up my alley. Quick wit was one of my strengths. I was a master at put-downs, but not with malicious intent. One needs to be careful how one wields the sword of humor. Many times I was simply defending myself. For example, one of the guys might jab me by saying, "Ernie, your face could stop a clock." My response might be, "Oh yeah, well yours would make one run!" They relished the comeback remarks. These were delicious moments and we all cracked up.

Sometimes one had to be funny and tough at the same time. In this neighborhood, you had to think tough, act tough, and hoped that no one called your bluff. One afternoon I was jabbering with some of the guys in front of the church when this rough-looking guy sauntered on up like he owned the place. He certainly had the look of someone you wouldn't want to mess with. The guys certainly knew and respected him as they gave way to his approach, akin to the parting of the Red Sea. He swaggered on up and got in my face. He realized I was new in the community and wanted to make sure I understood that he was one of the honchos at the top of the pecking order. They introduced him as "Bonneville." He looked me straight in the eye and proudly proclaimed: "Yeah, I'm Bonneville! Everyone's heard of Bonneville!"

What a setup. This guy had given me an opening I couldn't refuse. It was my turn to look him straight in the eye. This was all about vocal tone and body language. With a poker-faced expression I shot back: "Oh yeah, well I've been here for six months and I never heard of you."

There was an explosion of laughter. The guys were beside themselves. Of course, I was somewhat concerned as to how this tough icon was going to take this verbal slight. The situation was right, my timing was right, my tone was right, my delivery was right . . . but how would he take it? I almost wished the surrounding laughter had not been so robust. But this had been a make-or-break moment and I had taken the gamble. I firmly stood my ground and gave no hint of walking back the comment.

Fortunately, Bonneville rolled with the punch. He took it in stride although he looked a bit unbalanced by my brazen remark. He wasn't used to people talking back with sharp one-liners. But I was an unknown quantity and he hadn't yet sized me up. I talked like a big man and maybe I was as far as he knew. I stood at six foot one and my green "leather" jacket was on board. The uncertainty of it all gave him pause. Whatever the reason, he was willing to let the matter slide. I was relieved. My daring comment had paid off all the way around and my fragile nose was still in one piece. To ensure against hard feelings, I offered Bonneville a needed ride to his cousin's house. He and three of the guys piled into my 1964 yellow Mustang, and we were off. Speaking of cars . . .

As one might expect, none—and I mean none—of these "kids" had wheels. They were basically landlocked away from the affluent white neighborhoods that surrounded them. As a group of young teens, they were generally confined to their segregated district unless they drove out of the area with a parent or relative. This gave my Mustang special status and I took advantage of it. Whenever I got the chance, I'd pile four guys into the car and off we'd go. Many a day we drove to Playa del Rey, a beach along the California coast, about 25 miles from the church.

One evening, on a return trip from the beach, we all agreed to stop at a Taco Bell in Inglewood, an almost all-white community at the time. If you'll recall, I attended Inglewood High School. (Today, the entire area has racially reversed.) Anyway, the five of us approached the young lady standing behind the front glass (this was not a walk-in establishment). She and her coworkers were white.

I tend to be an extrovert and I advanced in my usual manner, friendly and smiling. She didn't smile. At that moment I didn't give it a second thought; I was too preoccupied trying to place my order. As the interaction between her and us continued, I became aware that she was cold and unresponsive with a very cautious manner. I saw something very unfriendly in her eyes. I joked a bit, as I usually do, but all I got back were looks of suspicion and a hint of contempt. It dawned on me that she thought I was black based on my tan coloring and the young boys that surrounded me. We had all gotten out of the same car. I was now getting a taste of the subtle, and yet not so subtle, attitude of racial prejudice directed against me. I was now being treated as a black person. It was most disconcerting. I will never forget that pretty face that was emanating the ugly vibes of bigotry. She wasn't trying to convey her bias. She was appropriately polite and filled our orders accordingly. I got a glimpse of what African Americans had to deal with.

I saw it again a few minutes later when a couple of jalopies filled with white teens pulled into the parking lot. Lord have mercy, there was an instantaneous rise of tension coming from all directions. Body language was heating up and verbal innuendos were obvious on both sides. They all strutted around like peacocks ready for the fight. Pride, intolerance, and ignorance were about to set off a firestorm. I had to get my guys out of there before all hell broke loose. I did. I was beginning to understand.

As a note of interest, my interactions and outings were almost always with the guys. The girls were usually under lock and key. They would come to the church dances, but that was it. The parents in that area were extremely protective of their daughters. I rarely saw them. I think unwanted pregnancies were a chilling concern. Also, it was a tough neighborhood, especially at night. I guess what I really ended up with was mostly a boy's club. That gender exclusiveness was certainly unique. Neither before nor after my Watts appointment did I ever have that gender gap experience with teens.

## Housing

I didn't want to live in the area I worked. I didn't feel comfortable. I could handle the daylight hours. But when the shadows came, the area felt ominous. Not surprisingly, then, I started looking for an apartment a few miles distant. I found a suitable place between Watts and my mom's home in Inglewood. This would do nicely.

Unfortunately, the D.S. was not pleased with this arrangement. Reluctantly, I recognized the wisdom and practicality behind his objection. I should have known better anyway. In ministry, especially with young people, availability is the name of the game. I needed to be near the action. I was back to square one. As it turned out, I found a nice little one-bedroom apartment about three short blocks from the church. This put the youth in walking distance to my home. Of course, I couldn't have them dropping over unexpectedly at all hours of the night. Accordingly, if they wanted to come by for a visit, I only had one rule of etiquette for them to follow: call me first! (They always honored that request.)

## Blood on the Street

You can't live in "Watts" very long before you discover some of the inequities therein. One evening I was scheduled to go visit my mom in Inglewood. Not less than a minute of having started my journey, I came upon a traffic jam on Florence Avenue. The cars in front of me were forming a single line and, ever so slowly, pulling off into the left lane. I followed suit. Everyone was rubbernecking to the right. Obviously, it was an accident scene. The streetlights were on but the darkness was not fully pierced. As I slowly followed the snakelike chain of cars that preceded me, I glanced to my right, as any good rubbernecker would do. I couldn't be sure of what I saw, but it looked like someone had hit a small object, possibly a dog. Whatever it was, it wasn't moving and there was no one around it. However, there was a small crowd of onlookers standing on the sidewalk. I thought it strange.

I was almost past the scene when I took another quick look at the small object lying on the roadway. I usually don't do this; that is, take a second look. Animals are precious to me, and I am almost emotionally incapable of dealing with dead or injured animals. I tried to avert my eyes. But what if the animal were injured and in need of assistance? Nobody on the sidewalk appeared to be engaged. Ok, another quick look-see before I escape this slowdown. What? OMG! That's not an animal; that's a child!

Why weren't any of these drivers stopping to assist? Why were the bystanders on the sidewalk immobile, like frozen popsicles incapable of movement? That child was alone, motionless, in the middle of the street, for heaven's sake. Even the car that must have hit that kid was nowhere in sight. Maybe a white driver had accidentally struck the child and was simply too frightened to stop in a black neighborhood where so much violence had recently erupted (inexcusable, but understandable). After all, whites had been murdered in this area with no provocation, and under benign conditions, much less this horrific scenario.

It mattered not. I immediately pulled my Mustang to the right and parked alongside the curb. I jumped out and ran back to where the youngster lay. The scene was unreal. There I was alone in a tough black neighborhood, in the middle of the street, with cars passing by in slow motion. The people on the sidewalk remained fixed in place as if they were part of an old photo. I did, however, hear someone sobbing as a man and a woman clutched each other in a bear hug. I surmised they were the parents. As I knelt down, I focused back on the little boy lying motionless on the cold hard pavement. He looked no older than five. He's gone, I thought to myself. But I couldn't be sure.

It was chilly that evening. The lad was uncovered except for his pants and short- sleeve shirt. One of his shoes was missing as a result of the impact. I removed my light jacket and covered him up as best I could, especially his arms and upper torso. I spoke to him as if he were awake and supplied him with words of encouragement and assurance. The severity of his injuries was obvious. There was blood oozing from the back of his head and also from his nose and mouth. There was so much blood draining onto the street that it ran all the way to the gutter from where he lay. His mouth, partially opened, contained an ominous looking thick mixture of blood and mucus. The boy remained motionless, but on closer inspection, I could tell that he was still breathing. I yelled over to the bystanders: "Did anyone call for an ambulance?"

'Shit!" came the sharp reply from one of the men. "We called about half an hour ago; where the hell are they?" His voice carried an obvious tone of frustration as it tailed off.

The popsicle bystanders started to thaw out. A couple of the men ambled on out to join me. One of them offered to pick the child up and move him over to the sidewalk. I nixed that idea by explaining that moving an injured person might do more harm than good. Better to wait for the paramedics. Everyone agreed.

In my state of naiveté, I couldn't understand why it was taking so long for the ambulance to arrive, until I heard one of the bystanders angrily blurt out, "If that was a white child, they would have been here 20 minutes ago!" There was a reflex groaning of agreement from the gathering crowd.

It took but a nanosecond to make sense of that telling sentiment. I had to conclude they might be right. I also became uneasily aware that I was the only white person around, and people were starting to exhibit disquieted body language. Maybe I should now make myself scarce. For the moment, I subdued the urge to skedaddle. No need to panic. After all, we were enveloped in semi-darkness, my skin color was a bit tan, and I was lending a helping hand. They couldn't know who or what I was. However, when the ambulance arrived, I gathered up my bloody coat and took a powder while everybody was momentarily distracted. I didn't want to be shuffling around with these strangers after the ambulance left. Better to make like the Lone Ranger and have someone say in afterthought, "Who was that masked man?"

By the time I reached home, my mom was freaked out. I was late and she was worried. It didn't help that my coat and trousers were all bloody.

"What happened? Are you okay?" she exclaimed.

I quickly gave account. She was relieved.

The next morning we listened to the news and searched the morning paper, but there was not one iota about the incident. In 1966 one would not expect otherwise. It was, after all, a black kid from a black community. I never did find out how that youngster made out. I'd be very surprised if he survived, especially with the head injury I witnessed.

## The Liquor Store Miscue

I was on the way home late one evening—can't remember where from—when I decided to stop at a liquor store and get some orange juice for my next day's breakfast. Parking was limited. Liquor stores in Watts were nightly beehives, replacing the general store of the past—and its potbelly stove—as the center of social activity. I could get no closer than a block and a half away. I locked the car and headed for wine country.

Uncharacteristically, I was not thinking clearly when I strolled into the place, which, I might add, was crowded with black youths (a good number of them just loitering around). I quickly became conscious of the numbers—one white, many blacks. I always felt the need to be aware of my surroundings, especially at night. In fact, venturing out at night was not a good idea in this neighborhood. I tried to act nonchalant as I grabbed 80 cents' worth of OJ and headed for the checkout counter. Reaching for my billfold—I always carried it in my front pocket as a safety precaution—I was very much aware that young men were standing beside me and in back of me. As I opened my wallet, my heart sank. What was I thinking? The smallest bill was a 20 (that was a good chunk of change in the '60s). I had no choice but to hand the clerk the 20, and then have him slowly dole back my change in multiple bills while everyone looked on. It didn't help that he vocalized the counting, apparently not caring that everyone within earshot was tuned in. What was he thinking? What were they thinking? Worse yet, it was almost a certainty that the guy on my right had seen other greenbacks in my billfold. I was now on high alert, pins and needles to the max. I grabbed the OJ and started to move on out. I felt everyone's eyes on me as I made my way toward the exit.

Easy does it, I thought to myself. Be cool. Don't let them see you sweat. Walk out of here like you own the street.

I was thankful for the green leather-like jacket that helped to mask my otherwise unimpressive physique. At least I had a decent height of 6'1". Albeit nervous, I actually strutted out of the place with an air of confidence. Body language was the key. I pretended not to care, as if to send a message, "don't mess with me."

In hopes of continuing this tough-minded false bravado, I proceeded down the block with a swagger in my gait. I hadn't gone but a few yards when I was overwhelmed by a sense of being followed. Real or imagined, I had to look. I turned my head slightly to the right and caught the shadow of a man on the periphery of my vision. I quickened my pace. He quickened his. I took the pace up another notch. He followed suit. There was no doubt now that he was in pursuit, and the distance between us was closing. I didn't want to panic, but I couldn't let him overtake me before I reached the car, which, at this point, seemed like a hundred miles away.

The heck with this, I thought to myself, and took off running.

That's when I really got scared because I heard his feet take flight. The race was on. As I neared my Mustang, I realized there was not enough time to get the car door open and get safely inside before he reached me (no automatic car door openers in those days). Short of collapsing on the sidewalk from a heart attack, I was left with only one option.

As we all know, we are wired with the inclination to take flight, or fight. Flight hadn't worked. It was time to fight. I had no other choice. Reaching the car, but too late for any evasive action, I spun around to face my would-be attacker.

He was black. No surprise there. In the darkness that surrounded us, he looked especially threatening. (I was affected by all the previous stereotypical images of my cultural upbringing.) His face remained partially hidden; a dark-shaped silhouette against the dim-lighted background emanating from the distant liquor store. From what I could see, he was a husky-looking dude. No doubt, he had the advantage.

In the blink of an eye, my worst nightmare became a reality. With his right hand he pulled a gun on me. He extended that gun-arm in my direction. OMG, you can't believe how frightened a person can get when looking down the barrel of a gun. I didn't lose any bodily fluids, but I was on the verge. With his right arm fully extended, he said: "Excuse me, sir, here's your wallet; you left it on the counter."

We had a good laugh after I explained the why of my hasty getaway. I knew that he totally understood my fear-related misperceptions when he said: "At night, we usually try to travel in pairs around here." I offered a reward for the return of my goods, but he graciously declined. I was fortunate that he was an honest and good-natured individual. Nevertheless, it was a lesson well learned.

## A Horse of a Different Color

The one time I think I almost got myself killed in Watts was the night when the fellows and I stopped off at McDonald's for a late bite. The guys had already ordered and I was now at the front window placing my order. I asked the girl behind the glass if the hamburger I was ordering—at that point in time I was not yet a vegetarian—came with lettuce and tomato. She answered with a negative: "Sorry, no, but you can order it special but it will cost you a little extra."

Her comment had barely reached my ears when I heard this grumbling, slurred like complaint coming from behind me. "God damn it, you fuckin' prick! Place your damn order or get out of the way!"

I'm not one to shirk away from conflict. Like any other boy growing up, I'd had my confrontational moments with a number of boys, most of them bullies. This is par for most males. But I've always stood my ground against those who tried to push me around. Even when I got to high school, I didn't back away from a fight (except on one occasion when I was to blame, so I couldn't see the point). If I knew for sure that I was outmatched, I would avoid fighting if given a choice, but I would take anyone on if backed into a corner.

As I contemplated my response to this obnoxious intruder—"asshole" is what I was thinking—I had it in mind to explain my right to ask questions and to make it clear that I wasn't going anywhere until my order was placed properly. I wanted lettuce and tomato on my hamburger. Period! Besides, I knew my guys had overheard his inflammatory remarks. They would be keyed to seeing how I responded. I would lose their respect if they thought me to be "yellow." This is the code of the jungle as far as men are concerned. In the iconic words incorrectly attributed to John Wayne, "a man's gotta do what a man's gotta do." I knew what I had to do. It was time to put up or shut up.

It wasn't like I had a lot of time to kick this all around in my thinking. Everything I've explained thus far and what I'm about to explain happened in a matter of nanoseconds.

Although my adrenalin was now flowing, I calmly turned around to face this nut and speak my peace. What happened next is fixed in photographic memory, as if it happened yesterday. As I faced my antagonist, I knew instantaneously that I was in trouble; I mean real trouble. Standing before me was a giant of a man. It was Arnold Schwarzenegger in black! He was about an inch shorter than me, but he was built like a Sherman Tank. He had so many muscles I couldn't see the people standing behind him. His eyes were glassy with drink or drugs but I couldn't tell which. It didn't matter. I knew that either way, stoned or drunk, he could squash me like a bug.

He was more than mad. He was in a state of sheer rage. He came across as extremely dangerous, ruthless, and cold-blooded . . . just looking for an excuse. This was my first real encounter with pure hatred. His eyes bristled with it. It spilled out from every pore of his being. There is no room for exaggeration here. Never before had I ever felt such a strong, odious touch of evil on my person. I was petrified.

You didn't have to be an expert in body language to recognize that he was primed to explode. I was definitely in harm's way, smack dab in the cross hairs of an irrational madman. Intuitively I knew this was a life-threatening situation. I had in some way triggered his rage, pushed his buttons, and I knew right then that he would kill me for sure if I uttered a word. So what did I say to him? I didn't say a thing. My brain was flooded with stop signs: don't move; don't say a word; don't do anything except slowly turn around, place your order, and get the hell out of the way. Without delay that's what I did.

I had no misgivings about backing away from this encounter. Even today I am perfectly comfortable with that decision. Any other move on my part would have led me to a lot of hurt and probably worse. My brain, at least on this occasion, had saved my bacon. It also saved my hamburger, albeit without lettuce and tomato.

When we left McDonald's that night, it didn't take long for one of the guys to challenge my inaction. "Hey, Ernie, how come you let that guy push you around?"

Even before he threw that question in my face, I knew they had been whispering and jabbering back and forth about my apparent cave. They needed an answer.

"Well," I said calmly, "I just didn't feel like getting myself killed tonight over a hamburger."

A few of the guys chuckled. A few disagreed. The debate was on.

"Man, I wouldn't let no Nigger talk to me that way," one of them echoed defiantly. (They sometimes used the "N" word but, of course, I never did.)

Another guy chimed in, "Are you crazy? Didn't you see the size of that jackass? Man, he could talk to me any way he wanted to."

The arguments went back and forth, but most of them came to agree that any other response on my part was an invitation to suicide. Nevertheless, I felt the need to make a closing statement. I will probably paraphrase my memory here, but this is the gist of what I said.

"Listen guys, there's an old saying that goes like this, 'Discretion is the better part of valor.' That means that sometimes it's wiser to retreat than to fight. In other words, there is no way I was willing to get myself killed or badly hurt by some drunken fool who didn't like the way I ordered hamburgers. My mama didn't raise no fool!"

I don't remember anyone disagreeing with that final assessment. In fact, it all turned into a jovial recount of the event, and the bad guy came out a sorry second. You can conclude that I was more than happy when those "kids" came around to my way of thinking. Maybe that's one of the reasons I have never second-guessed my decision that evening. I may be rationalizing, but I'm still here and my nose still works.

### The Alka-Seltzer Preacher

Our senior pastor at the EUB/United Methodist Church[79] in Watts was Jeremiah Rowe. He was a Jamaican by birth. By "nature," he was a jolly guy and very optimistic. He was a big man with a big heart. He was often a big hit at our summer camps, especially with the primary school ages.

Together we handled the worship service on Sunday mornings. Of course, he was the man in charge and I always enjoyed his style of preaching. Preaching was an energetic exercise for him as it was for many of the other black preachers in the area.

During one Easter season, I was asked to be one of the seven preachers invited to speak at a community-wide Good Friday service. The service was to be held at one of the larger churches in order to accommodate the hundreds of people that usually attended this Holy Week event. Accordingly, I would be one of the seven preachers speaking on one of the last seven words (or phrases) that Jesus spoke from the cross during his crucifixion. I accepted the invitation with a healthy sense of

---

[79]The Evangelical United Brethren (EUB) Church merged with the Methodist Church in 1968 to form the now larger United Methodist Church (UMC).

apprehension. If these preachers were as good as Jeremiah, I would certainly be outclassed. However, being the new kid in town, I really couldn't turn down the invitation. Besides, I thought to myself, I should be thinking of the importance of the message, and not my self-image.

Good Friday arrived soon enough. I found myself in a huge church filled with nothing but black folks. Nothing wrong with that except that I felt a little conspicuous because of my color and because of my age—all of the other preachers were much older. I sat up on the chancel with the other six ministers. I was in my best suit. Actually, I only had one suit (working in Watts was not a high-paying job).

It might have been my imagination, but no matter which way I looked, I found people staring back at me with expressions of: "Who is that guy, anyway? Is he white or what?" Well, they would soon find out.

Everything started off well enough. The singing was uplifting, as I had expected. I don't mean to come across with stereotypical assumptions, but these people could really belt out a song. The choir that was brought together from the various churches in the area would have given the Mormon Tabernacle Choir a run for their money. We joined in prayer. Scripture was read and an offering was taken up. So far everything was going as planned. But now it was time for the hard-hitters to come up to the plate. Shortly before the first preacher took the pulpit, it dawned on me that none of us would be preaching for less than 15 minutes, and some of these clergymen would surely take much longer. At 15 minutes a pop, we'd be here for at least another two hours. Little did I know that this concern would be the least of my worries.

I was to be the fifth speaker in the lineup that morning. My initial fear of being outclassed became evident when the first man up started the ball rolling. He was terrific. Perhaps the next three preachers would slow the pace. It was not to be. They weren't as good as Jeremiah Rowe; they were better than Jeremiah Rowe! Each man strutted back and forth across the chancel with the eloquence and bodily gyrations of a tent revival evangelist. They certainly weren't tied to the pulpit and they didn't use any notes. Where did these guys come from? Was this a Hollywood casting session for a new *Elmer Gantry* movie? Maybe this was all a plot, setting me up for a *Candid Camera* episode.

The congregation was rocking and rolling. With perfect timing the people shouted "amen" or "hallelujah" whenever the preacher gave them an opening. It was a beautifully choreographed dance between pastor and parishioner. The place was jumping. The verbal baton was passed from preacher to preacher, each one elevating the service to a higher pitch. We were in the process of crescendo. This evangelical train had a full head of steam. All of a sudden, it was my turn.

I made my way to the pulpit and looked out across the many faces that were still telegraphing their enthusiasm. With anticipation they patiently awaited my contribution. I was expected to further stoke the boiler of this fast-moving train. And so, looking down at my notes that I had set down on the pulpit, I began my sermon. I spoke in a calm, deliberate, and evenly-paced manner, as almost any young, white United Methodist minister might do. "This morning I would like to speak to you about the . . ."

Within seconds the congregation went silent. Noticeably, all of the amen and hallelujah shouts disappeared. The mood change was keenly obvious. I started to squirm. My heart was pounding. I got really nervous. I knew what had happened. I had just smothered the driving spirit that preceded my appearance. I had thrown water into the boiler; I had single-handedly derailed the train. I had stomped all over that old-time religion. I had turned Good Friday into Bad Friday.

I was mortified. I kept my head down and preached from my notes. When I finally mustered the courage to look up and eyeball the congregation, I was met with the wide-eyed stares of people who looked like they were watching a train wreck in slow motion. At that point we were all in shock. I broke out in a cold sweat. Eventually, I pulled myself together and forged ahead as best I could.

The worshipers that morning quickly came to the conclusion that I was white after all. To their credit, they evidently decided that they were going to help this poor white preacher, who was obviously out of his league, get through this ordeal. They kindly started to throw a few "amen" and "hallelujah" shouts my way, albeit at half the intensity previously noted. They were trying to sustain their fervor, but they had lost their mojo. But I knew these were sympathetic gestures and, eventually, they did help.

The entire experience was embarrassing for us all. The one good side effect of this humiliating nightmare was that I preached for less than 15 minutes. You couldn't get me out of that pulpit fast enough. In that respect, I guess I did everyone a favor. I crept back to my chair wondering if I had torpedoed the entire service, hoping that the next man up could salvage my blown assignment. I wouldn't have long to find out.

The next preacher grabbed the verbal baton and threw himself into the breach with gusto. He was not unaware of what had just taken place. He was a man on a fire, the religious Pied Piper of the moment. Mixing metaphors—as I like doing—he was going to right the ship.[80] As quickly as the excitement had faded with my appearance, it came roaring back with his silver-tongued rhetoric. His speech was strikingly powerful. The people responded with excited shouts of "amen," "hallelujah," "praise the Lord" and "thank you Jesus." I'm not at all sure that the shouts of "thank you Jesus" weren't in reference to having this follow-up preacher in the pulpit. That's why I gratefully nicknamed him the Alka-Seltzer preacher: "oh, what a relief it is."

## Black vs. White

If you were a teenager and didn't have enough money for a movie, there wasn't much else to do in Watts. I think that's why I focused on organizing outings for these youngsters. They were always eager to go some place, if nothing more than cruising. However, there was one activity that took center stage for many of the guys, and that was basketball. If nothing else, one could always wander onto a playground for a rip-roaring diversion. Shooting hoops was a local pastime. (I have no idea what the girls were doing).

When I was a teenager, our church got our youth involved in a church basketball league. It was city wide—Los Angeles—and incorporated numerous churches from all denominations. The teams were divided into three separate leagues—A, AA, and AAA (the latter being the most highly skilled). We never did win our A division. Nevertheless, we had fun.

---

[80]They say you shouldn't mix metaphors. I don't agree with "they." I love mixing metaphors.

I decided to provide this same opportunity to the guys in my church youth group. We had some pretty decent players. When I made the proposal, they jumped at the chance. Our first hurdle was making arrangements with the LA Basketball Organization; I took care of that problem. Our second hurdle was the entrance fee and the cost of any decent uniforms. Thankfully, some of our church members footed the bill.

Our third hurdle was trying to figure out a way to get the name of our church on the back of our uniforms: "The Community Evangelical United Brethren Church" just wouldn't fly. We finally pared it down to "EUB Church." We were set to roll. Yours truly would be the coach. Honestly, I really wasn't that knowledgeable about the game, but having played, I knew enough. Besides, these guys could practically coach themselves in terms of basketball tactics and execution. At the risk of stereotyping, I've got to tell you that some of these kids could play ball. As the adult in charge, I was only there to establish order, discipline, and substitution decisions, and so on.

After a couple of "practice" games, we were placed in the AA division. This was a tough division. Many of the teams consisted of grown men including some college players who were no longer playing college ball. All of our players were high-school age. At the outset, we heard it through the grapevine that the Lutheran team always won the AA City Championship. Whatever turned out, I knew our guys would give them a run for their money if, indeed, we ever got a chance to play them. Our schedule called for 12 games over a three-month period. If we were fortunate enough to win our league, we would than go into the semi-finals. If we won our semi-finals, the City Championship game was on the table. But first things first, our first league game was coming up.

We always played our games on Monday nights. Everyone was at courtside and eager to play that first evening, except for Frank. "Where is Frank?" I asked. Nobody seemed to know. This was a concern since Frank was one of our two best shooters. He played the forward position, and we really didn't have anyone of his stature on the bench. In fact, with the exception of one player, our bench was very thin. We basically relied on five very talented players with lots of stamina. Our center was no taller than 6'1 but all the guys were quick and that usually gave us an edge with rebounds. But we sorely needed Frank.

A few minutes before game time, Frank made his appearance. We all breathed a sigh of relief. As Frank approached our bench, I couldn't help but notice that his gait, his demeanor, was peculiar. I called him over. His breath reeked of alcohol and his eyes were glassy. I didn't have to ask him, it was obvious the kid had been drinking. He wasn't drunk but he certainly was impaired. He knew I knew. Frank assured me that he was able to play. By this time everyone had huddled around me waiting for me to send them onto the court. Everyone on the team murmured their disappointment when I benched Frank. I hated to do it because I thought it doubtful we could win without him. The other players were not pleased. But I had no choice. I couldn't have these guys thinking they could show up in this kind of condition. Church league or otherwise, there were certain principles to uphold.

We were losing at half-time. Everyone pleaded with me to allow Frank in for the second half. I really wanted him to play and almost rationalized my way to that decision. But something inside me told me to hold fast. In my opinion Frank had committed a serious infraction, and I could leave no doubt about this in the minds of these young boys. They weren't very happy with me, especially when we lost the game. This was a terrible blow to the high hopes we flirted with at the beginning of that evening. Was this a fatal blow to our championship aspirations? Who would they blame for the loss, Frank or me? It didn't matter. I did what I knew I had to do. Nevertheless, we had lost our first game and that was hard for all of us to swallow. There was also the possibility that Frank might walk. The guys told me he was pissed off (their words).

The answer came one week later when Frank showed up for the game, sober and all primed to go. No one ever again came to one of our games unfit to play. We won that game and almost every game thereafter. We finished at the top of our league and then went on to win the semifinal games that followed. We had fought our way to the AA City Championship playoff. As predictably noted, the Lutheran church had also made their way to the Championship playoff. They had won the City Championship game for the previous five years in a row, and were licking their chops for a sixth win. Of course, our team was hungry for this win, too. There was a showdown a-brewing.

A quick reminder. In 1966, we Americans were still segregated even though we pretended otherwise. The world we lived in was literally black and white in most areas. For example, our EUB congregations in California were white with the exception of this one black congregation that basically remained invisible to our other white churches. So, when I started taking my kids to an all conference youth rally, for example, it was like mixing 10 black beans in with 100 navy beans. I was the lone pinto bean. The contrast was obvious because these encounters were unprecedented for both black and white teenagers. This was always the case whenever I took these youngsters outside of their neighborhood. I bring this to your attention because in those early days of the Civil Rights Movement, there was a lot of apprehension and misunderstanding on both sides. Prejudice was the mainstay and it came from both directions. The point is, I had brought our kids into an all-white basketball organization. Accordingly, it became a racial issue of pride with my guys. They had many unresolved feelings about their place in American society. They knew—*and could feel*—that blacks had been regulated to second-class citizenship. Racial discrimination was healthy and rampant. This was their chance to strike back. They were going up against "Honkies" (to use one of their racial slurs). I'm sure the Lutheran team had issues of their own since they had never played against an all-black team. Keep in mind that the Watts Riot had occurred during the previous year. Black and white turmoil was still running high.

## The Game

The Championship was upon us. This was it. There was no doubt in all quarters that we were the underdogs. The Lutheran team was loaded with talent. These were grown men who had honed their winning ways over several years of championship wins. Their reputation preceded them.

On the other hand I knew we had a talented bunch, albeit high schoolers. We didn't have much depth on our bench, but our kids also had stamina and lots of pride. They wanted this game in the worst way.

Both teams came ready to play, and both teams had a good number of supporters sitting in the stands that evening. This was for all the marbles and everyone knew it. Parents, loved ones, friends, and congregants were all abuzz with excitement, not to mention the angst that hung in the air. I was nervous but remained stoic (I think). Both teams went through their warm-ups. They were also sizing each other up with a glance to the opposite end of the court every now and then. One couldn't help but notice that one team was all black and the other all white. People in the stands were equally conspicuous. I didn't sense any bad vibes from either side. It was more a sense of wonderment: how did this all happen and what did it mean? Of course, academic institutions that were virtually segregated (for example, high schools) had already experienced this type of racial confrontation in sports. But this game was more personal and street oriented.

The refs blew their whistles and the court buzzer sounded; it was game on! We broke our huddle, and five black kids matched up against five white men for the toss-up at midcourt. As one would expect, it was a fast-breaking game. Adrenalin had everyone running up and down the court like one of those old speeded-up Charlie Chaplin films.

I don't think anyone expected the kind of game that unfolded that evening. Both teams were in the zone, trading baskets with uncanny accuracy, back and forth, back and forth. Both teams must have been hitting 80% of their shots and 90% of their free throws. The game sizzled. I had never seen anything like it, before or since, in amateur competition. It felt like a Hollywood scripted movie and I hoped it would have a Cinderella outcome for our guys.

At half-time the scoreboard had us trailing by three. I think the Lutheran team was surprised that their marginal lead was minimal. Actually we were all amazed because the score of 53 to 50 was itself unbelievable. You'd be lucky to have that kind of a score at the end of a game, much less at the half. You only see that kind of scoring in college or the pros. I was so proud of our guys. They had taken that Lutheran team to the mat: matching them bucket for bucket, stride for stride, steal for steal, rebound for rebound, and tactic for tactic. Neither team was sloppy, cold, or slowing down.

I was also proud of myself for making key substitutions, taking crucial timeouts, along with other coaching decisions and encouragements. But make no mistake, the game would be won or lost by them. I just had to make sure I didn't make any mistakes in judgment that would cost them the game.

At the sound of the buzzer, the original players matched up again at mid-court. Down three points, it was important that we win the toss-up. We didn't. A few seconds later and we were down by five. I'll not bore you with all the details of the second half except to say that our team fought hard and long.

Fast forward: There was a little less than a minute left to play and our team had battled back to a one-point lead, 103 to 102! Again, no one had seen anything like this in any of the LA leagues. Neither the Lutheran players, nor the refs, and not the fans had ever witnessed such a display of gamesmanship. We, along with the Lutherans, had shattered every previous scoring record held by the LA Basketball Association. To the best of my knowledge, no team had ever registered more than 100 points, let alone two teams in the same game. Win or lose, we could walk away proud. Of course, neither team wanted to lose, but that goes without saying. (So why did I say it?)

They had the ball with less than a minute to play. With 35 seconds on the clock they scored the bucket that put them ahead by one, 104 to 103. We now had the ball with about half a minute left to play. We had one last chance to score. Pandemonium broke loose as our boys started their run toward the opposite end of the court. Everyone was up on their feet, screaming. Through the bedlam I frantically waved my arms and yelled to the ref for a timeout. Got it!!

We huddled together. As usual, the guys talked to each other with clarity and purpose. They knew what to do and they knew how to do it, if only they could execute. "Who's taking the final shot?" someone queried.

They weren't surprised when I decreed it should be Frank. "If Frank can't get open," I continued, "feed the ball to Tillman. If you see a chance for a layup, go for it. Whatever happens, don't let the clock run out on you!"

There was an uproarious crescendo from the stands as our players broke the huddle. The plan was simple; we would maneuver for one final shot leaving a few seconds to spare for a rebounded follow-up shot if necessary.

We inbounded the ball and passed it around looking for the open shot as the seconds ticked off. With about eight on the clock, Frank had a clear look from the outside corner. Not easy. He fired the ball up and the players crowded into the paint for a possible rebound. The ball's trajectory looked good but the outcome was uncertain. We held our collective breath. Swish! Nothing but net!

Our supporters went bananas, until they realized the game wasn't over. With three seconds left, the Lutheran team still had an outside chance. They inbounded the ball and quickly fired it to their best shooter who had broken free at mid-court.

With the clock expiring he shot a "Hail Mary" towards the basket. Everyone was transfixed as the ball glided effortlessly to its intended destination. The ball was in mid-flight when the buzzer sounded so the shot still counted; that is, the final score was still in doubt. A split second later the outcome was finalized. The ball hit the backboard and bounced harmlessly off the rim of the basket. We won (105 to 104)!

Thunderous cheering erupted. We were all ecstatic. The celebration was uninhibited. We took a few moments to respectfully greet our opponents and then continued to whoop it up. What a memorable night that was for us all. Pure magic!

Chapter 15

# YOUNG LIFE ORGANIZATION
## ORGANIZACIÓN DE LA VIDA JOVEN

*San Diego, California*
1968 – 1969

FOLLOWING TWO YEARS OF service in the Watts area of LA, I was approached by the Young Life organization. I was 28.

Young Life (YL) is an American evangelical Christian ministry that caters primarily to high school students. Presbyterian minister Jim Rayburn started YL in 1941.

As one might imagine, the Civil Rights Movement brought a great deal of attention to the black communities long ago abandoned by the white majority. Young Life was looking for youth workers that might help them with black youth in the inner city.[81] I'm not sure how they heard about my work in Watts, but they came knocking. They wanted me to start some YL clubs in the black high schools of San Diego. The matter was discussed over lunch with three YL managers. I

---

[81]Oxford Dictionary: "the area near the center of a city, especially when associated with social and economic problems." Generally considered to be a tough area, notorious for violence and crime. However, these areas vary widely according to geographical location.

was hesitant to accept any offers because I didn't want to work exclusively with black youth. Accordingly, they offered me two high schools: one in the "inner city" (Lincoln HS, primarily black), the other in suburbia (Helix HS, primarily white). I had to give their proposition some thought.

I knew YL was a great organization so the offer was tempting. Also, I felt my ministry had run its course at the EUB church I was serving. Additionally, YL offered the opportunity to be totally immersed in youth work without the ecclesiastical responsibilities of the wider church. I decided to accept the YL offer.

The governing board of the EUB California Conference was most understanding and granted me special assignment status. The decision to leave my Watts assignment wasn't that difficult but the actual leaving was. I had developed very close relationships with many of the local youth. There was a good deal of sadness in my departure and it wasn't all one-sided. I still harbor many fond memories from that very special experience. I regret losing touch with those young kids.

In the summer of 1968, at the age of 28, I drove down from LA to San Diego, the place of my birth, the city I had left at the age of four shortly after my dad had taken his last breath at the hands of a cold-blooded killer. It felt somewhat strange returning to San Diego 24 years later. I secured a one-room apartment for $76 a month and knuckled down to the task at hand.

Lincoln High didn't have a Young Life club. My job was to establish one. Imagine if you will, walking into a black high school, not knowing a soul, and starting a youth club. But I've always been good with young people so it didn't take me long to get acquainted with a few kids. Within two weeks we had a club of 30. We met in the homes of these young people and rotated our meeting place once every four weeks.

Helix High was a different animal; the students were predominantly white and their YL club was already established. I frequented many of their sports activities, especially their varsity basketball games. They had a player at center that was rather exceptional; his name was Bill Walton. At 6'11" he was easy to spot when he first walked into our YL club meeting one evening.

Some of you will recognize this fellow as the starting center for UCLA during part of that school's heyday. With Bill Walton at center they won the national title in 1972 over Florida State, and again in 1973 over Memphis State. Following his collegiate experience, he played center for the Portland Trail Blazers. During the 1976-1977 season, he led the Trail Blazers to the NBA title over the favored Philadelphia 76ers despite losing the first two games of the series. In 1993 he was inducted into the Basketball Hall of Fame. Had it not been for numerous injuries, some pundits believe he might have been recognized as the greatest center ever. If you look up his stats you'll understand why.

When Bill Walton walked into my Young Life club meeting one evening in 1969, he could hardly be missed. Aside from his vertical size, I had seen him play often enough. Of course, during those high school days no one except a scout could possibly know that he would go on to be such an athletic sensation. To me he was simply another high school "kid." Unfortunately, he did not stay for the meeting; I think he was looking for someone that evening and didn't see that person of interest, so then he left. Therefore, I never got to know him personally, only from a distance. The following is no big thing but I find it interesting.

Looking back on that brush with Bill Walton—and this is why I have raised this story—I sometimes wonder how I would have reacted to this young person had I known that celebrity status awaited him. As it was, I really didn't pay him any mind. I did this purposely. He was already receiving too much praise and attention for his talented exploits on the court. Jumping onto this bandwagon didn't seem right for either of us. But in hindsight, I'm sorry I didn't try to cultivate a personal connection.

Two events with YL remain memorable. The first centers on a required training program for any Young Life staffer who was scheduled to work in the inner city. Although I had previous experience in the Watts area of LA, a broader understanding of inner-city life was necessary. I was shipped off to the Lower East Side of New York City to mix elbows with YL workers and to get a taste of what it meant to live in the urban (downtown) area of the inner city. This would certainly be much different than the suburban (residential) areas I had previously encountered working with black youth.

United Airlines got me to NY City without a hitch. Armed with the address of my YL contact, I quickly caught a cab and sped off into the night. About five minutes into the drive the cab driver informed me that there would be an added charge.

"What for?" I enquired.

"This address is outside of my limits. We always charge extra when we cross certain boundaries," he responded.

"How much extra?" I asked suspiciously.

"Eight dollars," he shot back.

"Eight dollars! Are you kidding me? That's a lot of money."

I was not exaggerating; eight dollars was a hefty sum in 1969. This whole situation didn't seem right to me. This felt like a shakedown. Unfortunately, I was too young and too naïve to believe it actually was. I couldn't fathom the idea that this nice cab driver was trying to fleece me. Obviously I didn't know a whole lot about the shady side of NY City. Even so, I did manage to balk at the idea of this surcharge. But he quickly disarmed me by offering to call his boss if I thought he wasn't on the up and up. What could I say? I didn't want to insult him or hurt his feelings. I reluctantly gave him the okay to continue on.

Eventually we drove into the bowels of the inner city. It was close to 11 PM. In this part of town the streetlights made little headway against the dark quarters that surrounded us. Everything was old and dingy. This was Harlem or thereabouts, not a safe place to be, especially if you were white and didn't know your way around. I was thankful to be meeting someone at the YL headquarters. They were expecting me.

We finally came to a stop at the front of a long driveway, the end of which had been swallowed up by the darkness. The driver hoisted my luggage out of the trunk as I looked around for the address. The cabby quickly assured me that the dwelling was at the end of the driveway. But how could he know that since we couldn't see to its very end? It was plainly too dark to see anything that far back.

"I've been here before," he countered. "Not to worry, you'll be fine."

I paid him the fare with a tip. He thanked me and was gone in the blink of an eye. I grabbed my suitcase and headed down the driveway. Moving forward, my eyes strained against the darkness. I felt uneasy and was eager to get to my refuge.

It seemed like forever until I came to realize that I was standing in front of an empty lot. My heart sank. That cabby-rat had dropped me off in no man's land. I was alone in the concrete jungle—a white guy with a suitcase wandering around a predominantly poor, black neighborhood at midnight. I was scared. My first thought was to get to a phone . . . fast! Of course, cell phones were non-existent.

I made my way back to the street and strutted along as if I knew where I was going, although I hadn't a clue. I longed for my green, leathery-looking jacket from Watts (my Linus security blanket). I eventually stumbled across one of those phone booths that were so prevalent back in the day. I fumbled through my pockets for the cost of a phone call . . . my kingdom for a dime! Got it! A few minutes later I was rescued by a YL staffer. I was safe. A harrowing experience nonetheless. What transpired over the next week was no picnic either.

The plan laid out by YL was for me to spend a week in the inner city living the life. I was allowed $5.00 spending money, a one-room apartment in a multi-story building, and my legs as the sole means of transportation. The experience was an eye-opener. The only "grocery" store within miles charged me $1.50 for *one* egg. There were no veggies or fruits to buy. The apartment had no hot water and the bathtub was full of junk. It was winter. At night I was dreadfully cold in bed because the obsolete heater was insufficient and blankets were hard to come by. Then there was the rat that emerged from a hole in the wall; at first glance I thought it was a small dog. Scared the bejeebers out of me when I saw those long teeth.

If the plan was to help me get a better feel for the poor people living in slum areas, it worked. It was a tough week. However, knowing that I only had to endure this nightmare for seven days mitigated the trauma of it all. It sure was good to get back to California.

My second memorable event with YL occurred a few months later. They held a convention in Colorado Springs for all YL inner-city workers. We came from all over the United States; about 100 of us attended.

During one of our morning meetings the YL leader randomly pointed to a few of us in the audience and asked about our place of service. As an example, one person responded by saying: "I work in the inner city of Chicago." The speaker would then point to someone else, and on it went. I happened to be sitting in the front row with a bunch of other guys and I surmised that the odds of getting pointed out were slim to none. Nevertheless, the leader's fickle finger found its way to me. I quickly answered: "I work in the *outer* inner city of San Diego."

The speaker nodded his acknowledgement and turned away to select another person. He had only turned halfway around when I heard a voice from the rear: "What does he mean by the *outer* inner city?"

The leader turned back to face me. "Yes, what do you mean by the *outer* inner city?"

My answer was succinct and loud enough for everyone to hear. "Well, I do work in the inner city . . . but I stay out of it as much as possible!"

An explosion of laughter followed my comment. Everyone got it.

*Young Life Conference, Colorado Springs, Colorado (1969)*

Chapter 16

# THE GOOD SAMARITAN
# UNITED METHODIST CHURCH
EL BUEN SAMARITANO UNIÓ
IGLESIA DEL METODISTA

*Cupertino, California*
1969 – 1975

AT THE AGE OF 29, almost a year to the day I joined up with
YL, I received a telephone call from Rev. Roy S. Dunn. He
was a minister from our northern conference serving the Good
Samaritan United Methodist Church (aka the Good Sam
Church) in Cupertino, California (the town of Cupertino is
adjacent to San Jose, 48 miles from San Francisco by car). Roy
and I were well acquainted from our old EUB days, having
worked together in several summer high school camps. In fact,
I had asked him to be camp speaker at one of the summer
camps I directed at Idyllwild Pines, in Southern California.
He knew I had a way with youth and it didn't take him long
to make his point.

"Ernie, I'm looking for an associate minister. Specifically,
I'm looking for a Minister of Youth and I think you're the man.
What do you say?"

Roy and I had always hit it off. He was 20 years my senior, he was energetic and charismatic, and he had a thriving church. I thought we could be a dynamite team. This was one job offer I didn't have to think twice about. I accepted his offer on the spot, but not without insisting on one very important condition: I wanted my main focus to be youth work, period. I wasn't interested in all the administrative and committee meetings that swallow up much of a minister's good time. As an associate, of course, I didn't expect to dodge all of those responsibilities, but I wanted 90% of my time to go towards building a youth group, primarily high school. He agreed.

The next day I took off on Highway 101 headed north. Again, I was 29.

My departure from Young Life was rather abrupt. I should have given two weeks' notice but I was anxious to get moving. I stopped in LA for a couple of days to spend some time with my mom and grandmother before heading up north to Cupertino. The month was July 1969. That's when it happened—arguably one of the most amazing human accomplishments of all time.

On 20 July 1969 we had our first Moon landing. Two U.S. pilot-astronauts, Neil Armstrong and Buzz Aldrin, landed their Lunar Module safely on the lunar surface. On that historical day, most anyone who was over the age of five will surely remember where they were while glued to the flickering light of a black & white 21-inch television. The nation practically came to a standstill. I distinctly remember the absence of cars; the streets were almost deserted. It was quite eerie.

The following day I said my goodbyes to family and friends and headed north for Cupertino. Somewhere around this time I had already lost my 1964 Mustang to a thrown rod. I found myself driving a new four-cylinder 1968 Datsun from Japan. It wasn't as big or as powerful as my Ford Mustang; but for quality, endurance, and mileage, it beat American cars hands down.

## The Good Sam Church

At that time, the Good Samaritan United Methodist Church was not much to look at. Its nondescript outer appearance belied the fact that, for its size and looks, it was one of the most successful United Methodist churches in Northern California. The parishioners were middle to upper middle class, very white, and generally well educated. The church sat on the nearby corners of Homestead and Wolfe, directly across from the mega corporation, Hewlett-Packard. Orange groves still dotted the area and were not yet swallowed up by the upcoming population explosion and all the commerce that came with it. The City of Cupertino was simply another piece of a very prosperous suburban spread that included San Jose, Santa Clara, Sunnyvale, and so forth. It was a beautiful geographical area.

The congregation had been growing steadily under the leadership and charismatic personality of Rev. Roy S. Dunn. Its primary weakness, as was the case with most churches, was its dismal Senior High program. The Sr. High YF (Youth Fellowship) group totaled 13 kids. It was dismal indeed, but par for the course. My job was to turn that YF around.

There's no way to fully explain the phenomenon that happened over the course of the next six years. By December of 1969, just five months after my arrival, our high school group numbered around 80. By April of 1970, that number was up to 140. The majority of our youth came from three high schools: Fremont, Peterson, and Monta Vista. Eventually our numbers peaked at 346. I'm not guessing here; I kept very good attendance records. The numbers were so great that we ended up with three distinct YF groups meeting on separate nights of the week. To the best of my knowledge, there wasn't a single United Methodist church in the entire state of California that had more high schoolers in attendance every week. Furthermore, the Senior High YF group was larger than many of our California UMC adult congregations. The following video was created by one of my former YF members (Ted Larson), and chronicles the early years of the YF. The opening introduction reflects a 2013 interview between Rev. Dunn (92 years old) and me; he died a few months after this interview. He's the one who hired me in 1969. (See: http://youtu.be/GdF7kPSkp0E).

But the question remains, how did all this happen? I'll begin the answer to that question with the "me" factor. Without a doubt, I was the key. I'll not feign false modesty on this issue. In many respects I'm an extrovert with natural leadership skills. As I said earlier, I knew what to do, how to do it, and when to do it. When it came to youth work, I was in the zone. But I never heard it put so aptly as in the 1969 movie, *The Hustler*, starring the good-looking Paul Newman who tries to prove himself the greatest pool player of his time. He's talking to his girlfriend, attempting to express what it feels like to be at the top of one's game. The following is verbatim, but the ellipses (. . .) are not to be taken as omissions, but as pauses in his vocal nuances. [Brackets mine]

[This is] "what the game is like when it's great, when it's great, when it's really great. Like anything can be great, anything can be great. I don't care . . . brick laying can be great if a guy knows, if he knows, what he's doing and why . . . he can make it come off. When I'm going, when I'm really going, I feel like a . . . jockey speeding. Sitting on his horse he's got all that speed and power underneath him . . . and he knows, feels, when to let it go, how much, 'cause he's got everything working for him . . . timing, touch, it's a great feeling boy, it's a real great feeling when you're right and you know you're right . . . and you play the game like no one ever has."

I couldn't have said it better. Those were my sentiments exactly when it came to working with young people. "The proof is in the pudding." No one was paying these kids to come to YF. I was competing against everything that might pull them away from the church. I was competing against their outside world which included school activities, movies, parties, sporting events, you name it. I had to provide a better time than they could find elsewhere. Not unlike TV producers, I always thought of myself as competing with all the other channels of teenage life that were available. I had to provide a program that was not only compelling and entertaining, but also included a myriad of activities—activities that would outclass any other outside happenings.

In addition to the fun-packed Sunday night YF meetings I conducted, we had Friday night get-togethers at the church, complete with dancing, volleyball games, refreshments, and plenty of time to visit and relax with each other. Study groups were offered during the week for the more seriously minded. Annual events included snow trips, Disneyland trips, summer camp, bike rides, and cross-country backpack trips into Yosemite. Sometimes it took two or three rented buses to carry the kids that signed up for the Disneyland trip or snow trip. Our youth group was so large we could rent an entire 24-lane bowling alley for an all-night bowling event. We also had fundraisers for charity. Our all-night bowling event earned close to $3000 for UNESCO (big money for the early '70s). Monthly paper drives also fattened up our YF coffers to help further promote and support activities. We were constantly innovating, constantly on the move.

Music was another YF drawing card. Our *Good Sam Singers* was an ensemble group of about 30 teenagers that contributed to the Sunday worship services. We also sang at nursing homes, prisons, and rest homes. A couple of these young people were musically gifted, especially JoAnne Avery (Neish). She was majoring in music at De Anza Community College. Eventually, I put her in charge of the entire music program and suggested that the church hire her part-time (they did). In the spring of 1975, JoAnne and I put together an original musical. With the *Good Sam Singers* in tow, it was played out at the Fremont High School auditorium where a sold-out audience gave us a standing ovation.

A smaller group of seven, that I dubbed *Homestead and Wolfe* (H&W), consisting of myself and six youth, toured the nation.

JoAnne and I were primarily responsible for putting H&W together. Our group was so good that I contacted my old musical friends, the *Wrecking Crew* (see pp. 136–137), and with their instrumental backing recorded an album in the mid '70s at the pre-eminent Gold Star Studios in Hollywood with Stan Ross on board as our engineer. The album was titled *Our Times*.

Thirty years later (2004), the album was reissued by Anopheles Records. Anopheles's write-up ensued (see sidebar below).

"Originally released in 1975, Homestead & Wolfe's lone and unknown privately pressed LP is an artifact so lost to time, it has never appeared in any discography, list of rare records, or catalog, anywhere. However, exist it does, and now their story can be told.

Homestead & Wolfe was a folk-harmony group based around the United Methodist Good Samaritan Church in Cupertino, CA (near San Jose). Comprised of two female lead vocalists, one male lead vocalist, and buttressed with superb male and female harmonies throughout, H&W performed original material in a rich, melodic folk-rock-country style that is well executed, as well as earnest and personal. The patriarch, producer and lyricist of the group, Ernie Bringas, had dabbled in the record biz as one of two founding members of the "surf hot rod" early 1960s vocal duo, the Rip Chords . . . . As a Minister of Youth and master planner and motivator at Good Sam from 1969-75, Bringas assembled and encouraged this ensemble of counselors and students, eventually offering them an opportunity to record an album and have a shot at "making it" as artists. He gave them the ultimate "leg up" in the business, producing this finely crafted recording using his old Hollywood connections.

These 15 tracks were recorded at the legendary Gold Star Studios in Hollywood between 1973-75. Engineered by Stan Ross, these recordings feature top flight studio musicianship from legendary "wrecking crew" drummer Hal Blaine, guitarist Ben Benay (Goldenrod, Darius), acoustic guitarist Al Casey, monster bass player Ray Pohlman, not to mention one of the world's most renowned and respected pedal steel guitar players, Jay Dee Maness . . . . The harmonies and arrangements of H&W recall both the Mamas and the Papas and the Carpenters at times . . . . Homestead & Wolfe represents a highly unusual and strikingly original blend of unproven but talented young vocalists, top quality session players and engineering, and a truly rare chemistry that makes this one of the great folk-rock discoveries of the last 10 years." (see: ripchords.info)

Having said all this, I must point out that the H&W singing group was a very small facet of our youth program. As already stated, there were numerous outlets for participation. But the last thing I wanted was for these kids to feel pressured in any way. Although I was the Minister of Youth at Good Sam, my goal was not to convert these kids to Christianity, but to provide a safe haven for fun, fellowship, education, and a place where love could be experienced, a place where we could become family. If thereafter faith developed, as it did with some, so be it.

But for all this to have happened, there had to be more than my personal input. Not unlike a football team, the players surrounding the quarterback will make or break any game plan. I didn't build this youth group in a vacuum; that is, I wasn't alone. I may have been the glue that brought it all together, but without the right pieces, the end result would have been less impressive. Suffice it to say, the young people that joined up were exceptional; they were bright, friendly, and talented. You couldn't ask for a better bunch of "kids." They put the icing on the cake. I have one final observation about these exceptional young people.

In hindsight, I am struck by the educational and vocational excellence of the YF members. They eventually earned nearly 100 college and university degrees that included 17 Associate of Arts degrees, 33 Bachelor of Arts degrees, 23 Bachelor of Science degrees, 17 Master of Arts degrees, 6 Master of Divinity degrees, and 4 Doctor of Philosophy degrees (Ph.D.).

In the year 2000, thirty-one years later, we had our first YF Reunion. The gathering was prompted by the premature death of a YFer; she was only 45.

Our reunion numbered close to 150 in attendance. They came from all over the USA and from countries as far away as Peru. Since that time we have gathered together once every five years to celebrate our rich and unique heritage. During each reunion I conduct an old-fashioned YF meeting. The electricity and excitement of those long-ago YF years come flooding back, and we continue to upgrade that legacy with new innovations of thought and evolving experience. Lifelong friendships that began at Good Sam remain potent. I just returned from a 2015 YF reunion (August 7-9). We had another smashing good time with an attendance of 111 (46 years after our 1969 beginning).

Yes, 1969 to 1975 were amazing years. But all good things must come to an end. (In Buddhism, it's called the "philosophy of impermanence.")

In 1975, after serving as Minister of Youth for six years, I decided it was time to move away from Good Sam. I needed to spread my theological wings. To do so in my present position

*I'm leading a YF Reunion (2010). (Photo by Sue Larson)*

would not have been possible without creating waves for the conservative senior pastor. I've often found the following biblical verse to be so apropos: "For everything there is a season, and a time for every purpose under heaven." (Ecclesiastes 3:1) Purpose under heaven or not, it was time to go.

The United Methodist Church (UMC) is wide-ranging in its theological makeup. It is inclusive because it is based on pluralism (a condition or system in which theological differences willingly coexist). In other words, the Church as a whole is comprised of conservative, moderate, and liberal congregations or a combination thereof. Conveniently, ministers can be assigned to churches that are in keeping with their theological inclinations. After spending nine years in youth ministry, I was assigned a small church (par for the course as a first assignment) in Vallejo, California, about 75 miles north of Cupertino. Supposedly, it was a church that would match up with my progressive theological perspectives.

Chapter 17

# THE WAYSIDE UNITED
# METHODIST CHURCH
LA IGLESIA METODISTA UNIDA WAYSIDE

*Vallejo, California*
1975 – 1978

I WAS NOW 35 years old. My experience at the Wayside UMC
was a good one. Inevitably my ministry there prospered, but not
without some controversy (as you will soon see). Of course, that
ministry also included the resuscitation of a high school group
that was, at that time, basically stifled. Building a youth group
had always been my forte and Wayside was no exception.

It wasn't exactly the church in the wildwood, but it did
sit on the outskirts of town. I had asked for an "open pulpit,"
which are code words for a more progressive church. I wanted
a church in which I could share what I had gleaned from my
education without getting crucified on first hearing. I was,
however, savvy enough to tread carefully. My opening sermons
were strictly G and PG, so to speak. I spent the first six months
of my ministry just getting to know my congregation and vice
versa. In the process, I discovered that most of my parishioners
were quite conservative (not what I had asked for). No matter, everything was going great. Our rapport was wonderful

and the congregation doubled in size during those opening six months. It was time to ratchet up my sermons.

I can honestly tell you that my message on that fateful Sunday morning was quite benign. It certainly wasn't one of my X-rated, or even R-rated, sermons. But it doesn't take much to draw fire when the people you're addressing are sporting conservative antennae. Following the close of the service, I knew something was terribly wrong when some of my congregants descended on me like a flock of starving vultures looking for a fast meal. Evidently, during the course of my sermon, I had made a verbal misstep (at least in their thinking). One question led to another, and before I knew it, they wanted to know if I believed in the Virgin Birth (which had nothing to do with my sermon). I answered directly and honestly, "I don't take it literally."

My answer was too blunt. In a blink of an eye, friendship was out the window and all bets were off. I had answered like a minister, not a politician. I should have answered like a politician.

My Virgin Birth "miscue" spread quickly like the rumor about dead rats in Kentucky Fried Chicken's meat.[82] Containment was impossible as my congregants continued to jabber away. Soon after, they called in my D.S. (District Superintendent) for a special meeting of the Administrative Board (the governing body of the local church). It was during this meeting that someone stood up, pointed me out and shouted, "He's the anti-Christ!" When the D.S. supported my views (based on the pluralistic nature of the UMC), my accuser stomped out of the room. This whole affair split the church in half. Fortunately,

---

[82]As a word of caution, the rat rumor was totally wrong.

we had grown sufficiently strong enough to absorb the loss of those disenchanted members.[83]

Incidentally, not all Administrative Board meetings are that memorable, but sometimes they're unpredictable and crazy things can happen. We were mulling over my reluctance to live in the Wayside parsonage (that's a house owned by the church and provided for the minister). The house was too old and too big for a bachelor. I preferred a condo, or an apartment, or even a smaller house in a nicer neighborhood. But if I didn't stay in the parsonage, that would create an additional housing expense for them, and what would they do with an empty parsonage anyway? Finally, an elderly man came up with an equitable solution. "Here's what we can do," he stated. "We'll rent out the parsonage," he continued, "and that will provide Rev. Bringas with plenty of rental money so that he can move into a *condom*!"

During my first two months at the Wayside Church, I met Lyndon and Yvonne Lafferty. They lived right around the corner from the church, a delightful couple in their early forties. Following a church service one Sunday, they invited me over for dinner. I accepted. We hit it off right from the start. During the following weeks and months we became close friends (and still are today).

## On Patrol With the Highway Patrol

At that time, Lyndon Lafferty was a CHP officer (California Highway Patrol). He had an excellent record with the CHP. He devoted 27 years to law enforcement with many

---

[83]The previous three paragraphs were paraphrased from another one of my books: *JESUSGATE: A History of Concealment Unraveled*, 2013, pp. 192-93.

commendations. He was best known for crushing the hood and top of a patrol car as he and fellow officers used it as a platform to rescue 38 injured and trapped passengers on a commercial bus in November of 1976.

One night he offered to take me on patrol and I took him up on it. CHP cruisers were very striking. The Dodge body was all black with the exception of the white top and doors. The doors carried the image of a gold CHP badge with a blue coloring in the center. Above the badge inscribed with gold capital letters: HIGHWAY PATROL. Getting into a California Highway Patrol car felt adventurous.

We had just merged onto Interstate 80 when Lyndon spotted a speeder. He pushed the pedal to the medal and we took off in hot pursuit. Flying down the freeway in the middle of the night at 90 miles an hour with flashing lights had me sitting up straight. My adrenal glands pumped out the adrenalin and my heart took flight (or should I say fright). Cars were swinging out of our way as we ran up their tailpipes. While trying to maneuver through traffic, Lyndon lost sight of the vehicle and started to slow down.

"There he goes, Lyndon! He's pulling off the freeway at the next exit!" I shouted.

"Good eyes, Ernie," Lyndon said, as he sped up once again.

We were on him in a flash. I could see him looking in his rearview mirror. There was no way he couldn't know he was being stopped. He slowed way down as he took an off-ramp and made a right turn into street traffic and then made another quick right onto a street that was not well lit. He pulled over. We found ourselves in an isolated area: no homes, no businesses, or streetlights—just vacant lots. And it was awfully dark. We were now below the freeway and I could see and hear the cars rushing by. I started feeling edgy about this encounter.

Lyndon exited the patrol car. As he did, he cautioned me to remain in the car. Instinctively I had a sense of foreboding. I watched Lyndon calmly approach the vehicle.

As I watched Lyndon converse with the driver, my brain was scrambling for what I might do if this traffic stop went south. I kicked myself for not asking Lyndon what I should do if something went wrong. I glanced over to the left side of my left knee. The squad car was equipped with a formidable looking shotgun fastened vertically to the dashboard. Unfortunately, I had no idea how to release the mechanism that held it fast. I looked around for a smaller firearm in the glove compartment but to no avail. My paranoia was peaking when Lyndon suddenly opened the door and got in.

"What happened?" I asked quickly.

In a calm voice he answered: "Nothing. He seemed like a good kid so I just gave him a warning."

It must take a certain kind of nerve to be a police officer, something that is totally outside of my psychological makeup. It's more than a tough job. (To view the CHP–Officer Down Memorial Page, Google: www.odmp.org/agency/504-california-highway-patrol-california.) I was shocked to discover that since the inception of the CHP, hundreds of these officers have been killed in the line of duty. As one example, in 1978, California Highway Patrol officers William Freeman, 35, and Roy P. Blecher, 50, had been shot and killed execution-style on this very same Interstate 80. Blecher was shot with his hands cuffed behind his back.[84] But let's get back to my ministry in Vallejo.

## The Zodiac Killer

Aside from being called the "anti-Christ," and some scary rides in a police car, nothing unusual occurred during my tenure at the Wayside UMC, with one monumental exception; an exception I am now at liberty to divulge. The information I now reveal had been held back for almost 40 years before its recent release. Although the revelation in question really had nothing to do with my church, it did involve one of my congregants. At my suggestion, he accepted my willingness to get involved with one of the most intense manhunts regarding a serial killer known as *The Zodiac!* Before recounting my involvement, a little historical backdrop in the sidebar below will be necessary.

"The *Zodiac Killer* was a serial killer who operated in northern California in the late 1960s and early '70s. The killer's identity remains unknown. The Zodiac murdered victims in Benicia, Vallejo, Lake Berryessa, and San Francisco . . . Four men and three women between the ages of 16 and 29 were targeted . . . Although the Zodiac claimed 37 murders in letters to the newspapers, investigators agree on only seven confirmed victims, two of whom survived."[85]

[84]According to Wikipedia referencing the *Sacramento Bee* newspaper, Luis V. Rodriguez was convicted of the Dec. 22, 1978 murders. He was initially sentenced to death, but his sentence was later reduced to life without parole. Presently, Rodriguez is incarcerated at R.J. Donovan Correctional Facility in San Diego.
[85]Taken from Wikipedia

Authorities also suspected the Zodiac of five additional victims, stretching all the way down to southern California, that included Cheri Jo Bates, 18, who was stabbed to death on October 30, 1966, at Riverside City College in Riverside.[86] The majority of murders, however, took place in northern California. As already noted, some of the Zodiac murders occurred in Vallejo. Here's what happened. Just before midnight on July 4, 1969, Darlene Ferrin (22) and Michael Mageau (19) ". . . drove into the Blue Rock Springs Park in Vallejo . . . . While the couple sat in Ferrin's car, a second car drove into the lot and parked alongside them but almost immediately drove away. Returning about 10 minutes later, this second car parked behind them. The driver of the second car then exited the vehicle, approaching the passenger side door of Ferrin's car, carrying a flashlight and a 9 mm Luger. The killer directed the flashlight into Mageau's and Ferrin's eyes before shooting at them, firing five times. Both victims were hit, and several bullets had passed through Mageau and into Ferrin. The killer walked away from the car but upon hearing Mageau's moaning, returned and shot each victim twice more before driving off."[87]

Most of the above sidebar was unbeknownst to me in 1975 when I arrived at the Wayside United Methodist Church in Vallejo. Of course we all had heard about the Zodiac killer. But Vallejo was a good 75 miles north of Cupertino. I had no

---

[86]Ibid.

[87]According to Wikipedia in referencing Robert Graysmith's book, *Zodiac*, pp. 26-28.

idea that in 1969—six years before my arrival—the Zodiac had killed two young people in the parking lot of the Blue Rock Springs Park, not too far from the church I would now be serving. It wasn't until I took some of my new YF teenagers to that park that I learned of the gruesome details. They were well versed on the Vallejo killings that took place at Blue Rock Springs that fateful night. Nerves remained on edge. The Zodiac was still on the loose, and this was the beginning of my Zodiac education. That education was to be furthered by my good friend, Officer Lyndon Lafferty.

At some point early on, I learned from Lyndon that he was actually working on the Zodiac investigation in concert with Naval Intelligence Officer Jerry Johnson and Vallejo Police Detective James Dean, albeit unofficially. All were dedicated to this mission with passion and determination; Officer Lafferty was the lead investigator. But little did I know that I, too, would be engaged in this clandestine operation. I'll start at the beginning.

In 1970, while on patrol, Officer Lafferty stopped at a rest stop between the cities of Vallejo and Fairfield on Interstate 80 (Fairfield is almost 18 miles by car north of Vallejo; Sacramento was another 43 miles north of Fairfield). In the parking area of the rest stop he noticed a man in a white Chevrolet that vaguely matched descriptions of the Zodiac killer. He became even more suspicious because of the man's facial expressions. Lafferty states: "I looked into a quivering, snarling face like I was looking into the face of death. It scared the hell out of me."[88] Evidently, the man had the stare of a crazed individual. This hateful glare of the suspect would come to be known

---

[88]FRONT PAGE, *Fairfield Daily Republic*, August 30, 2011, by David DeBolt.

by those who encountered him as "the look." Of course, you can't arrest someone based on the way they look at you, and the Zodiac sketches were somewhat unclear. However, those hateful stares emanating out from that individual could not be ignored. In Lafferty's opinion, not only were these stares highly unnerving, but they also personified evil. Accordingly, Lafferty ran the man's license plate and that's how the whole investigation started. In the months that followed, the investigation indicated that this suspect could, indeed, be the Zodiac killer. But the proof of the matter (the smoking gun), as required by the judicial system, was lacking.

As I later learned, the authorities did possess some evidence obtained from a pay telephone that the Zodiac had used to taunt the police after the Lake Berryessa killings (September 27, 1969). The call was traced, and when detectives arrived at the scene, they only found the receiver dangling from the phone. It was dusted for fingerprints. The result was negative, but a partial palm print was successfully lifted. This was a significant clue. Thereafter, the palm print of any Zodiac suspect became the gold standard for proving guilt. But unless a suspect was willing to walk into a police station to give up a palm print, the odds of getting one was nigh to impossible. Another point of evidence was the numerous ciphers (coded notes) that the Zodiac had written to authorities.

Fast forward to 1975. During my ministry at the Wayside UMC, as mentioned earlier, I became close friends with the Lafferty family. Consequently, most of what I learned about the Zodiac case came from Officer Lyndon Lafferty including the ciphers, and the suspect that the Lafferty team had in mind—a middle-aged man who was a real estate agent living in the city of Fairfield just north of Vallejo.

At some point, Lyndon devised a plan to secure much-needed handwriting samples from the real estate office where the suspect worked. A search warrant was out of the question. So, Lyndon asked if I'd be willing to risk a clandestine raid with him. The plan was to make our way to the back of the real estate office around 2 AM when no one was around. With a large plastic bag in hand, we would empty the trashcan and flee the scene before anyone knew the difference. In so doing, we might gather important handwritten documents from the suspect.

The legality of this move was in question, but not the ensuing embarrassment should we be caught messing around on private property by the authorities. One could imagine the headline in the Vallejo or Fairfield newspapers: "Police Officer and Minister Arrested for Trespassing." Fortunately, that didn't happen. We made a clean getaway. I was glad to get back home that evening. I hit the sack. Lyndon stayed up all night going through a mound of trash that yielded a few enticing clues, especially some handwriting samples that proved helpful in breaking the Zodiac cryptograms/ciphers (a text written in code). During his years in the Air Force, Lyndon had been trained in deciphering such codes. According to him, the FBI believes his work is in the ballpark and could be right.

One evening shortly thereafter, while sitting around the dinner table, I asked Lyndon if I could be of further assistance in the investigation of their prime suspect. He thought for a moment and then responded in the affirmative. They had plenty of information on the suspect, but they didn't have boots on the ground, so to speak. They knew he attended AA meetings (Alcoholics Anonymous) and suggested I might attend these meetings as a means of observation. Lyndon gave me fair warning of what he thought could be a very dangerous undertaking on my part. He actually feared for my life. I kidded with him that if anything drastic did happen to me, they'd know for sure that they had the right man.

Anyway, I decided to participate, but not until I agreed with Lyndon that I should carry or have a firearm close at hand. On his insistence, I bought a 9-shot .22 Standard Magnum. Great! I was now a United Methodist minister who carried and was loaded for bear. Lyndon went so far as to advise me to carry the gun into the pulpit on Sunday mornings. I almost took his advice until I realized that any such emergency in the middle of a Sunday worship service might lead to unintended consequences—like accidentally shooting a couple of my congregants. My parishioners would never forgive me if I got blood on that expensive sanctuary carpet.

My first objective was to become a part of AA. This, of course, would require me to create a cover story and attend these meeting under false pretenses, that is, as a recovering alcoholic. I would have to play-act my way through the meetings. I was confronted with the dilemma of unethical misrepresentation with people who were struggling with very serious life issues and, God forbid, that I might run into one of my church members. I decided the ends justified the means.

So it was that I started driving the 18 miles to Fairfield every Tuesday evening to attend AA meetings. Of course, I maintained anonymity. HB was my handle for the ensuing six months. At every meeting I would introduce myself in the required confessional mode: "I'm HB and I'm an alcoholic." On one occasion I nearly blew my cover when I lost focus and *almost* blurted out: "I'm Ernie Bringas and I'm an alcoholic." That was close.

Over the course of the six months that I was involved with AA, I was able to gather some information that proved helpful to the Lafferty team. For example, I was able to secure more handwritten papers that the suspect unwittingly would toss into a wastebasket. Overall, my contributions did help to fill in a few pieces of this very complex Zodiac puzzle. My involvement is well documented in the 2005 publication, *The Zodiac Killer Cover Up: The Silenced Badge* by Lyndon E. Lafferty. I will, however, leave you with a small excerpt from that work in the sidebar below and, thereafter, make two qualifying statements. [Brackets mine]

"Ernie has been a dear and close friend for many years, and on occasion, would spend time with me on patrol. Ernie volunteered his services in our investigation, and he soon became a member of the Mandamus Seven [the investigative team]. His dedication and commitment was exceeded only by his bold courage and calculated risk-taking. Very few men would have faced the challenge or danger as Ernie did. Ernie's a person the poet Lisa Pelzer wrote about when she said:

'As we walk the path of life, we meet people everyday. Most are simply met by chance, but some are sent our way.'

Everyone who meets Ernie feels the same way. The information he provided on the case was invaluable. He had been walking a razor's edge for a long time when his secret identity was revealed. When Ernie's safety was compromised by Graysmith's first book in 1986, he decided to leave the state. Had I been in his shoes, I would have done the same. Ernie is convinced, without a shadow of a doubt, our suspect was, and is the Zodiac."[89]

The above comments from my good friend, Lyndon, require some modification. First, I did not leave California because of Graysmith's book. In fact, I had left the state three years prior to Graysmith's 1986 publication.

Second, if Lyndon's comment is correct that *Very few men would have faced the challenge or the danger as Ernie did ...* then we're in serious trouble. Truth is, I just reckoned that serial killers are very calculating and, therefore, are not likely to kill someone sitting next to them. Almost always, their victims are strangers. I figured the closer I got to this guy, the less likely he would do me in (by continuing this sentence I have nullified ending it with a preposition).

The Zodiac case remains open. Proof positive was never achieved although most of our circumstantial evidence remains compelling. Unfortunately, our suspect is no longer with us; he fell down and broke his neck (February 2, 2012). Thus, we'll never know for sure unless more evidence surfaces.

Sadly, my good friend Lyndon E. Lafferty died of cancer on March 5, 2016. The family asked me to conduct the funeral service. It was an honor to serve in this manner on March 10, at the Wayside United Methodist Church in Vallejo, California.

---

[89]Lyndon E. Lafferty, *The Zodiac Killer Cover-up: The Silenced Badge.* Parker, CO, Outskirts Press, Inc., 2005, pp. 363-64.

# The ZODIAC Team

**JERRY JOHNSON**
Naval Intelligence Agent

**LYNDON LAFFERTY**
CHP Officer

**ERNIE BRINGAS**
United Methodist Minister

**DAVE FISTER**
CHP Officer

**JAMES DEAN**
Homicide Detective

**ROBERT JERNIGAN**
Historian-Investigator

**NEAL McCASLIN**
District Attorney (Deceased)

**LESLIE LUNDBLAD, SR.**
Investigator Sergeant
(Deceased)

**CHUCK FORREST**
Naval Intelligence Agent
(Deceased)

Chapter 18

# LEAVE OF ABSENCE
## PERMISO PARA AUSENTARSE

*San Jose, California*
1978 – 1979

AT THE AGE OF 38, in the summer of 1978, I left the Vallejo church to take a one-year leave of absence from the United Methodist Church. We can't call it a sabbatical because I did not receive paid leave. Nevertheless, I had saved enough money to buy a new Toyota Corolla, and to take a year off for the purpose of working on a writing project that I felt needed my full attention. I rented an apartment in San Jose and got to work.

Since seminary days I had promised myself to put into writing the information I had garnered through my educational journey. Although my writing endeavor was partially accomplished during that year, believe it or not, it would take another 17 years to get it completely finished and then published. I kept shelving the project and then coming back to it at haphazard intervals. It was finally published in 1996 (*GOING BY THE BOOK: The Past and Present Tragedies of Biblical Authority*). It was basically a compilation of destructive Christian behaviors throughout the centuries that had been prompted by ignorance, dogmatic belief, and the misunderstanding of biblical revelation. This 1996 publication was not my last. I'll say more about this later. Before we get back to 1979, I'll leave you with an additional thought.

One night I imagined myself having died and gone to Heaven. Saint Peter greeted me at the Pearly Gates. He offered to show me around the celestial grounds. Not unlike Disneyland, Heaven was divided into different theme parks. I didn't see any "Pirates of the Caribbean," but we did come across a theme area called "Angels of Heaven." We entered a long hallway leading to many rooms where angels were involved in various activities. As we passed the first room, one could hear the numerous angels singing their favorite hymns. Another room featured angels that had an interest in painting, and their portraits were beautiful. Every room we passed had plenty of angels engaged in some form of favored activity. We finally came to a room that was filled with boisterous laughter. I couldn't help but wonder what all the excitement was about.

"Why are these angels laughing so hard?" I asked inquisitively.

St. Peter answered: "This is the Reading Room and they're browsing through one of your books."

Chapter 19

# THE DIXON UNITED
# METHODIST CHURCH

## LA DIXON IGLESIA METODISTA UNIDA

*Dixon, California*
1979 – 1983

IN THE SUMMER OF 1979 I returned to the ministry. I was 39 and I had been appointed by the California United Methodist Conference to a small church in Dixon, a small bedroom community about 36 miles north of my previous church in Vallejo. Nearby was the California State University of Davis, only 8 miles north of Dixon, and Sacramento was another 15 miles north of Davis. All of these cities were on a nearly straight line up Highway 80: Vallejo—Fairfield—Dixon—Davis—Sacramento. Outside of Dixon and Davis, farmlands stretched in all directions.

Dixon was a quaint little town with a population of about 5000. The church was picturesque and originally had been built in 1866. It looked the part of a typical small frontier church, with a white steeple whose old bell was no longer usable. Directly across from the church—about 250 feet—were the shiny rails that carried the numerous freight trains that were slowly pulled through the town by their noisy locomotives. Don't get me wrong; I love trains. Sometimes I'd come out of the church office and count the boxcars as they passed by. Since the age of four, when I was at my aunt's house in San Diego and spotted one of these majestic iron giants piercing the night with light and whistle, I became permanently captivated by them.

The parsonage—the pastor's house owned by the church—was situated directly behind the church. That old wooden house would literally shake and rattle when those trains with their throttles wide open would come rumbling along in the middle of the night. Every evening for the first few days I would jump out of bed from a deep sleep thinking I was in the middle of a California earthquake. After a while, my mind adjusted and I didn't hear them anymore.

## The Dark Side

During my first week in Dixon, a young married man had been shot and killed by a so-called friend. I can't recall what led to the argument between the two. In any case, I was called in to counsel with the surviving widow and her four-year old son. It was impossible not to draw a comparison between myself and this child; our fathers had been abruptly and violently taken from us at this tender age. And yet, because of my own experience, I felt I could counsel with some authority on the travesty at hand.

Premature deaths and violent endings of any sort were always the most difficult part of ministry for me. On the one hand, it was an honor and a privilege to facilitate the grieving process. On the other hand, one was not immune to the emotional free-fall endured by survivors who were the closest to the departed. This was acutely true in the case of premature and unexpected deaths, accidental or otherwise. The death of a child had no equal. Along these lines, my most difficult funeral remembered is that of a 12-year-old boy who had committed suicide. No words could, or would, suffice in that depressing atmosphere. Let's move away from this morbid subject.

**The Lighter Side?**
On the lighter side of things, and this is not exaggerated, ministers tend to draw the attention of the opposite sex. The ministerial platform creates the illusion of purity, which in many instances has its unique advantages. Tom Cruise may have great looks, but ministers have the *illusion* of purity and righteousness going for them. However, a minister with Tom Cruise's looks, combined with purity, can, if he chooses, run the table (to coin a pool game metaphor).

Of course, I was single and I never dated anyone who was married, and rarely anyone from my congregation. The problem arose, however, when I drew the attention of a married woman; it was really nothing more than her infatuation with the clerical image. But that can be a most disruptive problem—flattering, but disruptive nevertheless. The following example will suffice.

It was close to noon. I was alone working in the church office when I was interrupted by one of the young married women from my congregation. I knew "Jane Smith" and her husband well. He was a successful self-made entrepreneur. They had the advantage of youth, a beautiful home, and money to spare. Indeed, they were one of our church's biggest contributors.

Jane was obviously troubled that day. I asked her to sit down and gently probed for an explanation. With a slight hesitancy in her voice and shaky body language, she quietly clarified. I gleaned from her explanation that I meant more to her than just a friend. She didn't know exactly why she felt so attracted to me, but her emotions were deep seated. Indeed, she actually used the word "love" in trying to define her feelings toward me. I was absolutely dumbfounded! I had no clue.

I quickly searched my mind for any word or action on my part that would have misled this woman. I came up with absolutely nothing. How could this be? True, they had invited me to dinner and she had worked on the Board of Christian Education. But so what? I could only conclude that she had conjured up in her mind some kind of "Knight in Shining Armor" image of me.

Suddenly, the jangling ring of the telephone rudely interrupts my thinking. In some small way I am thankful for the infringing relief. My relief is short lived; it's her husband on the line. The one time this man calls me happens to be at the very same moment his wife is smack dab in front of me with confessional drippings of the heart (talk about Murphy's Law).

"Is my wife there?" his agitated voice demands.

"Why yes," I answer with all the innocent transparency I can muster.

"I thought as much," he states with an accusatory tone. "Don't think I don't know what's going on," he continues, as if to say "aha" to a child caught with his hand in the cookie jar.

"Wait a minute!" I respond with a hint of indignation. "I don't like what you're insinuating."

I can't remember my exact words, but the gist of my evolving conversation with him was to help him understand—as best I could—that his wife and I were not engaged in any romantic dalliance. Indeed, until that very moment I was totally oblivious to this unsolicited soap opera. But without alienating him, how do you tell a man that his wife is no more appealing to you than a sponge, and how do you do that without hurting the sponge sitting directly in front of you?

Sure, we got this whole mess straightened around but not without consequences. The embarrassment of it all was a bit too much for them; soon after, Jane and her husband left my church. That was par for the course.

❊

Dr. Sam Nader was the senior pastor at the First United Methodist Church in Lubbock, Texas. In 1979, this church was the ninth largest UMC in the world, with a membership of over 6000. At that time they were on a national hunt for a minister of youth who could help them with their high school program. Unbeknownst to me, my reputation as a youth minister had drifted across state lines, and my name ended up at the top of their list. Accordingly, Dr. Nader called me by phone and expressed a desire for me to come interview for the job. But the timing wasn't right. I had just started working at the Dixon UMC in 1979. It was nevertheless a tempting offer. If I auditioned for the job and got it, I would be leaving a small rural church of 100 members for a 6000-member mega-church in Texas. Moreover, it provided the opportunity to work in my specialty, youth work. But in my heart of hearts, I really didn't relish the idea of moving to Texas. My answer to Dr. Nader was a polite "thanks, but no thanks."

For the next couple of years I truly enjoyed my ministry at Dixon. The people were extremely friendly and it was an open pulpit; in other words, the folks were open-minded and my progressive sermons did not lead them to open revolt. Therefore, I had plans to remain in Dixon. I even bought a house, and it wasn't anywhere near the railroad tracks. But I love trains, so I did miss them.

## Leroy

I can't neglect to mention Leroy. I met him through one of the girls who was attending the University of Davis. He turned out to be one of the great loves of my life; we became inseparable. He was a strong and handsome specimen, one of a kind. My friend could no longer tend to Leroy the dog, and asked if I would be willing to look after him. He was already five years old. I told her I would, but only as a temporary measure. Of course, it didn't take long for this German shepherd to win me over. We never parted company. The bond between us became incredible. We were so tight that one of my close friends once said, "Here comes a dog and his man."

## Dr. Sam Nader on the Line

In the spring of 1983, I was in my fourth year at Dixon and everything was going smoothly. Working on a sermon at my house one afternoon, I was interrupted by a phone call. It was Dr. Sam Nader on the line once again. He wanted to fly out to California and meet with me. He said: "I'm going to make you an offer you can't refuse." Of course we both chuckled because that line carried ominous connotations as depicted in the 1972 movie, *The Godfather*. I continued the banter with, "Ok, but we meet on my turf, and you come alone."

A few weeks later we met at Tia Maria's Mexican restaurant in Sacramento. We had a good meal, he picked up the check, and we eventually got around to business. We started off with small talk.

"What is your main racket in Texas?" I asked.

"All," he responded quickly.

"All?" I inquired.

"Yes, that's right, all," he repeated.

"I'm sorry, but I don't understand. What is all?" I politely asked.

"You don't know what all is?" he shot back.

"No, I don't know what 'all' is." I started feeling a bit nervous at this point. Was I stupid or something? Adding to my mounting tension was the look of dismay on his face.

"All is all," he said with irritation. "Everyone knows what 'all' is!"

I emphatically stated: "Well I don't!"

By this time I was beside myself. What was this guy talking about? Was he pulling my leg? What was I missing? And then it dawned on me!

"Oh, you mean oil!"

"Yes, that's what I said, all!" he blurted out with what I then recognized as a very strong Texas accent. He was saying "oil," and I was hearing "all." We both had a good laugh.

Thereafter, our conversation narrowed to the significant. He wanted to fly me out to Lubbock and interview with the ministerial committee for the position of youth minister. They would pick up the plane fare and all other expenses regardless of what I decided. The interview, of course, was just a formality because if the senior pastor wanted you on staff, the committee was simply a rubber stamp of approval (assuming you were somewhat competent).

But dragging me off from the Golden State to some city in the middle of an expansive desert crawling with scorpions and rattlesnakes was not my idea of a fun time. It would take a herculean effort on Dr. Nader's part to convince me to do otherwise; or, as he had intimated, he would have to make me an offer I couldn't refuse.

Our conversation was somewhat "cat and mouse," shifting those roles as we went along in the dialogue. I held back discussing the issue of salary because I didn't want to give the wrong impression. Unavoidably, however, we eventually got to the nitty-gritty question of compensation. I took the lead.

"What's the going salary for this position?" I asked with a calm monotone voice, but with enough body language for him to know it better be a good offer.

As that 62-year-old gentleman sat across from me in that restaurant, I got the impression he knew something I didn't. He reached into the inside pocket of his coat and retrieved paper and pen. He then made a notation on the paper, folded it in half, and slowly shoved it across the table. My mind flashed back to *The Godfather*, Don Vito Corleone. I reached out and placed my hand atop the folded slip. I looked him in the eye for a few moments with just a hint of a smile. There was no need to appear anxious.

Prior to this meeting I had already determined two things: First, I was not really interested in going to Texas. That's one of the reasons I didn't consider the first invitation four years earlier. Second, I would only reconsider the matter if the salary offered were at least $6000 higher than my present earnings as a senior pastor. "Show me the money!" I surmised that a $6000 increase in salary was virtually prohibitive. That was my psychological insurance against having to move to Lubbock, Texas.

I unfolded the slip of paper and focused on the dollar amount. I was mentally bushwhacked for what my eyes were telling me. The offer was $12,000 above my current salary. Adjusting for inflation in today's market that would be the equivalent of a $24,000 raise! This was way beyond anything I thought they would offer. I froze but maintained my composure. I didn't want him to think he overshot the runway. Quite the opposite; you want the individual to feel he made the right call, and that anything less wouldn't have sealed the deal. The last thing you want to say is: "Wow, you could have gotten me for $6000 less." That would cause him anguish and simultaneously devalue me. I paused for a moment as if to give the impression of thinking the matter over. That's when he went for the jugular.

"By the way," he continued, "that figure doesn't include your free housing allowance and an extra $200 a month contribution into your pension program."

That was the killer. He had sweetened the deal to the max. The seduction was complete. My brain was tripping out. I wasn't about to turn this bonanza down, but I didn't want him to think he had just bought me like a piece of meat, even though he had.

The reader may think me somewhat materialistic or monetarily crass. But I was 43 years old and had worked most of my adult life in the church for meager wages. For example, when I worked as the minister of youth at the Good Samaritan Church in Cupertino for six years, my wages were minimal. We had around 100 teenagers participating in the worship service every Sunday morning and that triggered an influx of adults. During the week we had an average of 200 high schoolers at our meetings with a record high of 346. The majority of

American churches could only dream of such numbers. Things were really humming and church growth exploded. But I was only paid $7,200 a year while the senior pastor was making over $45,000. I never thought the arrangement was equitable, but I loved working with the "kids." Therefore, I accepted the salary gap and went along to get along. However, I was older now and still running "against the wind."[90] But today was a different story. I had already paid my dues and it was time to look out for my future interests.

"This is a very generous package," I stated earnestly, but with a tone that suggested I was not a donkey in pursuit of a carrot. I moved the conversation away from finances to pragmatic issues; for example, how much control would I have over the youth program? If I had the green light on that last question, I'd accept his offer. He assured me in no uncertain terms that I would have total control. With that assurance, it was a done deal. Leroy the dog and I would be Texas bound. I didn't want to sell my house so I secured a real estate office to handle it as a rental. In June of 1983, Leroy and I hit the road in my Toyota Corolla. When we arrived in Lubbock, I came to the realization that I was only about 350 miles from El Paso, the city where my infant mother and her family had landed after crossing the Mexican border in 1916.

---

[90]According to Wikipedia, "Against the Wind" is a song by Bob Seger & The Silver Bullet Band from the 1980 album *Against the Wind*. "Against the Wind" is the highest ranking single from the album, peaking at #5. Glenn Frey of the Eagles sang background vocals on this song.

Chapter 20

# THE FIRST UNITED
# METHODIST CHURCH
## LA PRIMERA IGLESIA METODISTA UNIDA

*Lubbock, Texas*
1983—1986

THERE'S NO PLACE LIKE TEXAS. It's a paradox; that is, it is a part of Americana, but it also carries a distinct identity unlike any other state I've seen. It's a real hoot to watch the ladies and gents, sporting boots and cowboy hats, do the Texas Two-step at a respectable honky-tonk club on a Friday evening. Then again, Texas has the highest U.S. execution rate, numbering over 500 since the Supreme Court reinstated the death penalty in 1976. Oklahoma follows with 112 executions (according to the Death Penalty Information Center [DPIC]).

I was 43 when Leroy the dog and I arrived in Texas during that summer of '83. I rented a small apartment adjacent to a big, open field where Leroy would have some room to run when I took him out (four times a day with never a miss). At 60 pounds he was small for a shepherd dog, but he needed some space outside of that apartment. We'd go out early morning before I left for the church, then again at lunchtime, late afternoon, and again at night before we retired. I slept on the floor in the bedroom and he slept in the open closet nearby. He was my alarm clock. Every morning at sunrise he would rudely awaken me with his cold nose on my face, his way of telling me it was time to start our morning stroll. On my days off, if I were still sleepy when he woke me, I'd simply say: "Not now, Leroy."

He would slowly turn away looking dejected and come back a few minutes later with another nudge to my face. I didn't have the heart to say "no" twice. This ritual continued through the hot days of summer and the cold, snowy days of winter. Sometimes it got very cold, and it seemed like the wind blew year round in Lubbock, but Leroy the dog didn't seem to mind the wind chill factor.

My job as Minister of Youth turned out to be less than ideal. Although we started off with a bang, pulling in 100 youth within six weeks, a serious problem arose. I had been promised complete control of the youth program (you need that control to establish loyalty and continuity). Unfortunately, that was not the case. There was already a large youth choir led by a professional music director.

Aside from singing every Sunday during the worship service—and they were very good—they also had their own social gatherings, summer and winter camp outings, and so forth. It was like having two youth groups in the same church, each going their own separate ways. I tried to integrate the kids but they played one group against the other, depending on what suited their particular whims at any given moment. The old axiom proved true: "A house divided against itself cannot stand." As a consequence, I never came close to achieving my previous successes.

Leroy and I stayed the course for three years. During that time an additional friend was added to our family circle. There was a 28-year-old youth counselor at the church who helped me diligently with the youth program. One thing led to another and eventually Teena and I became engaged. She had her own apartment and I had mine. This led to a unique set of problems. We thought it might be a good idea if we lived together for a short while before taking a stroll down the matrimonial aisle. This idea of premarital cohabitation was an almost universally accepted practice in our society by the 1980s (thanks to the sexual revolution of the 1960s).

However, West Texas in the 1980s still possessed a 1950s moral mentality. In fact, they still practiced the blue laws (known also as Sunday laws). These laws were designed to restrict shopping, sales, or ban any or all activities that might conflict with Sunday as a day of worship or rest. Most everything shut down on Sundays including shopping malls and car dealers. West Texas—at least in Lubbock—would not even sell bottled alcohol inside the city limits, regardless of what day it was. If you wanted liquor, you had to drive a good ten miles out to purchase it. I didn't drink so that wasn't a problem.

Most blue laws have been repealed in the United States, and I think they have been scaled back in Texas since 1985, but not completely. Be that as it may, these blue laws were well entrenched when I arrived in Lubbock. I was from California where everything was wide open; I'd never even heard of the blue laws before coming to Texas. This reminds me of an old blue joke that has nothing to do with Texas. Question: What do you do with a blue whale? Answer: You try to cheer him up. (Sorry, I couldn't resist; back to the blue laws.)

My point here is that I was now living in one of the most conservative regions in the country. Trying to live with Teena and being found out would be the equivalent of striking a hornet's nest with a baseball bat. That's putting it mildly. After all, how would it look if a 43-year-old minister, in one of the most prestigious United Methodist churches in the country, decided to shack up—that's what they would call it—with a 28-year-old youth counselor from said church? We'd probably make the front page of the *National Enquirer*. How would it be possible for Teena and me to share the same apartment without causing this kind of an uproar?

Additionally, I recognized that church members would be outraged if their minister of youth set this kind of an example for the young people he or she were leading. This would be true in every region of the country. Ministers are always held to a higher standard. Such behavior would never be condoned. I certainly did not want to cause this kind of harm to the church as a whole, and especially the youth. Prudently, Teena and I kept our separate apartments.

Teena and I were married October 5, 1985, with Leroy's approval, of course. My marriage to Teena reminds me of an early poem I wrote as a teenager. It makes for a good metaphor when experiencing the overpowering impact of love.

When I was young and brassy just the age of 22,
I signed up as a buccaneer to sail the ocean blue.
Tis heaven to be moving, 'twas adventure that I sought,
But home is what you make it and I guess I never thought.

A sleepless night came to an end when through a stormy gale
I heard the captain yell to me, "hey boy bring down that sail."

I felt the spray of water, heard the wind and thunder sound,
and before I knew what happened I fell overboard and drowned!

(No more poems, I promise.)

In the summer of 1986, I terminated my ministry at First
UMC in Lubbock. It was back to California. To be precise, it
was back to my house in Dixon that I had rented out before
leaving for Lubbock.

Chapter 21

# AN OCCUPATIONAL DEMARCATION
## UNA DEMARCACIÓN OCUPACIONAL

1986 - 1992

IN THE SUMMER OF 1986, I was 46 years old. Teena and I, and Leroy the dog, made Dixon our home for the next few years. I did not petition the California UMC for a church assignment. I felt it was time to take another sabbatical, not realizing at the time that I would never return to full-time Christian ministry. The truth is that it was getting more and more difficult to speak truth to my congregants. Theologically, I tend to be quite progressive (liberal). Besides, I wanted to continue writing. But how would I make a living?

Basically, we were on our own. There was no longer any job security, something I had enjoyed throughout my ministry. I had to get a job and provide some income for my family (which, of course, included Leroy the dog). With Teena on board, that responsibility became more acute. The monthly mortgage on the house alone was close to $900, a hefty sum in those days.

Unfortunately, I couldn't always depend on Teena for support in this area. She was beginning to suffer from severe bouts of Bipolar depression. We often joked that being married to me would depress anyone. But it was a malady that started during her early 20s and had been progressively getting worse. Most of her time and energy were now spent on keeping herself together. Suicidal tendencies were apparent. She encouraged me to remove all firearms from our house. I did. Psychiatric help came into play on several occasions. That created a substantial drain on our finances. Whatever money I had saved from my Lubbock days was dwindling down faster than a snow cone in a microwave. I had to make money and I had to make it fast. I turned to sales.

## From Minister to "Carnie"

Believe it or not, I became an encyclopedia salesmen; I started working for World Book Encyclopedia (WB) in the fall of 1986. I chose WB because it had a strong reputation for creating reader-friendly educational materials for all ages. It was a strange feeling going from the professional status of a United Methodist minister to that of being a "car salesman," so to speak. Not because there's anything wrong with sales people, but they get a lot of bad press (based on a few bad apples). As a consequence, my status rating fell to zero. I was still the same person, but strangers didn't interact with me in the same way. My ministerial platform was gone. I was now a salesman, a carnie, not a minister. The respect so freely accorded me in the past was completely absent. It took some getting used to. Q. – Why did the car salesman bring his car to a screeching halt when he saw the snake crossing the road directly in front of him? A. – Professional courtesy.

Teena was not totally incapacitated by her Bipolar disorder and joined with me in the sales venture whenever she was able.

For example, every year we worked the California State Fair together in Sacramento. That was a blast. During our breaks, it was great sport walking around to see all the exhibits on hand.

Between the two of us, we could actually sell a couple of those sets each day we were there. They ranged from $500 to $800 depending on the binding. Our commission was around $100 per set. I can still hear myself in shotgun rhythm yelling out to folks who walked by our exhibit stall: *"Hurry, Hurry! Step right, up ladies and gentlemen, and sign up for a free drawing of the World Book Encyclopedia! World Book is the world's #1 selling encyclopedia. The World Book outsells Americana, Britannica, Collier's, Book of Knowledge, you name it. World Book will sell more encyclopedias in 7 weeks than all the other encyclopedia companies combined! It is the only encyclopedia most highly recommended by the American Library Association and the American Teachers' Association. There's no obligation to sign up for this free drawing. Don't be afraid folks, step right up!"* There was hardly a breath between those statements.

When passers-by signed up for the drawing, it gave us an advantage to lead them into a conversation that, on occasion, led to a sale. However, we were never pushy with the product, simply honest in our explanations. Even if they didn't purchase, the sign-ups provided ample leads for follow up.

Aside from the few times that Teena and I worked together, I carried the job on a full-time basis. In fact, I became the #1 salesperson in the Northern California WB division. In a business where the average closing rate was 25%, I had a closing sales rate of 84%! I suspect that was the highest WB closing rate in the nation. As a consequence, I won every selling award offered by World Book, including an award given for the highest number of sales within a seven-week period; I sold almost

100 sets. My closing rate was unprecedented, and it drew attention. I was soon promoted to division manager.

## Leroy's New Journey

Leroy took ill in early October of that same year (1986). Fortunately, the University of California Davis School of Veterinary Medicine was only eight miles north of Dixon by freeway. This was no fly-by-night facility; it was akin to that of a regular multi-storied hospital. It was literally a teaching hospital for training future veterinarians. The UCD School of Veterinary Medicine is the largest veterinary school in the United States and is currently ranked #1 in the USA by *US News & World Report*. It also has the distinction of being ranked #1 in the world by the 2015 *QS World University Rankings*.[91] Leroy could not have been in a better place. After a few exams and some X-rays, Leroy was suspected of having cancer.

On the evening of October 29th, Teena and I had just visited Leroy in the Davis hospital and we were on our way back home to Dixon. It was almost midnight by the time we entered our home. Suddenly, a strange feeling of apprehension overtook me.

"Teena," I said quietly, but with serious overtones. "Something is wrong. I'm not sure what it is but I've got to go back and see Leroy."

"But why?" she asked. "It's really quite late. Besides, we just left Leroy and he was okay," she stated with a look of uncertainty.

---

[91] *QS World University Rankings* is an annual publication of university rankings by the British Quacquarelli Symonds (QS) company.

I could see that Teena was all played out and ready for bed. I told her not to worry and that I would call her from the hospital if anything was wrong. But I needed to go back. We had two cars. She could join me later if necessary. I jumped into the Toyota Corolla and headed back up the eight miles to Davis. The ominous feeling that poured over my body and mind was unrelenting as I sped up the freeway. Never in all of my life had I ever felt this intuitive emotion that was now driving me back to a place I had just left a half-hour earlier, smack dab in the middle of the night no less.

When I arrived at the hospital, the parking lot was dark and desolate but for a couple of night lights. I parked the car, rushed up to the entrance, and pushed hard against the red button adjacent to the locked doors. A questioning voice rang out from the call box. I identified myself. The locking mechanism gave way as I pushed through the entrance doors. I had a pretty good idea of Leroy's whereabouts unless they had moved him elsewhere. Bypassing the elevators, I quickly made my way upstairs to the second floor and started down the corridor. I was moving with some urgency but I wasn't sure why. I just felt this strong sense that Leroy had summoned me in some mystical way, although my rational approach to life would not allow me to fully embrace that theory. Nevertheless, the feeling of urgency was undeniable and irrepressible. What was all this about? My thought process was interrupted as I noticed someone approaching from the opposite end of the corridor—it was one of Leroy's doctors.

"Ernie," she exclaimed, "we've been trying to reach you by phone. I just talked to your wife and she is on her way over here. Leroy's had a heart attack! He's still alive but it doesn't look promising."

My heart sank. She led me to a room where I found Leroy sprawled flat on his side atop a shiny silver table. He was motionless except for the slight rise and fall of his multi-colored body hair. Aided by an attached breathing apparatus, he clung to life. Standing nearby were three solemn-faced student practitioners in white coats. I spoke Leroy's name softly as I moved towards him. I gently kissed him on the middle front of his long nose, and tried to let him know I was there. About twelve minutes later, Teena was on scene. Leroy lay unconscious through the remainder of the night. We stayed with him.

Decision time came with the rising sun. The doctors gave us a few options, but they were very blunt about his chances for survival if we made any attempt to bring him back from the clutches of the Grim Reaper. It didn't take us long to figure it out. Neither Teena nor I were willing to drag Leroy through a painful so-called healing process that offered little chance of success. To begin with, Leroy was nine years old and German shepherds don't have a reputation for long lifelines. We wanted to do what was in his best interest, not ours. The decision was difficult, to say the least, but we knew we had to let him go.

On the morning of October 30, 1986, we sat on the floor next to our beautiful, four-legged companion, wished him well on his next journey, and allowed the doctor to inject him with the necessary drug that peacefully ended his life. Even in the throes of death he looked majestic. My final words to Leroy: "We love you, Leroy. Save us a place on the other side; we'll be along soon enough."

Halloween was upon us the following day. We had already purchased a good number of full-size candy bars for the expected youngsters that evening, but we really didn't feel like celebrating. We were heartbroken over the loss of our family member. What to do? Was it our imagination, or was Leroy the dog whispering in the background, "Don't disappoint the kiddos on my account."

Whatever the reason, Teena and I prepared for the evening onslaught (that area was full of children). With her creative skills, Teena made us up for the occasion. When she was finished smearing that white and contrasting black paste all over our faces, we looked pretty scary.

We sat on the front porch that evening and handed out the candy bars as the kiddies came by, many of them too young and thus accompanied by a parent. One incident remains memorable. A mother and her small son approached our house, but the boy balked at the edge of our driveway; he would go no further. He was obviously frightened by the two grotesque looking characters he spotted on the porch. Encouraged by his mother to step forward, he remained immovable even as we waved candy bars in his direction. Unable to be coaxed, the mother finally left him at the driveway's edge and came forward to retrieve his candy bar. As they departed for the next house, the little boy slowly walking along the sidewalk, turned as he walked by and very politely said: "Thank you, monsters."

## Divorce American Style

We continued to work for WB over the next few years. During this time period, Teena was having more and more difficulty coping. This was not an easy time for either of us. For many other reasons that I'll not go into, our marriage became less viable over time. By 1992 we decided to separate. Teena headed back to Texas and I stayed in Dixon. Strangely enough, we discovered that we were better at being friends than we were spouses. Although those attributes are not mutually exclusive, they are for some relationships. That's the way it was for us. As a result of our mutual respect and concern for each other, our separation and ultimate divorce was very amicable, and we remain very close friends to this very day. In fact, we make it a point to have a reunion once a year with a few of our other friends. We had our yearly reunion last March of 2015, and will continue to do so.

Chapter 22

# TRANSITIONAL YEARS
## AÑOS DE TRANSICIÓN

1992 – 2016 (and counting)

In September of 1992 I would be 53 years old. Time was getting away from me. The book I had started back in 1979 remained unfinished. I was determined to press ahead with that goal. But I still had to make a living. I was offered a lucrative position as associate pastor—United Methodist—but decided not to re-engage with that side of my life. Instead, I branched out further into sales. I left WB and started selling health insurance and, eventually, selling Trusts for attorneys in the Sacramento area (about 30 miles north of Dixon). I didn't get rich but it paid the mortgage and put food on the table.

### Good News/Bad News
In 1995 I received the good news from Hampton Roads Publishing Company that they were interested in publishing my work. Let me emphasize here that this was no simple accomplishment. Trying to get published by a legitimate publisher proved to be more arduous than my original quest for a recording contract back in the '60s. I kid you not. Unless you've

swum through these turbulent waters, believe me, you have no idea. As I noted earlier, the book was actually published by Hampton Roads in 1996 under the title, *GOING BY THE BOOK: The Past and Present Tragedies of Biblical Authority.* The book never reached the NY Best Seller list—these types of books rarely do—but it was well received, and got good reviews. Although the book is now out of print, used copies can still be purchased on Amazon.

*The bad news* also came in 1996. On a routine dental X-ray, my dentist discovered what appeared to be a cyst on the right side of my mandibular jawbone and suggested I see an Otolaryngologist (ears, nose, and throat doctor). I took his advice. The cyst had to be removed; it was infected and had to be checked for cancer. I was put on antibiotics and scheduled for surgery. Even if the cyst was benign, it was eating up the mandibular bone and, in time, the bone would break and cause all kinds of problems, including disfigurement. Speaking of bones getting eaten, I read an article in the paper a few days ago about a man who had eaten most of the left side of his body. According to the article, the doctor said: "Not to worry, the man is going to be all right!" (If you didn't get the punch line, read it again.) Let's get back to reality.

No one I know looks forward to surgery. I was no exception. It had been over 40 years since my last surgery (nose reconstruction). I was so young back then I really never gave surgery a second thought. Most of us are impervious to the dangers surrounding us in the early years of our naiveté. But this time I was older and wiser. The idea of surgery unnerved me. The doctor sensed my apprehension.

She told me not to worry. I asked her what the fatality rate was for this type of operation. She told me that only one out of every 30,000 died on the operating table, and she herself had never had a fatality. I asked her how many of these operations had she performed. She said: "29,999." :)

Although I was a person of faith, I was a progressive thinker and I had long given up on prayer as a form of petition. It was perfectly clear to me that nothing failed like prayer if one started asking for favors. I know it's almost a reflex action to reach out to God when one faces dangerous issues, health or otherwise. But I had determined not to play that game. The traditional view of God's intervention within the natural order had long since faded from my sense of plausibility. And even if I were wrong, it's hard—at least for me—to conceive of a God whose mercy is dependent on the cries of some desperate soul. I did, however, offer up one prayer: I prayerfully explained to God why I wouldn't be praying for any special favors during this ordeal. Go figure.

I didn't realize it at the time, but this would be the first of three operations trying to rectify the mandibular cyst. Following my first surgery at the Sacramento Medical Center, the right side of my face was swollen to the max; it made Quasimodo, the hunchback of Notre Dame, look handsome. It took several weeks to reach normality again. Having said all that, the success of my first surgery was only partial. They were not able to excise the cyst because it was embedded in the bone. Future remedies would be needed. At least for the present I was in stopgap mode.

A more serious problem arose in 1996. My mother had remarried in 1965 to Thomas Gibson. They lived in Thousand Oaks (about 30 miles north of Los Angeles off of Highway 101). He was about ten years her senior and had taken ill. My mom needed help. I decided to take a few months off from my sales work to see if I could help. I left Sacramento and headed down to Thousand Oaks. Without going into too much detail, I will summarize the remaining six months of that year. My stepdad died. My mother sold her house and bought another house in Mesa, Arizona (Mesa is adjacent to Phoenix). She purchased the home across the street from my sister and her husband (Virginia and Don Robbins). My mom's home rested on one side of the Red Mountain Golf Course that ran right up to her back yard. It was a beautiful setting. How far removed she was now from that little shack of a house in El Paso, Texas. Her Mexican roots had been planted in American soil as far back as 1916 and every year since, there had been nothing but a continuing evolution of the American dream for all of us.

My 1996 September birthday had notched me up to 57. When we arrived in Mesa, it was the middle of October so we were lucky to have missed the summer heat. My intention was to get back to California after getting my mom settled. As it turned out, I came to realize that my mother should not be living alone, even though my sister was directly across the street. My mom was a diabetic and just seemed too vulnerable at the age of 81 to be living alone. I decided to remain with her. She was overjoyed. My mom and I always got along famously and it was one of the best decisions I ever made. Simply stated, I was devoted to my mom. It was an honor and a privilege to share life with her and to watch over her.

During the following year, 1997, my previous bout with the mandibular bone resurfaced. It was infected once again. A second surgical round was imminent. Fortunately, the Mayo Clinic was in nearby Scottsdale (also adjacent to Phoenix). Unfortunately, my surgery at the Mayo Clinic/Hospital was no more successful than the first one in Sacramento because the infection came back a few weeks later. I was back on antibiotics.

It seemed that the only remedy was to excise the bone. But that radical solution would lead to facial deformity. God knows, on that score, I was already alongside the 8-ball; I didn't want to get behind it. There had to be another way. There was.

The answer to my complication arrived in the person of Mark L. Urken, MD, who was Professor and Chairman of the Department of Otolaryngology at Mt. Sinai Medical Center, in NY City. Dr. Urken had pioneered a method for replacing the excised portion of a jawbone by excising and reshaping the fibula (the thinner of two bones between the knee and the ankle) to replace the excised jawbone. Microvascular surgery was also part of this reconstructive technique. After several long distance conversations with Dr. Urken, I headed to NY City in 1997, hoping to resolve this menacing irritant.

Honestly, this operation and its aftermath was a hellacious ordeal. It all began with X-rays, CT scans, blood tests, intravenous (IV) therapy, catheters, and that's the good news. This sarcasm has nothing to do with Dr. Urken; it's just the nature of the beast. The surgery itself kept me on the operating table for almost six hours. Remember, they had to excise the jawbone and the fibula, reshape the fibula, and reconnect it to the remaining jawbone. Taking out the fibula required an incision from my knee all the way down to the ankle. I couldn't even stand on that leg for a couple of days. Of course they had to cut through the inside of my mouth to reach the bone underneath my teeth. Reaching that bone was no easy task. They approached it from both sides; that is, they also had to cut the outside of my neck from my ear down to my Adam's apple as well as the inside of my mouth. This also allowed for the microvascular surgery to connect the blood vessels that would supply the proper blood nutrients to the reconstructed bone. When they cut through the inside of my mouth, they unavoidably damaged a vein that had to be replaced by removing a vein from my right leg to replace the one that had been cut. My body was playing a scripted game of Whack-A-Mole!

I woke up in ICU with my mouth wired shut. I couldn't open my jaw. This was necessary to keep my upper and lower jaws from becoming misaligned. My mouth was locked up tight for seven days (a preacher's nightmare). You can still talk with your mouth wired shut, but it's all in murmurs and guttural sounds. Everything you eat has to be taken in through a straw, nothing but liquids. The one fear you have is what might happen if you become nauseated. You could choke to death on your own vomit. I guess that explained the wire cutters next to my bed.

I spent 7 days in the hospital and the next 25 days in a halfway hotel near the hospital. They wanted me close by to monitor the healing process. I couldn't shave because of the incision along the side of my neck. It wasn't long before I started looking like a mountain man. I couldn't see the incision because of the beard, but I could tell it was seeping blood. A few weeks later when Dr. Urken saw me, he was a taken aback. He told me I had to shave or risk an infection at the site. Very easy for him to say, but of course, I had no choice. I gingerly slid the razor across the incision as best I could and eventually made it so.

Most of my food intake was still liquefied. On entering the hospital I weighed 180 lbs.; I now weighed about 160 lbs. I wasn't very spry because my leg wasn't up to par, to say the least. I felt rather weak most of the time, and was totally stranded without transportation, not that I could drive anyway. The television became my sole companion. It was a lonely time. On top of all this, I developed a UTI (urinary tract infection), generally the result of the catheter that is inserted into your penis during a hospital stay. I was back on antibiotics. I was also worried about my mother who was home alone in Mesa worrying about me (that's what mothers do).

Finally, after 33 days of this misery, it was time to go home. Because of my leg and my weakened condition, I was in no shape to travel alone. Teena, my ex, was kind enough to assist me (we continue to help each other through the years). She met me at the NY airport and got me back to Arizona all in one piece. Well, not quite: part of my original jawbone was gone, and my fibula was nowhere to be found, except for that small segment that was now part of my jawbone.

## Back to College and a Major Detour

Looking after my mother was time consuming but not a full-time job. She was not an invalid although she needed help with meds, transportation, doctor consultations, paying bills, and various other matters. Nevertheless, I had some time to spare. Although I was teaching a seminar every Sunday morning at the Velda Rose UMC, I needed something more. I had previously obtained from the State of California, a community college teaching credential for Philosophy and Religion. I was hoping that it would transfer across state lines. It didn't. Not to be deterred, however, I took the necessary steps— including some mandated courses—to acquire that Arizona credential. All I needed now was a part-time teaching position at one of the local colleges.

In early August of the year 1999, about a month short of my 60th birthday, I was offered a position at the Glendale Community College in Glendale, AZ (about 45miles from our house in Mesa), teaching World Religions for the fall semester. Although I was very familiar with Christianity, and had a smattering of World Religions in seminary, I was nonetheless inadequately prepared. Nothing short of a self-oriented crash course in the religions of Hinduism, Buddhism, and the like, would suffice. By the time I entered my first teaching assignment in late August of that year, I was sufficiently prepared to handle the course material, albeit still trying to negotiate the learning curve.

Although I had been teaching all my life through the church's venue, this educational platform was different, but equally enjoyable. Importantly, the students enjoyed me. I had found another career to explore. What I didn't realize in those opening weeks of my new career was that Murphy's Law was about to pounce on me like a tick on a hound dog.

During my childhood years, doctors had discovered a heart murmur caused by what they called a bicuspid aortic valve disease (BAVD). According to the Cleveland Clinic web page: "Normally, the aortic valve has three small flaps or leaflets that open widely and close securely to regulate blood flow . . . .In bicuspid aortic valve disease (BAVD), the valve has only two leaflets. With this deformity, the valve doesn't function perfectly, but it may function adequately for years without causing symptoms or obvious signs of a problem.... About 2% of the population has BAVD, and it is twice as common in males as in females."

I had been jogging since the age of 28. Recently, however, I was feeling some discomfort in the upper chest area while running. I went to my cardiologist at the Mayo Clinic. He ran some tests and, sure enough, my aortic valve had calcified to the point of needing replacement; in other words, open heart surgery. Yikes! That was my first reaction.

My second reaction was one of dismay. I had only been teaching for a couple of weeks at the college, and now it looked like I would have to bail out on my students and the college. I wasn't even sure the college would give me another shot after this quick exit, or if a teaching position would even be available after my recovery from surgery. But I had no choice. I reluctantly gave up my newly acquired teaching position and started looking for the best doctor I could find.

One of the best lessons I learned from my recording experience in Hollywood was how important it was to always surround oneself with the best people; that is, the foremost musicians, arrangers, studio engineers, producers, and so forth. Always surround yourself with the most gifted talent you can find. So, I went looking for the best medical facility and cardiologist in the country. That turned out to be the Cleveland Clinic (rated the #1-ranked Heart & Vascular Institute in the United States by *US News & World Report* every year since 1995), and cardiovascular surgeon and Chair of the Cardiology Department, Delos M. Cosgrove (presently the CEO of the Cleveland Clinic). My aortic valve replacement was scheduled for December 22, 1999. I couldn't think of a better Christmas present (assuming I survived, of course). Do I have to tell you I did? :)

Although this surgery was much more serious than any previous operation I had, it was a piece of cake relative to what I had expected. Aside from my age and otherwise good health, Dr. Cosgrove performed what they call a "keyhole" surgery. A small incision in the chest precludes the necessity for a more invasive procedure that requires an incision down the center of your sternum (breastbone). I was headed back home from the hospital in a matter of five days. Nevertheless, I do not want to minimize the intricate aortic valve replacement that I received. The medical notes alone scared me half to death when I read them later. Furthermore, three months of rehabilitation still lay ahead.

## Back To College

Eventually, life came back to normal. In the middle of 2000, I reapplied for the teaching position that I was forced to abandon the previous year. Much to my surprise, they gave me another chance. I started teaching three World Religions classes in the fall semester of 2000 at the Glendale Community College in Glendale, Arizona. Getting my feet wet that first semester was a challenge. I felt sorry for my students because I had not yet mastered the material. It takes a couple of semesters before you really start feeling comfortable. But I had personality—lots of humor—and that got me through in good stead, including the spring semester of 2001.

I started my second fall semester at the college in August of 2001. My classes for that fall semester were scheduled for Mondays and Wednesdays. So I was home that Tuesday morning of

9/11/2001 having breakfast with my mom. The morning meal was interrupted when I got a call from my sister telling me to turn on the TV. The tenor of her voice gave notice that this was not the time for chitchat. I acknowledged her call, hung up, and quickly turned on the set. As I stared unbelievingly at the television, I felt relieved that I didn't have classes that day. I was free to absorb this catastrophic event that consumed me in all respects. According to Wikipedia, here is how the events of that day unfolded:

> "The *September 11 attacks* . . . were a series of four coordinated terrorist attacks by the Islamic terrorist group al-Qaeda on the United States in New York City, New York, and Arlington County, Virginia, on the morning of Tuesday, September 11, 2001. Four passenger airliners which all departed from the U.S. East Coast to California were hijacked by 19 al-Qaeda terrorists to be flown into buildings in suicide attacks. Two of the planes, American Airlines Flight 11 and United Airlines Flight 175, were crashed into the North and South towers, respectively, of the World Trade Center complex in New York City.
>
> Within two hours, both 110-story towers collapsed with debris and the resulting fires causing partial or complete collapse of all other buildings in the WTC complex, including the 47-story 7 World Trade Center tower, as well as significant damage to ten other large surrounding structures. A third plane, American Airlines Flight 77, was crashed into the Pentagon (the headquarters of the United States Department of Defense) in Arlington County,

leading to a partial collapse in its western side. The fourth plane, United Airlines Flight 93, was targeted at Washington D.C., but crashed into a field near Shanksville, Pennsylvania, after its passengers tried to overcome the hijackers. In total, 2,996 people died in the attacks including the 245 civilians, a law enforcement officer, and the 19 terrorists aboard the four planes. It was the deadliest incident for firefighters and law enforcement officers [first responders] in the history of the United States, with 343 and 72 killed respectively." [Brackets mine]

As we all know, 9/11 was the catalyst that led us into the wars of Afghanistan and Iraq. The fallout from 9/11, and the presidential decisions that followed, continue to be problematic to this very day. I need say no more.

Seven years later in the fall of 2008, at the age of 69, I was still teaching at the college and still taking care of my mom who was now 93 years old. When the fall semester came to an end in early December of that year, I was looking forward to a six-week break before the spring semester of 2009. Little did I know—as is often the case for us all—how personally turbulent December of 2008, and the year of 2009, would be for our family.

On December 22, 2008, I came down with a dangerous blood infection called *Staph aureus.* The source was unknown. When something like this hits you—you know you're sick. I drove myself to the ER exhibiting symptoms of a high fever, and flu like symptoms that were manifestly worse. Those symptoms came on fast and furious. The ER staff didn't seem too concerned about my obvious complaints until the blood results came back telling them I was in serious trouble. I was so sick I took a turn for the nurse (dumb joke). Staph could also lead to endocarditis (the infection of my aortic valve replacement). That's when I got the royal treatment.

Generally speaking, I really like hospitals. I think this is a byproduct of being in the ministry for so many years; people are taking care of you rather than you taking care of them. However, this hospital stay was not as pleasant because the blood infection I had, necessitated numerous blood draws from a phlebotomist (these are medical technicians trained to draw blood for testing, transfusions, or research). I hate needles, probably a leftover fear from my childhood trauma at the Children's Hospital back in the 1940s.

Since this staph was blood oriented, the phlebotomists would come in every few hours and poke me in order to monitor my status. It wasn't long before my arms were all black and blue. The needle tracks on my arms would give an outsider the impression that I was a drug addict. (I wonder how porcupines make love.) I eventually started calling the phlebotomists, blood-sucking vampires; all in good fun, of course. I remained in the hospital until December 30th (a period of 8 days). This was a longer stay than my heart surgery. Anyway, I managed to escape the hospital one day ahead of New Year's Eve.

## The Dreadful Year Of 2009

The opening day of 2009 was innocent enough. It felt good to be home, away from Phlebotomy-land. Nevertheless, I would have to report back to the hospital every morning for 30 days to receive an infusion of antibiotics; this was done through a PIC line that had been inserted into my right arm for the extended antibiotic therapy. It was painless and did not require additional puncture wounds. Therefore, I was basically free to engage the New Year with little concern. I did, however, notify the college that I would not be available for the spring semester.

On January 1, I happily faced my yearly ritual of watching our national football extravaganza. This was a holiday addiction that was irresistible. As far back as our first television set when I was thirteen, January 1st was the day of the Rose Bowl, and I don't remember ever having missed one of those games. In this particular Rose Bowl, the Pacific-10 Conference Champion University of Southern California (the USC Trojans)— my favorite college team—defeated the Big Ten Conference co-champion, the Pennsylvania State University Nittany Lions, 38-24. Everything was coming up Roses (that was definitely a pun). Having been in the hospital the week before the big USC win at the Rose Bowl, brought back to mind the old axiom: "Behind every cloud there's a silver lining." However, you don't get to live this long without realizing that behind every silver lining there's another cloud.

The first ominous sign indicating that this New Year might go awry came on January 17. I ended up back in the hospital for a heart condition known as *atrial fibrillation* (a rapid, irregular, heart rate). It was probably brought on by the stress endured from the previous run-in with *Staph aureus,* and the army of blood-sucking vampires that had me up in arms. (Was that a pun?) I won't labor the point here. Suffice it to say I was in the hospital another couple of days. But the *atrial fibrillation* persisted until January 30.

Most of February provided a brief respite. But before the month ended, whatever roses were left in the picturesque year I had envisioned, would soon fade away. My mother, at the age of 93, took ill. She came down with a UTI (urinary tract infection). This UTI was only one of many she had experienced in the past, so we didn't become overly concerned. However, within a few short days, even with the help of antibiotics, the infection proved to be more serious, and it became obvious she required a hospital stay. Almost one week later we brought my mom home from the medical center and placed her on hospice. About 4 days later she died. If there is any such thing as a good death, this was it. She died on March 5, at 9:50 PM during a peaceful sleep. I was fortunate to be by her bedside, holding her hand, as she slipped away. I will always be grateful for what seemed to be an effortless exit on her part, and for the wonderful privilege of having shared the final years and final moments of her life.

I am not unusual in thinking I had the best mother that ever lived, the best mother that anyone could ever possibly have. Over the span of my life many people have died that I've been close to. But the loss of my mother has been the hardest one to bear.

Ruth Arellano-Bringas-Gibson was interred at the world-famous *Forest Lawn Memorial Park* in Glendale, California, alongside her late husband Thomas, her dear sister Mary Arellano, and her mother, Guadalupe G. Arellano. Her father, Francisco Arellano is also buried within a stone's throw of those I have just mentioned. My sister Virginia and I, and a few other family members and friends, attended the service.

According to Wikipedia: "There are more major Hollywood stars buried at *Forest Lawn Memorial Park* than at any other spot in the world. It's a place that must be seen to be believed. The park's sheer size is overwhelming, a seemingly endless vista of rolling green hills; over 300 acres dotted with white sculptures and quaint English chapels . . . Forest Lawn isn't your ordinary, run-of-the-mill cemetery. Far more than just a memorial park, it's also an architectural showcase, a Hollywood tourist site, and a religious retreat. Even Pope John Paul II stopped here, during his visit to Los Angeles . . . Hollywood stars buried here include some of the biggest names in the history of Hollywood: Clark Gable, Carole Lombard, Jimmy Stewart, Jean Harlow, Humphrey Bogart, Mary Pickford, Errol Flynn, Spencer Tracy, . . . George Burns . . . Disney . . . Red Skelton . . . Robert Young . . . Lon Chaney . . . Alan Ladd . . . Dick Powell . . . Robert Taylor . . . ."

I mention the above Sidebar because I find it interesting that my mother, my grandmother, my grandfather and aunt, all of whom were born in Mexico and crossed the border in 1916, are now buried near some of the most famous Hollywood celebrities in one of the most famous world cemeteries. This could only happen in a place like America.

### Dreadful 2009 Continued

My mother had a parakeet named Chulita (Cutie). Chulita was a free bird. She could fly around the house because her wings weren't clipped and she was not confined to a cage. The abundance of little poops kept me on the run. During daylight hours she would often perch on our shoulders as we walked about. Not unlike most animals, Chulita felt a sense of loss when my mother died. Fortunately, I had also bonded with her and so we both carried on in good spirits. She continued to fly around the house unabated.

In August of 2009 I was into my fall semester at the college. On September 19th I hit my 70th birthday. Shortly thereafter, I ran into some stormy weather; another dark cloud was fast approaching. After taking my yearly sonogram, the cardiologist informed me that my aortic heart valve needed to be replaced once again. I was facing another open-heart surgery. I wanted to finish the fall semester because I didn't want to disappoint my students. My cardiologist gave me the okay, so I postponed the surgery until the third week of December. Sound familiar?

The fall semester of 2009 ended around the middle of December. One week earlier, Chulita had become seriously ill. Within hours of becoming symptomatic, I took her to the Arizona Exotic Animal Hospital and discovered that she had cancer in the reproductive tract. The vet told me she had a 50-50 chance with surgery. Unfortunately, she died on the operating table. It was December 7th (an easy day to remember). I brought her home and buried her in the backyard. It was terribly hard to say goodbye.

A few more weeks and I, too, would be facing surgery back at the Cleveland Clinic. This time around I would be facing a full-blown invasive procedure that required the sternum (breastbone) to be split wide open. What if I didn't survive either? That would be incredibly ironic if my mother, Chulita, and I all died during the same year.

It was back to the Cleveland Clinic. For this procedure I carefully selected Dr. Sabik as my surgeon, the new Chairperson of the Cardiology Department (the best, in my opinion). I survived my second open-heart surgery with flying colors. I did, however, end up with one humongous keloid scar down the middle of my chest. Most importantly, I made it home again to see the Rose Bowl game on January 1, 2010. My unbroken ritual remained intact. USC wasn't in it that year so I can't remember the score, or who was playing. I just Googled it: Ohio beat Oregon 26 – 17.

We're getting close to the end of this book, and probably my own life. As I tell my students: "We have to make way for you young whippersnappers!" But before I end this tome, I need to discuss three points: (1) my collegiate teaching experience, (2) family contributions to American society and vice versa and, (3) personal comments.

## 1. Collegiate experience

As already stated, I have been teaching at the college level for the past 15 years (2000 - ?). Presently I teach Religious Studies—World Religions and Introduction to the New Testament—at Glendale Community College in Glendale (adjacent to Phoenix) in Arizona. Under their auspices, I also taught these courses at Arizona State University (ASU) for several years. It has been a great joy and honor to serve in this capacity, and I hope to continue until ill health or some unforeseen event prevents it.

People often ask me about the youth I encounter. Too often our young people get a bum rap in our social media. I can assure you that these youth, aside from all their electronic gadgets and computer savvy, are really no different than those of my own era (and that goes way back). Are they all "good kids?" Of course not, but that's always been the case. Sure, they face different challenges in this "new" world and their music is a bit off target from the old rock & roll I relished, and their sexual values have loosened up. But those are the same adult criticisms I faced as a teenager. The concept of "morality" has always been a moving target.

Truth be known, young people have always been criticized throughout history. Consider the following well-known quote attributed to Socrates from his student Plato: "The children now love luxury; they have bad manners; contempt for authority; they show disrespect for elders and love chatter in place of exercise." (Actually, we really don't know where this quote, in its present form, originated. It's been attributed to Socrates, Plato, Cicero, Puff the Magic Dragon, and Winnie the Pooh.) The point is, however, that every generation tends to downgrade the upcoming generation. All I can say is that my experience, for the most part, does not bear out those criticisms.

Here is a humorous note for you. At the beginning of my World Religions class I ask my students to write a short statement—anonymously—that expresses where they stand in terms of their religious affiliation (or lack thereof). Here are a few of the verbatim responses I got back with lots of misspellings:

a) Raised as Cathalic/Jehovah Witness don't agree so I'm an unknown Protestant.

b) I do not belong to a denomination. I do not believe in the existence of Gods due to the lack of scientific evidence. I do believe in a high power.

c) Agnostically aetheistic to the point of being Panentheistic. . . . (confused).

d) I don't know. I thought I was Christian but I didn't even know what that was.

e) I'm non-religion. But I'm interested in knowing what the religion Is.

f) Agnostic Christian except when I'm scared or hurt. . . then theist or traditional belief of Christianity.

g) Catholic – practicing if my grandmother asks.

h) I am an atheist who believes in God.

I know that some of the above responses sound convoluted. But don't fool yourself, some of these youngsters are quite sharp.

## 2. Family contributions to American society and vice versa

So here we are 100 years after my grandparents on my mother's side (the Arellano clan) crossed over the border with five children in 1916. On the Bringas side, it was my father's father that crossed the border ca. 1903. Although this memoir has focused primarily on my life, which didn't begin until 1939, I'll make note of what kind of a difference those crossings have made to our family, along with the contributions we have made in return. I begin with the benefits derived.

There's an old song title that captures the significance of those crossings, "What a Difference a Day Makes." I can't even begin to imagine what life would be like without those immigration milestones. Indeed, I wouldn't even exist, and neither would my sisters, cousins, nephews and nieces, and all of their offspring. Actually, my father never would have come into being if his father (my grandfather) hadn't crossed the border ca. 1903; he never would have met Maria, my dad's mother (my other grandmother). If you got dizzy on that last one, you're not alone.

Furthermore, as we all should know, America is the land of opportunity and much more. So, from my perspective, the positive advantages of migrating to the USA are seemingly incalculable. This insight is driven not only by the fortuitous encounters mentioned above and the resulting progeny of those encounters, but also by the opportunities afforded within the borders of the real magical kingdom we call the USA.

Accordingly, over the past 100 years, our family has expanded, has adapted, has adopted, has integrated, and has been assimilated. My mother, aunts and uncles, all became U.S. citizens. Like any other American family, we have been a part of the journey called the American experience. Although this work highlighted the single journey of my life, other members of our family have made significant contributions. The following is a partial summary of those contributions.

I served as a United Methodist minister for almost 20 years and am presently into my 16th year as a college professor. My two sisters, Martha Lawrence and Virginia Robbins, served as registered nurses (RNs) for numerous years; my cousin, Frankie Arellano, served as an educational counselor at USC; my cousin, David Arellano, served 32 years as an elementary and junior high teacher in Los Angeles; my uncle, Gene Arellano, served on a destroyer in the Pacific during WWII, followed by a 30-year career at General Mills; my 19-year-old cousin Xavier Arvizu served in the U.S. Army and was killed in Vietnam; my second cousin, Karen (Moss) Willner, served as a college instructor; my nephew, David Lawrence, serves as the General Manager of the "Swiss Federal Institute of Technology" (like MIT except in Switzerland); my nephew, Paul Lawrence, serves as a field operator for Pfizer Pharmaceuticals; my nephew, Tim Robbins, served in the United States Air force

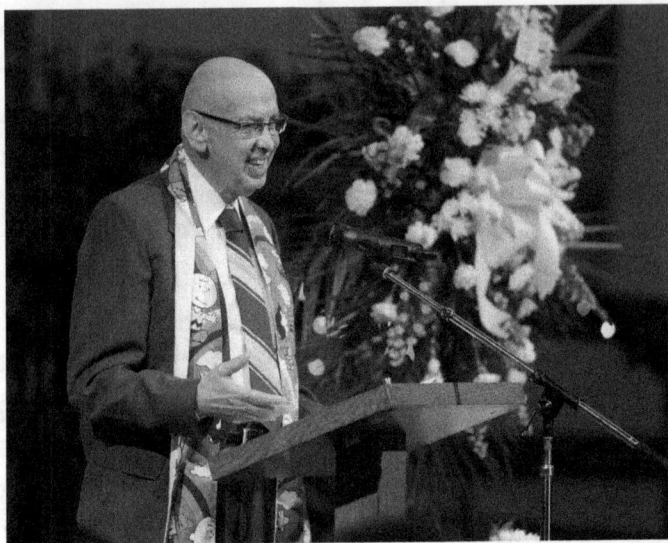

*I'm speaking at a friend's memorial service (2013). (Photo by Sue Larson)*

and is now the manager for an Apple online customer support company; my niece, Doreen Zimmerman, serves as a middle school science teacher; my niece, Sharon Kouba, has been a U.S. Postal letter carrier for the past 22 years; my niece, Judy Reeves, is a writer and entrepreneur; and so forth.

Again, this is a very short list of our family's résumé. Many other cousins, nieces, and nephews could be mentioned. Take, for example, my 23-year-old great niece Cassidy P. Bringas, who is presently studying to be a pediatrician.

This limited presentation profoundly illustrates what can happen to immigrants, and their progeny thereafter, who make it into the crosshairs of the American culture; provided, of course, that the host country is willing to embrace them.

My story, and that of my family, is not an isolated anecdote by any stretch of the imagination. Almost always, immigrants become the renewing bloodline for the continued health and prosperity of their host country, provided they are allowed the same opportunities to participate, and provided they are not suppressed to the point of becoming inefficient, or worse, kicked out of the country. When I think back to that 1930s Mexican deportation fiasco (see pp.17–18), I can only be thankful that our family was not caught up in that bigoted round up. (Where in the heck was the ACLU during those civil rights violations?) I'm not sure how my grandparents, my mother and her siblings escaped that illegal American dragnet of deportation in Los Angeles (it was massive).[92] None of the above-mentioned family members, including myself, would exist today had they been deported. That would also be true if the Bringas family members in San Diego had been ousted.

On the other hand, newcomers must be willing to adopt or embrace new patterns of thought and behavior, even at the partial expense of their previously held traditions. The failure to do so will have grave implications for us all.

IN SUMMARY – We have now come full circle. I will reiterate my reasons for writing this chronicle. First, to help all Americans view and understand immigrants as an essential part of a healthy nation, and to thereby recognize the contributions made by immigrants as advantageous to the American way of life. Historically, it is impossible to deny this reality.

My second point was in trying to help immigrants understand that without integration and assimilation, they will fail to become part of the American mainstream. Failing to do so, they will forfeit the advantages and benefits thereof. The good news is that the second and third generations are almost certainly integrated and assimilated. Case in point: The children of my nieces and nephews are virtually oblivious to their Mexican

---

[92]See Wikipedia: Mexican Deportations.

roots. That may be a sad consequence, but it's par for the course. Those last three sentences provide the perfect segue.

My third purpose for writing was to provide the present and future generations of my family with a short historical ancestral background. Obviously, much of our family history is missing here. I leave it to others if they are so inclined. I have, however, provided as much information as I could about our family background.

### 3. Personal comments

I'm closing this composition with some personal observations, conclusions, and sundry remarks. At the present time we are in the midst of a huge national immigration debate. Perhaps the word "debate" is inappropriate since most opposing arguments are delivered through an acidic atmosphere that resembles more of a shouting match than a debate. I won't labor the point; I covered these problems in the introduction. One can only hope that in the near future—I'd even settle for the far future—that this divisional conflict is resolved in the most amicable way.

To be clear here, no rational person is advocating for open borders; we can't absorb everyone. Nor can we allow immigrants to enter our country without being vetted. We need a reality-based approach for solving the thorny issues surrounding immigration, including the path to citizenship. It will take considerable effort on the part of well-intentioned, well-informed, and well-educated compassionate leaders to resolve this issue fairly. But an equitable solution will be impossible if ignorance and ethnic bias rule the day.

As for me, I will continue to teach at the college until I can no longer stand and deliver. And if my life should come to a screeching halt tomorrow, I would have no complaints. Wait, that's not exactly true. I really don't want this to end; it's been a great ride thus far. I suspect a final exit might be appreciated if one were in great physical pain, depressed by hopeless circumstances, or very dissatisfied with life in general. That's not my situation but one never knows. At some point in time, we all have our "veil of tears." That said, I can certainly be thankful for all the privileged years I have enjoyed compared to those poor souls on this violent planet that have not been as fortunate. Sadly, that has been the case for most people during humankind's history.

Aside from my inevitable death, I don't know what the future holds. I'm not sure how close I am to becoming just another casualty at the hands of the Grim Reaper, but at the age of 76, I can certainly hear the approach of his footsteps. Even so, I readily remind myself that I have been most fortunate throughout these many years. Of course, I am eternally grateful that 100 plus years ago my ancestors had the vision for a better life, and had the tenacity to make that better life possible by crossing the Mexican/American border. I still marvel at their courage and foresight.

Conversely, I am grateful to all the Americans that welcomed our family with open arms and helped us not only aspire to the American dream, but also helped us to achieve that American dream. In the words of President Obama: "Whether our forebears were strangers who crossed the Atlantic, or the Pacific, or the Rio Grande, we are here only because this country welcomed them in."[93] In other words, this country provided the educational means, and various opportunities

---

[93]Michael D. Shear, *New York Times*, November 20, 2014

afforded to all others who came together underneath the Stars and Stripes. As a result of that generous opportunity, I feel that my family has responded in kind, and has made a positive contribution to the fabric of American culture on many levels, including the sacrifice of blood on foreign battlefields.

Today, we Americans may have Italian, Irish, Vietnamese, Chinese, Japanese, German, English, French, or Mexican handles (to name a few). But in time, those handles are jettisoned like the spent fuel tanks of a spacecraft reaching orbit. When that happens, we are simply Americans, one and all, period! Nevertheless, we must always remember that we have been nurtured in American soil and, hopefully, we have enriched that American soil in return. Thank God! Thank America! Thank you! Thank us!

Before I say good-bye, I will leave you with my personal code of behavior. I can't pretend to live by this code 100% of the time, and sometimes I don't even come close. But this is what I aspire to:

Respect all life,
Live love,
Pursue knowledge,
Have fun along the way.

As my mother always said: "Que Dios te bendiga." ("May God bless you.")

—Ernie :)

*My mom at age 51 (1961)*

# EPILOGUE
## EPÍLOGO

### Integration and Assimilation

I have been Americanized (fully integrated and assimilated into the American culture). Before we take another step, we need to define what it means to be *integrated* and *assimilated.*

*Integration* is the intermixing of people or groups previously segregated for whatever reason. The lack of integration is the most difficult and limiting obstacle that new immigrants face.

*Assimilation* simply means to "take in," to absorb, and be absorbed; to understand fully, mainstream information, ideas, concepts, and the societal nuances of one's own culture (be it native or adopted). Realtors will tell you that the most important factor in real estate is: Location, Location, Location! In immigration, the most important factors are: integration and assimilation.

The Point is*: Without integration, assimilation is hard to achieve, if not impossible. You cannot assimilate if you do not integrate. Without this tandem correlation, trouble ensues.* That is why today, for example, the Muslims in France are so alienated from the general French population. Muslims have not been assimilated because they have largely remained in Muslin communities as opposed to integrating into the larger culture.[94]

---

[94]On January 7, 2015, two Islamist gunmen entered the Paris headquarters of the satirical magazine, *Charlie Hebdo,* and massacred 12 of the staff members. Also, the terrorists attacks in Paris on November 13, 2015, will exacerbate the current divide between the Muslim and French communities; that is, anti-Muslim sentiment will continue to simmer until Muslims are integrated and assimilated into the mainstream.

## The Seeds of Bigotry

But even when there is integration and assimilation, discrimination seems to rear its ugly head. But why is this so?

I will preface the answer to that question with some specific comments about *xenophobia* (intense or irrational dislike or fear of people from other countries, especially when physical characteristics differ); *ethnocentricity* (judging other cultures relative to the values and standards of one's own culture); and what I call *in-house discrimination.* In-house discrimination will manifest itself on two levels.

*First,* we have the bias directed against people with opposing values or opinions, even though they come from the same cultural frame of reference. A prime example of this intolerance would be the hostile attitudes directed against gays in America, which has nothing to do with outsiders.

*Secondly,* in-house discrimination is exemplified by the bigotry directed against Mexican Americans, African Americans, Muslim or Jewish Americans even though they are American-born citizens. Remember those deportations of U.S. Mexican Americans in the 1930s? This is in-house discrimination.

I'm not a sociologist, but I would venture a fair guess that xenophobia, ethnocentricity, and in-house discrimination are common knee-jerk reactions for the majority of people in all cultures. That is, *we prefer our own kind.* We need not beat ourselves up for what seems to be a "natural" inclination. Most anyone outside of one's cultural, physical, religious, or social norm tends to be suspect.

But all too often this dislike or suspicion of strangers—or those who are different—is exacerbated by misinformation and/or disinformation. In other words, we become prejudiced through social conditioning. Consider, for example, how minority groups have been stereotyped through the media, cartoons, films, and other creative expressions. Minorities are often portrayed in exaggerated, ridiculous ways so as to create a comic or grotesque effect. During WW II, the Japanese were portrayed with squinty eyes and buckteeth. Up until the '60s, blacks were portrayed—especially in film—as stupid, subservient, lazy, and cowardly (shaking involuntarily with their mouths and eyes wide open). With few exceptions, western films have typically portrayed Mexicans as these ugly, double-dealing, semi-toothless, dirty, half-witted banditos or as plump, jolly interlopers with nothing better to do than take a siesta. Jews have been stereotyped with long noses, and have been called conspirators, greedy wealth-seeking misers, murderers of the prophets, and Christ killers. Muslim Arabs have been stereotyped as belly dancers, terrorists, religious fanatics, and anti-American. Is it any wonder that Americans are brainwashed into unfavorable thoughts about these people even though they may suspect that these accounts and images are obviously exaggerated? Come on, we've all been a little bit brainwashed by these portrayals.

On the other hand, some of us just might have an irrational fear or uncomfortable feeling in the presence of those who are different, even though we may not have any malice or prejudicial leanings toward them. Whatever the case, xenophobia, ethnocentricity, and in-house discrimination, combined with societal indoctrination, must be understood and controlled personally and collectively. Failure to do so can lead to injustice. Take, for example, the practice of racial and ethnic profiling of minority groups in our country; that is, singling out African Americans (racial) and Hispanics (ethnic) in punitive ways. It is no secret that our judicial system imposes stricter penalties on persons outside of mainstream America. Information regarding the racial or ethnic disparity in sentencing is overwhelming.

## Other Examples of Ethnic Discrimination

Here's yet another instance of ethnic discrimination. In July of 2013, the conservative Republican Congressman from northwest Iowa, Steve King, speaking with the conservative outlet *Newsmax*, acknowledged that some Hispanics had done well. But then he said: "For every one who's a valedictorian there's another hundred out there that, uh, they weigh one hundred and thirty pounds and they've got calves the size of cantaloupes because they're hauling seventy-five pounds of marijuana across the desert." In all fairness to Rep. King, he claims to have been misunderstood and that his "characterization was exclusively to drug smugglers." Even so, his speculation that Mexicans are using their children (130 lbs. – 75 lbs. of marijuana = a child's weight of 55 lbs.) to smuggle drugs across the border reflects an attitude of animus against the Mexican people.

On July 1, 2014, the immigration issue exploded in Murrieta, California, when three buses carrying undocumented Central American immigrants, mostly children, were surrounded and stopped by 200 to 300 angry protesters. It was an ugly demonstration that put Murrieta on the map for all the wrong reasons. It was a disheartening scene, and certainly more so for the little ones and their parents who were seeking shelter from the terror and turbulence created by the drug lords in their homeland (similar to my grandparents who fled the Mexican Revolution). In any case, these immigrants were not allowed to reach a Border Patrol station in the Riverside

County city. The buses were detoured to a Border Patrol facility in San Diego County.

Donald Trump's scathing criticisms, as he started to run for the presidency in 2015, is another perfect example of misguided exaggeration, xenophobia, and ignorance. He declared that Mexico was sending people across the border that were bringing drugs, crime, and were rapists. No doubt that there is some truth in what he proposes. However, like so many others, he has merely cherry-picked his sources. The words of Mark Twain ring true: "A half-truth is the most cowardly of lies." In my opinion, a half-truth is also the most insidious of lies.

## Immigrant Exceptionalism

But discrimination has many faces. In other words, *the intensity of discrimination is sometimes proportional to the physical, ethnic, or racial differences between the parties.* For example, one can hardly avoid noticing the treatment of Japanese Americans living in California during WW II. Physically, they certainly didn't look like the majority of Americans. As I noted previously, caricatured representations of the Japanese certainly didn't help (although these distorted portrayals were understandable in the face of Pearl Harbor). Nevertheless, as a consequence, these poor souls were illegally rounded up like enemies of the State and shipped off to internment camps; incarcerated for the duration. Aside from suffering humiliation and injustice, these Americans also suffered the loss of freedom, not to mention the loss of property and financial earnings.

It should be noted that this incident that occurred with the Japanese is not the equivalent to what happened with Mexican Americans in the 1930s, *neither in numbers nor in consequences.* By far, Mexican Americans suffered not only displacement, but for the majority, loss of country and American citizenship.

So why didn't we round up German Americans as we did Japanese Americans? Aside from not attacking us directly—as was the case with the Japanese at Pearl Harbor—weren't we also at war with Germany? Perhaps we didn't entertain the same mental and emotional bias against German Americans because they looked very much like the rest of us. You think? This is not to deny the fact that there wasn't some discrimination aimed against German Americans, especially if they had an obvious accent. But compared to what happened to the Japanese, not so much.

The point is, the further one is outside the norm—be it racial, ethnic, or social—*the more one is apt to be singled out for discrimination.* Conversely, the more one approximates the norm, *the less likely* one will be discriminated against. This reminds me of the old saying: "If you're white, you're all right; if you're brown, you can hang around; if you're black, stand back."

Exceptions to that old saying have occurred. The Irish and Germans were certainly white. But when they migrated in droves to the U.S. during the 1800s, they encountered extreme hostility because most of them were Roman Catholic. The U.S. population was predominantly Protestant. Discrimination was also driven by politics and the fear that the American labor force would be undermined by cheap labor.

Conveniently, however, prejudicial attitudes against minorities are sometimes set aside in the face of exceptional talent or some other attractive human characteristic. For example, geniuses, great athletes, musicians, and good-looking people—be they ever so foreign or different—are usually exempt from any overt, prejudicial hostility (at least on the surface). Success is generally assured in America for anyone who is gifted, regardless of his or her race, ethnicity, or country of origin. Consider, as one example, the movie industry in Hollywood that, in spite of the anti-Semitism of that time, was successfully developed by *Jewish immigrants*. The majority of these men—such as Samuel Goldwyn, David O. Selznick, and Darryl Zanuck—came from poor Jewish backgrounds in Eastern Europe and promoted film making during its infancy. The same holds true for the Russian born Jew, Louis B. Mayer. These men offered moviegoers an irresistible product. Leave them alone, already.

As another example of favoritism based on prized characteristics, consider Jackie Robinson (#42) who broke the baseball color line when the Brooklyn Dodgers started him at first base on April 15, 1947. The Dodgers were the first major-league team to field a black man since the beginning of the Negro Leagues in the 1880s. They ended racial segregation that had relegated black players to the Negro Leagues for six decades. Because of Robinson's exceptional talent, white America eventually came around to making him an exception to the rule—an exception to an otherwise prejudicial society (evident by the racial taunts and slurs he originally endured at the games). This historic move by the Dodgers didn't eradicate racism, but it was a start in the right direction. Although that opening serve was not an ace—to use a tennis metaphor—the positive fallout has been tremendous (especially since the Civil Rights Movement of the 1960s).

That, of course, reminds me of Martin Luther King. Talk about prized characteristics. Here was a charismatic black man with high intelligence and oratory skills second to none. That made him an unstoppable and influential force among whites; ergo, the Civil Rights Movement. But if you still believe that racism in America is not a serious problem, only a casual look at what President Obama endured over his tenure will tell you otherwise (it wasn't just about politics). That's the bad news. The good news in that story, of course, is that he was re-elected for a second term. We're getting better.

In the case of Hispanics, this accepting inclination repeats for those who are gifted. But what if you're not Ricardo Montalban or Eva Longoria (from TV's *Desperate Housewives*)? What about "everyday" Mexican Americans? Why is so much hostility directed against them?

Of course, much of the hullabaloo revolves around the immigration issue and the vast number of Hispanics now living in America. In California, for instance, the Pew Research Center correctly projected that Latinos would become the largest single ethnic group in 2014, making up 39% of California's population and second only to the state of New Mexico.

## Whose Country is this, Anyway?

When mainstream America hears about the upcoming possibility of racial, ethnic and religious parity, they begin to feel like their country is being taken over by foreigners. *Well, it is! It has always been taken over by foreigners. We are*, and always *have been*, a nation of immigrants. President Obama uses the future tense: "We are and always *will be* a nation of immigrants." But through the means of osmosis (the gradual or unconscious process of assimilation), almost all immigrants become Americanized, regardless of their differentiating backgrounds. (By the way, what happened to our poor native Indians cannot happen to our general population. Their numbers and scientific knowledge were inadequate relative to their invading European counterparts. With our present stability, that inverse scenario cannot be repeated.)

With the exception of the indigenous peoples of this geographical plane we now call America, we can all trace our roots back to that honorable distinction—immigrant! America's soil has been—and continues to be—seeded by outsiders; that is, the Japanese, Chinese, Irish, Italians, French, British, Spaniards, Arabs, Jews, Germans, Scandinavians, Africans, Russians, Romanians, Poles, Vietnamese, and many others streaming here from almost every corner of the planet (not to mention Latin American countries). Sometimes they come in small numbers and sometimes they come in droves. It's when they come in droves, as we have seen, that some Americans become paranoid. That's when things get ugly. But whether people coming from other cultures are small or numerous in numbers, it matters not—bias rears its ugly head, especially if the immigrant doesn't fit the Anglo norm. Or, there is a perceived threat between border-states.

It should be noted, however, that Mexicans were indigenous to these lands long before there was a border to cross, and even before the Thirteen Colonies were established. Actually, that border wasn't defined until after the American—Mexican War (1846-1848). Up until that time, Texas, New Mexico,

California and other western states were part of Mexico's territory. After the war, many Mexicans remained and became part of the new American landscape. I am aware that the immigration quandary goes beyond the security of our southern border. However, at the moment, it holds center stage.

This problem is exacerbated by the fact that many of these foreigners have been illegally crossing the border for decades. Legal or not, the numbers are so great that the deportation of the many appears to be virtually impossible. Furthermore, draconian (harsh) deportation measures might lead to unintended consequences since many Americans are unwilling to do the hard labor needed should some of these undocumented workers disappear. Nevertheless, many Americans continue to clamor for their expulsion based on irrational fear and illogic. Thus, the bias continues unabated.

**Border Security**

In closing, I wish to repeat what I consider to be a most important comment I made in Chapter 22:

> *To be clear here, no rational person is advocating for open borders; we can't absorb everyone. Nor can we allow immigrants to enter our country without being vetted. We need a reality-based approach for solving the thorny issues surrounding immigration, including a pathway to citizenship. It will take considerable effort on the part of well-intentioned, well-informed, and well-educated compassionate leaders to resolve this issue fairly. But an equitable solution will be impossible if ignorance and ethnic bias rule the day.*

# APPENDIX

*Rip Chords Discography*

## Singles

1962–63: "Here I Stand" (Bringas on lead vocal) backed with "Karen" (Stewart on lead)

1963: "Gone" (Bringas on lead) b/w "She Thinks I Still Care" (Bringas on lead)

1963–64: "Hey Little Cobra" (Melcher on lead) b/w "The Queen" (Melcher on lead)

1964: "Three Window Coupe" (Melcher on lead) b/w "Hot Rod U.S.A." (Melcher on lead)

1964: "One Piece Topless Bathing Suit" (Melcher and Bringas on lead) b/w "Wah-Wahini" (Melcher on lead)

1965: "Don't Be Scared" (Melcher on lead) b/w "Bunny Hill" (instrumental by The Wrecking Crew)

## Albums
### *Hey Little Cobra and Other Hot Rod Hits*

"Hey Little Cobra" (Melcher on lead)

"Here I Stand" (Bringas on lead)

"The Queen" (Melcher on lead)

"409" (Bringas on lead)

"Trophy Machine" (Melcher on lead)

"Gone" (Bringas on lead)

"Little Deuce Coupe" (Melcher on lead)

"'40 Ford Time" (Instrumental by The Wrecking Crew)

"She Thinks I Still Care" (Bringas on lead)

"Shut Down" (Bringas on lead)

"Drag City" (Melcher on lead)

"Ding Dong" (Stewart on lead)

### Three Window Coupe

"Three Window Coupe" (Melcher on lead)

"Bonneville Bonnie" (Stewart on lead)

"Gas Money" (Bringas on lead)

"This Little Woodie" (Melcher on lead)

"Hot Rod U.S.A." (Melcher on lead)

"Old Car Made In '52" (Stewart on lead)

"Surfin' Craze" (Bringas on lead)

"Beach Girl" (Melcher on lead)

"My Big Gun Board" (Melcher and Bringas on lead)

"Surf City" (Melcher on lead)

"Summer U.S.A." (Melcher on lead)

"Big Wednesday" (instrumental by The Wrecking Crew)

# ABOUT THE AUTHOR

Presently, as an adjunct faculty member, Ernie Bringas teaches Religious Studies (Two subjects: *World Religions* and *Introduction to the New Testament*) at Glendale Community College in Arizona. Under their auspices, he previously taught these classes at Arizona State University.

Ernie received his B.A. at the California State University, Long Beach. His graduate studies led to a Master of Divinity degree from United Theological Seminary, Dayton, Ohio, in 1966. Further religious studies were briefly pursued at the Pacific School of Religion, Berkeley, California.

After graduating from seminary, Ernie was ordained as a minister of the United Methodist Church. He served the Church for almost 20 years before venturing into academic studies.

During the early 1960s, while pursuing his university and seminary education, Ernie and his partner Phil Stewart founded a rock group that came to be known as the RIP CHORDS. The group, recording for Columbia Records, placed five hit singles on Billboard's Hot 100 singles chart, 1962-65 (see: ripchords.info or Wikipedia).

Other Books by Ernie Bringas

*GOING BY THE BOOK:*
*Past and Present Tragedies of Biblical Authority*

*CREATED EQUAL:*
*A Case for the Animal-Human Connection*

*JESUSGATE:*
*A History of Concealment Unraveled*